For Margaret,

With deepest gratitude for your interest, support and friendship, and with much love as always,

Julie

Palgrave Macmillan Memory Studies

The nascent field of memory studies emerges from contemporary trends that include a shift from concern with historical knowledge of events to that of memory, from 'what we know' to 'how we remember it'; changes in generational memory; the rapid advance of technologies of memory; panic over declining powers of memory, which mirrors our fascination with the possibilities of memory enhancement; and the development of trauma narratives in reshaping the past.

These factors have contributed to an intensification of public discourses on our past over the last 30 years. Technological, political, interpersonal, social and cultural shifts affect what, how and why people and societies remember and forget. This groundbreaking series tackles questions such as the following: What is 'memory' under these conditions? What are its prospects, and also the prospects for its interdisciplinary and systematic study? What are the conceptual, theoretical and methodological tools for its investigation and illumination?

Aleida Assmann and Sebastian Conrad (*editors*)
MEMORY IN A GLOBAL AGE
Discourses, Practices and Trajectories

Aleida Assmann and Linda Shortt (*editors*)
MEMORY AND POLITICAL CHANGE

Brian Conway
COMMEMORATION AND BLOODY SUNDAY
Pathways of Memory

Richard Crownshaw
THE AFTERLIFE OF HOLOCAUST MEMORY IN CONTEMPORARY LITERATURE AND CULTURE

Astrid Erll
MEMORY IN CULTURE

Anne Fuchs
AFTER THE DRESDEN BOMBING
Pathways of Memory, 1945 to the Present

Irial Glynn and J. Olaf Kleist (*editors*)
HISTORY, MEMORY AND MIGRATION
Perceptions of the Past and the Politics of Incorporation

Yifat Gutman, Adam D. Brown and Amy Sodaro (*editors*)
MEMORY AND THE FUTURE
Transnational Politics, Ethics and Society

Amy Holdsworth
TELEVISION, MEMORY AND NOSTALGIA

Jason James
PRESERVATION AND NATIONAL BELONGING IN EASTERN GERMANY
Heritage Fetishism and Redeeming Germanness

Mikyoung Kim and Barry Schwartz (*editors*)
NORTHEAST ASIA'S DIFFICULT PAST
Essays in Collective Memory

Emily Keightley and Michael Pickering
THE MNEMONIC IMAGINATION
Remembering as Creative Practice

Philip Lee and Pradip Ninan Thomas (*editors*)
PUBLIC MEMORY, PUBLIC MEDIA AND THE POLITICS OF JUSTICE

Erica Lehrer, Cynthia E. Milton and Monica Eileen Patterson (*editors*)
CURATING DIFFICULT KNOWLEDGE
Violent Pasts in Public Places

Motti Neiger, Oren Meyers and Eyal Zandberg (*editors*)
ON MEDIA MEMORY
Collective Memory in a New Media Age

Anna Saunders and Debbie Pinfold (*editors*)
REMEMBERING AND RETHINKING THE GDR
Multiple Perspectives and Plural Authenticities

V. Seidler
REMEMBERING DIANA
Cultural Memory and the Reinvention of Authority

Evelyn B. Tribble and Nicholas Keene
COGNITIVE ECOLOGIES AND THE HISTORY OF REMEMBERING
Religion, Education and Memory in Early Modern England

Forthcoming titles:

Owain Jones and Joanne Garde-Hansen (*editors*)
GEOGRAPHY AND MEMORY
Exploring Identity, Place and Becoming

Palgrave Macmillan Memory Studies
Series Standing Order ISBN 978–0–230–23851–0 (hardback)
978–0–230–23852–7 (paperback)
(*outside North America only*)

You can receive future titles in this series as they are published by placing a standing order. Please contact your bookseller or, in case of difficulty, write to us at the address below with your name and address, the title of the series and the ISBN quoted above.

Customer Services Department, Macmillan Distribution Ltd, Houndmills, Basingstoke, Hampshire RG21 6XS, England

---

Remembering and Rethinking the GDR

Multiple Perspectives and Plural Authenticities

Edited by

Anna Saunders
Bangor University, UK

and

Debbie Pinfold
Bristol University, UK

palgrave
macmillan

First published 2013 by
PALGRAVE MACMILLAN

Palgrave Macmillan in the UK is an imprint of Macmillan Publishers Limited, registered in England, company number 785998, of Houndmills, Basingstoke, Hampshire RG21 6XS.

Palgrave Macmillan in the US is a division of St Martin's Press LLC, 175 Fifth Avenue, New York, NY 10010.

Palgrave Macmillan is the global academic imprint of the above companies and has companies and representatives throughout the world.

ISBN 978–0–230–36057–0

This book is printed on paper suitable for recycling and made from fully managed and sustained forest sources. Logging, pulping and manufacturing processes are expected to conform to the environmental regulations of the country of origin.

A catalogue record for this book is available from the British Library.

A catalog record for this book is available from the Library of Congress.

10 9 8 7 6 5 4 3 2 1
22 21 20 19 18 17 16 15 14 13

Contents

List of Figures vii

Acknowledgements viii

Notes on Contributors ix

Introduction: '*Wissen wie es war*'? 1
Anna Saunders and Debbie Pinfold

Part I Theoretical Reflections

1 The GDR and the Memory Debate 19
Silke Arnold-de Simine and Susannah Radstone

2 Selective Memory: Channelling the Past in Post-GDR Society 34
Patricia Hogwood

Part II Narrative Frameworks of Memory

3 Reframing Antifascism: Greta Kuckhoff as Author, Commentator and Critic 51
Joanne Sayner

4 Community and Genre: Autobiographical Rememberings of Stasi Oppression 67
Sara Jones

5 Doppelgänger in Post-*Wende* Literature: Klaus Schlesinger's *Trug* and Beyond 83
Elke Gilson

Part III Beyond Nostalgia

6 '*Ostalgie* doesn't fit!': Individual Interpretations of and Interaction with *Ostalgie* 101
Claire Hyland

7 Reflective Nostalgia and Diasporic Memory: Composing East Germany after 1989 116
Elaine Kelly

8 Colour and Time in Museums of East German Everyday Life 132
Chloe Paver

Part IV Past Memories for Present Concerns

9 Memory Matters and Contexts: Remembering for Past, Present and Future 149
Anselma Gallinat

10 The Politics of Memory in Berlin's *Freiheits- und Einheitsdenkmal* 164
Anna Saunders

11 'We were heroes.' Local Memories of Autumn 1989: Revising the Past 179
Alexandra Kaiser

Part V Memories in Private and Public

12 Re-Imaging the Niche: Visual Reconstructions of Private Spaces in the GDR 197
Gabriele Mueller

13 Memories, Secrets and Lies: The Emotional Legacy of the GDR in Christian Schwochow's *Novemberkind* (2008) 214
Owen Evans

14 Life in the Army: Reported, Represented, Remembered 229
Mark Allinson

Index 245

Figures

7.1 Bredemeyer's transformation of Schumann's formal structure in *Aufschwung OST* 126
8.1 Display of objects at the DDR-Museum 'Zeitreise' in Dresden-Radebeul (Chloe Paver; image reproduced with the permission of Hans-Joachim Stephan) 134
10.1 2011 open air exhibition on the designated site for Berlin's *Freiheits- und Einheitsdenkmal* (Anna Saunders) 169
11.1 Candle display on Augustusplatz, Leipzig, at the 2009 'Festival of Lights' (Alexander Schmidt/PUNCTUM) 181
12.1 Familie Brun: Marcel Brun, 59, Schriftsteller; Ingrid Brun, 40, Lektorin; Stephan Brun, 11, Schüler. Copyright: Bernd Lasdin 200
12.2 Familie Helminiak: Carsta Helminiak, 24, Wirtschaftskaufmann; Sebastian Helminiak, 3. Copyright: Bernd Lasdin 201
12.3 Reconstructing the material world of the GDR. Screen shot from *Jenseits der Mauer* (Fromm, 2009, Ziegler Film GmbH + Co.) 210

Acknowledgements

The essays presented here emerged from the concluding conference of the 'After the Wall' interdisciplinary research network, held at Bangor University in September 2010. We would like to thank the Arts and Humanities Research Council for its generous funding of the 'After the Wall' Network (2009–2011), and our respective institutions, Bangor University and the University of Bristol, for their support in hosting the Network's events. We are also grateful to our colleagues in the School of Modern Languages in Bangor and the German Department at Bristol for their interest, support and encouragement throughout the project; the Bangor University web team deserves special thanks for its help in setting up the 'After the Wall' website (http://afterthewall.bangor.ac.uk/). We would particularly like to thank our contributors, whose prompt, patient and cheerful cooperation with our editorial requests made editing the volume a real pleasure, but also those other members of the Network, keynote speakers and presenters at the final conference who are not formally represented here, but whose contributions to our wider discussion informed and enriched our thinking at every stage. Thanks are also due to the DAAD for financing Debbie Pinfold's study visit to Berlin in early 2012, to Matthew Linehan for his sterling work on translating Chapter 5, to Georgina Leighton for her assistance in preparing the index, and to the editorial team at Palgrave for their advice and efficiency during the final stages.

Contributors

Mark Allinson is Senior Lecturer in German History at the University of Bristol and has focused most of his research career to date on the political, social and economic history of the German Democratic Republic (GDR). His first book, *Politics and Popular Opinion in East Germany 1945–68* (2000), explored the development of communism in post-war Thuringia. He is currently working on a history of the GDR in the 1970s. His other publications include *Germany and Austria 1814–2000* (2002). He has supervised and examined master's and doctoral dissertations on a variety of areas of modern German history and politics.

Silke Arnold-de Simine is Lecturer in German Studies in the Department of European Cultures and Languages, Birkbeck, University of London. Her research interests lie in nineteenth- and twentieth-century German literature and early film, gender studies, cultural memory and museum studies. She is the editor of *Memory Traces: 1989 and the Question of German Cultural Identity* (2005). Currently she is working on a monograph with the provisional title *Mediating Memory in the Museum Landscape: Empathy, Trauma, Nostalgia.*

Owen Evans is Professor of Film in the Media Department at Edge Hill University. He has published widely on GDR literature, German film and European cinema, including monographs on Günter de Bruyn and German literary biography, and recent articles on *Das Leben der Anderen, Sophie Scholl: Die letzten Tage,* the European Film Festival and *Sight and Sound*. He is the co-founding editor of the international journals *Studies in European Cinema* and the *Journal of European Popular Culture* and co-founding director of the European Cinema Research Forum (ECRF).

Anselma Gallinat is Lecturer in Sociology at Newcastle University. She holds a PhD in social anthropology and has conducted several periods of field research in eastern Germany, working on questions of cultural change, identity and narrative. Her most recent work is on the memory and history-writing of socialism and questions of belonging, citizenship and government. She has published in *Ethnos*, *Social Anthropology* and *Identities* and is currently working on a book project on her latest research. Methodologically she is interested in ethnography and has published a volume with Peter Collins entitled *The Ethnographic Self as Resource* (2010).

Elke Gilson studied Germanic languages and literature in Ghent and Berlin. She is currently Postdoctoral Fellow of the Flemish Research Fund attached to the Department of Literary Studies at Ghent University, and was formerly Visiting Fellow of the Institute of Germanic and Romance Studies, University of London. She has published on GDR and Berlin literature, memory, masculinity and gender issues; recent publications include articles on urban self-encounters in the works of Inka Parei, old age in the novels of Monika Maron and Judith Hermann's relationship to Kleist. She is also co-editor of *Literatur im Jahrhundert des Totalitarismus* (2008).

Patricia Hogwood is a reader in the Department of Politics and International Relations at the University of Westminster. She writes on aspects of democracy, identity and well-being in united Germany. Her current projects include the 'inner unity' project and the politics of behaviour change; consumer culture and consumer behaviours in the development of post-GDR identities; and subjective well-being in united Germany. She also works on constitutional and cultural identities in Germany as a 'country of immigration' and on German and EU policy strategies of immigration control.

Claire Hyland has recently completed her doctorate with the University of Bath, and is currently working as a Research and Teaching Fellow at the University of Bristol. In her research she draws on qualitative interviews to explore processes of identity construction among 1970s-generation East Germans in Berlin. She focuses specifically on how this group negotiates dominant discourses and stereotypes when constructing perceptions of the self and of other easterners.

Sara Jones is Research Fellow at the University of Birmingham in the departments of Political Science and International Studies, and Modern Languages. She has published on East German cultural policy and the involvement of GDR writers with the Stasi. Her first monograph, *Complicity, Censorship and Criticism: Negotiating Space in the GDR Literary Sphere,* was published in 2011. Her current research analyses portrayals of the Stasi in different cultural media. She has published articles emerging from this project on memorials and museums in Eastern Europe, and on the use of online discussion forums for social and cultural remembering.

Alexandra Kaiser is a cultural anthropologist and works for museums. She studied Art history and Empirische Kulturwissenschaft at the University of Tübingen and was a fellow of the DFG-Sonderforschungsbereich 'Kriegserfahrungen', where she completed her doctorate on the history of the German People's Day of Mourning (*Von Helden und Opfern. Eine Geschichte des Volkstrauertags*, Campus, 2010). From 2009 to 2011 she worked at the Zeitgeschichtliches Forum in Leipzig. Her publications have focused on German memory culture, regional studies and popular religion.

Elaine Kelly studied music at NUI Maynooth and Queen's University Belfast and is currently Lecturer in Music at the University of Edinburgh. Her research interests span a range of issues relating to music, cultural history and politics in nineteenth- and twentieth-century Germany, with a particular focus on the GDR. She has published in journals such as *19th-Century Music, Music & Letters, 19th-Century Music Review* and *Kritika: Explorations in Russian and Eurasian History*, and is co-editor with Amy Wlodarski of *Art Outside the Lines: New Perspectives on GDR Art Culture* (2011).

Gabriele Mueller is Associate Professor of German Studies and affiliated with the Canadian Centre for German and European Studies at York University. Her research focuses mainly on contemporary German cinema and German film history. She has published on various aspects of post-unification cinema in Germany, in particular on cinematic contributions to memory discourses. She is the co-editor of *Cinema and Social Change in Germany and Austria* (with James M. Skidmore, 2012).

Chloe Paver is Senior Lecturer in German at the University of Exeter. She is the author of *Refractions of the Third Reich in German and Austrian Fiction and Film* (2007) and other work on post-1989 German fiction. Since undertaking research as a Humboldt Fellow at the University of Konstanz in 2006–07 she has published a number of articles on historical exhibitions and aspects of cultural memory. She is preparing a monograph on the recent museum and exhibition boom in Germany (and, to a lesser degree, Austria), analysing what motivates and influences the public display of the history of dictatorships.

Debbie Pinfold is Senior Lecturer in German at the University of Bristol. Her research focuses on post-war German literature and culture and on memories of the GDR. She is the author of a monograph on literary representations of childhood in the Third Reich and is currently working on a project about childhood as it appears in the political and literary discourses of the GDR.

Susannah Radstone is a professor in the School of Arts and Digital Industries at the University of East London. She is currently working on the relationship between localism and internationalism in memory studies and on new approaches to trauma. Recent publications include (co-edited with Bill Schwarz) *Memory: Histories, Theories, Debates* (2010); she is currently completing a book titled *Getting over Trauma*.

Anna Saunders is Senior Lecturer in German at Bangor University, Wales. Her research interests include questions of history and memory in eastern Germany, memorialisation in contemporary Germany, and socialist and post-socialist youth culture. Her publications include *Honecker's Children* (2007) and articles on *Ostalgie*, the memory of Rosa Luxemburg, and monuments in post-*Wende* Berlin. She is currently working on a monograph about memorialising the GDR.

Joanne Sayner is Lecturer in Cultural Theory and German Studies at the University of Birmingham. Her research focuses on the politics of remembering the Nazi past in Germany since 1945. She has published on life writing, antifascism and memory. Her publications include *Women without a Past: German Autobiographical Writings and Fascism* (2007).

Introduction: '*Wissen wie es war*'?*

Anna Saunders and Debbie Pinfold

Saturday 14 January 2012 saw an estimated 5,000 visitors from Berlin and beyond swarming over the precincts of the former Stasi headquarters on Normannenstraße (Fuchs, 2012), which had been reopened following extensive renovations. The date for the event had been chosen to coincide with two significant anniversaries: the twentieth anniversary of the law which first granted German citizens the right to examine their Stasi files (2 January 1992) and the twenty-second anniversary of the storming of the Stasi headquarters by East German civil rights activists (15 January 1990). Visitors were able to participate in a full day's programme of walking tours of the precinct, visits to the archive and back-to-back talks, culminating in the first ever podium discussion between all three heads of the Stasi files authority: the present incumbent, Roland Jahn, and his predecessors, Joachim Gauck and Marianne Birthler. The event included contributions from many prominent actors from 1989–90 and was conducted under the title *Wissen wie es war* ('Knowing how it was').[1] Quite coincidentally, that same evening a group of five cabaret singers from the group named 'Chansonwerkstatt', four of them born in East Germany during the 1970s, presented the final performance of a show titled *Ostpaket: Wendekinder packen aus!* (lit: 'Package from the East: Children of the *Wende* unpack') (see Chansonwerkstatt, 2012).[2] This took place in a theatre-café and featured young people dressed in army and youth organisation uniforms, singing everything from Pioneer songs to popular *Schlager* (hits) from the GDR in a playful manner with a strong ironic undercurrent. Some of the songs were sung with a quasi-earnestness that betrayed a certain nostalgia for the sounds of childhood and youth; others were defamiliarised in ways which harked back to the group's earlier experience of singing Brecht in such a way as to demonstrate the distance the performers felt from the ideology underlying the songs. The audience, numbering approximately

100, greeted the melodies with chuckles of recognition, handclapping and attempts to sing along, but also showed appreciation for the more satirical elements of the show.

That two such different events should have taken place in the same city, on the same day, over 20 years since the *Wende* says much about the continued relevance of GDR remembrance in united Germany. First, it is significant that interest in the GDR is genuinely ongoing. Time and again at the Normannenstraße event it was emphasised that no-one had expected interest in the files to last more than ten years after the *Wende*. And yet, as Birthler pointed out, a new wave of interest has begun; many people have only just mustered the courage to apply to see their files, largely because their children want to know more about their family history. The fact that the performers of the Chansonwerkstatt were born in the 1970s also testifies to the interest of this younger generation in the GDR past. Second, it is important to note the very different forms that these engagements with the same past took. On the one hand, the reopening of a national museum and archive promised a path to enlightenment and reconciliation; the fact that the Stasi archive allows individuals to access documents about their own pasts was presented by numerous speakers as ultimately liberating, for the individual and for society itself. Indeed, the very title given to the open day presented the museum as offering no less than a path to truth. The cabaret production made no such elevated claims for itself, yet still offered emotional and cognitive means of accessing a lost past. Audience reactions in different locations suggest that the show is open to many different interpretations: some audience members have left in tears, overwhelmed by memories of a happy childhood, whereas others have found the show deeply provocative, owing to the much less pleasant memories that the songs evoked for them.[3] Third, the staging of these events lends weight to the suggestion that Germany's political elite has a vested interest in maintaining a certain narrative about the GDR. Various speakers at the Normannenstraße event stressed that the day was a testament to united Germany's democratic credentials: that the openness, transparency and speed which had characterised the new Germany's decision to open the Stasi files were proof of the country's success in working through its GDR legacy. In contrast, the difficulties the Chansonwerkstatt has had in finding places to perform *Ostpaket* suggests an ongoing anxiety within certain public institutions, lest their association with such a project lead to them being branded 'ostalgic'. Certain views of the past are clearly still officially deemed more acceptable than others.

These issues concerning periods of remembrance, memory media, and the dominance or marginalisation of certain narratives inform the contents of this volume. They were the central concerns of the 'After the Wall' Network from which this volume has grown; its activities (2009–2011) were timed so as to enable participants to reflect not only on the GDR 20 years after the *Wende*, but also on the anniversary celebrations themselves as an integral part of the remembering process (see Chapter 11). Such commemorative events were in no way restricted to Germany, with a large amount of scholarly activity taking place beyond its borders in 2009.[4] Our Network and this volume thus fit alongside – but also reflect upon – a variety of resulting publications from beyond Germany; its interdisciplinary nature and focus on processes of memory, however, mark it out as distinct. Indeed, the Network bore the subtitle 'Reconstructing and Representing the GDR' to reflect its interest in a wide range of cultural and political representations, some of which are more conscious of their constructed quality than others. Svetlana Boym's distinction between two broad tendencies in relating to a national past, 'restorative' and 'reflective' nostalgia, is key here; while the first of these tendencies suggests an attempt to reconstruct and protect a past home, the second focuses rather on the complex ongoing processes of remembrance. Boym (2001: 41, 49) argues that while restorative nostalgics 'believe that their project is about truth', reflective nostalgia focuses 'not on recovery of what is perceived to be an absolute truth, but on the meditation on history and the passage of time'. While the Network considered artefacts and narratives that might be considered typical of both tendencies, its own focus on multiple disciplinary and personal perspectives in productive dialogue enabled precisely the kind of 'new flexibility' which Boym sees as characteristic of reflective nostalgia (ibid.: 49). Thus the resulting volume is explicitly not about knowing 'wie es war': rather, the various contributions from political science, history, anthropology, museum studies, musicology, literary and media studies explore the diverse ways in which the GDR is remembered over 20 years on, and the agendas which underlie those different memory products. Multiple disciplinary perspectives not only allow plural authenticities to stand alongside and complement one another in the present, but also leave the way open for continued dialogue and development in the future.

After the Wall: Memories and media in flux

As the GDR recedes ever further into the past, it has become increasingly clear that memories of this past remain in flux, partly in response to shifting political, social and cultural agendas, but also as a result of the passing of time, the coming of new generations and the exploration of new media. If anything, the place of the GDR within German collective memory has become increasingly complex; as Martin Sabrow (2009: 15, 20) claims, the East German past has become 'a battleground of memories' in which knowledge of the GDR can no longer be taken for granted as a self-evident part of the eastern German experience, but has rather become a 'site of projection' which is increasingly questioned and contested. The past 20-plus years have, indeed, seen the development of multiple forms of remembrance, incorporating political and legal processes, as well as historical, literary, filmic, museal and other popular media forms.

In the first years after unification, however, public understandings of the GDR were dominated by official attempts to rework the East German past. Most notably, the Bundestag's two special enquiry commissions into the GDR past, from 1992 to 1994 and 1995 to 1998, clearly highlighted the totalitarian nature of the GDR. Moreover, by using this narrative to legitimise the democratic present, the commissions worked towards establishing a 'didactic public history' (Andrews, 2003: 51). As the aims of the second commission read, for instance: 'The special enquiry commission should contribute to the consolidation of a democratic self-awareness, a sense of justice rooted in freedom and an anti-totalitarian consensus' (Schlußbericht der Enquete-Kommission, 1998: 11). Legislation passed in the early 1990s also worked to provide compensation and rehabilitation for victims of injustices committed by the GDR regime, as well as the prosecution of individuals identified with such injustices, such as leading party functionaries and border guards accused of shooting to kill at the border. Above all, the illegitimacy of the GDR was highlighted through the crimes and corruption of the Stasi, particularly following the Stasi Files Law mentioned above. Throughout this period, the emphasis on the repressive power structures of the state inevitably highlighted parallels with the National Socialist state, and provoked references to Germany's 'dual past'.[5]

As the 1990s progressed, however, narratives began to emerge which challenged the emphasis on totalitarian structures of power and instruments of repression, and a number of social history approaches suggested alternatives to the totalitarian paradigm, developing notions such as *Eigen-Sinn*, the 'welfare dictatorship', or the 'modern dictatorship'.[6] Greater emphasis on aspects such as the GDR's social welfare system, its comprehensive childcare system, or women's emancipation also went hand in hand with a growing interest in the everyday, and the notion that it was possible – in contrast to Adorno's dictum – to lead 'a right life within the wrong one'. Within this context, however, personal biographies could not neatly be divided from the power structures of the dictatorship, for the two regularly intertwined. The growing importance of the everyday was also highlighted in the expert commission headed by Sabrow in 2005 and 2006, whose recommendations that the everyday and spheres of resistance should receive greater attention met with the criticism that the commission was promoting a homeopathic version of the GDR dictatorship (for more detail, see Sabrow *et al.*, 2007). Commonly – yet often inaccurately – associated with *Ostalgie*, the notion of the everyday clearly gained ground during this period, as evidenced by the many museums to everyday culture which opened from the late 1990s onwards.

With time – and particularly since the millennium – more complex representations of the GDR past have emerged, whether in literary, filmic, documentary, artistic, musical or digital form. Indeed, the numerous media available today are doubtless significant here, for not only are the voices of professional historians and public figures to be heard, but also those of individuals and diverse interest groups through blogs, social networking sites, web pages and YouTube, as well as popular publications and the mass media; multiple fora allow for a multitude of competing memories. The influx of publications on a large variety of media dealing with the GDR bears testament to the increasingly serious engagement with concepts such as writing history – and exploring memory – 'from below' and investigating the complex interplay between memories of political realities and everyday experience, whether through material culture, political, geographical, ethnic or cultural perspectives (see, for example, Leeder, 2009; Balbier, Cuevas-Wolf and Segal, 2011; Clarke and Wölfel, 2011; Fuchs, James-Chakraborty and Shortt, 2011; Hodgin and Pearce, 2011; Rechtien and Tate, 2011). The increasing variety of media used to represent different memories of the GDR has become an important topic not only for our understanding of contemporary east Germany, but also for memory studies in general (Erll and Rigney, 2009: 1). Indeed, with this focus has come the understanding that media are not mere transparent vessels, but help condition the form of memory produced (ibid.: 2–3). For example, museums, traditionally sites where reliable, objective information is conveyed to the general public, tend to be perceived as more authoritative than literary fiction about a historical period. The increasing prevalence of 'memorial museums' (Williams, 2007), however, adds another layer to the museum's traditional authority as a source of information, for memorial museums ask the visitor not simply to learn about the past, but to enter into an emotional relationship with it. Where possible, such museums exploit the advantages of the auratic site to the full, as in the case of the museum at Hohenschönhausen (the former Stasi remand prison), where the use of former inmates as tour guides creates the potential for what Alison Landsberg (2004) terms 'prosthetic memory': the possibility that a visitor who has not experienced this past will be able to enter emotionally into the experience of others and experience a change in his or her own consciousness as a result (Jones, 2011: 215).

Museums on both sides of the still polarised museum landscape in Germany all emphasise their claims to authority through the use of authentic sites, objects or stories, but as the GDR recedes into the past, eyewitnesses die out, and authentic sites and objects lose their resonance for post-1990 generations, other media with less claim to historical reliability are inevitably coming to the fore. Since 2000 the GDR has proved, perhaps surprisingly, successful at the box office, with films such as *Good Bye, Lenin!* (2003) and *Das Leben der Anderen* (*The Lives of Others*, 2006) achieving not just domestic but international acclaim. The success of this medium may be explained not only by the voyeuristic desire to watch representations of the second German dictatorship, but also in terms of Landsberg's prosthetic memory, where the ability of the mass media to facilitate emotional identification is perceived as a valuable means of allowing memories to be passed on transgenerationally and transculturally.

The increasing prevalence – and popularity – of films alongside museums may indicate a shift from the need to find out about the GDR to a need to experience it more viscerally, especially in the case of younger generations. A similar phenomenon may be observed in the sphere of literary production. Individuals began writing narratives of their lives in the GDR almost as soon as the state ceased to exist; however, the nature of such accounts has – logically – shifted over time, particularly from around 2000, when the generation born in the 1970s began to record their experiences of life in the GDR. These accounts not only had the subjective individual focus characteristic of autobiographical writing, but in many cases they contravened the by then reasonably well-established narrative of the GDR as an *Unrechtsstaat* (illegitimate state) simply because the nostalgia for the securities of childhood implied in texts like Jana Hensel's *Zonenkinder* (2002) was all too frequently misunderstood as pure, uncritical *Ostalgie*. Such autobiographical texts are almost by definition limited in scope and appeal, and their longer term contribution to the broad cultural memory of the GDR thus seems doubtful. However, the shift from visual to textual memory media since the GDR's demise (Geier, 2011: 102) is complemented by a second shift from monolinear, autobiographical narrative to polyvocal, multi-perspectival fictional texts which, by inviting the reader to invest emotionally in multiple characters and voices, allow him or her to experience vicariously a more complex image of the GDR. It is perhaps in such texts that the ongoing cultural memory of the GDR will be located.

Greater temporal distance from the GDR is creating increasing confidence in producing not just potentially more durable and complex narratives in the form of literary texts, but also, ironically, more durable and arguably simplistic narratives in the form of memorials (see Chapter 10). Simplistic, unified narratives obviously prove highly attractive to those with specific agendas in the present, and the mobilisation of memory for the purposes of state legitimation is far from a new concept. Yet contemporaneous technological developments and the ever-expanding use of social media suggest that for all the attempts to establish straightforward summative narratives of the GDR and its demise, this past will continue to be contested at an individual and state level for as long as there are former GDR citizens living in united Germany; multiple perspectives will continue to produce plural authenticities. Indeed, the apparent insistence on traditional perpetrator–victim or Stasi–*Ostalgie* dichotomies – perhaps on the surface encapsulated by the two events that took place on 14 January 2012 – have increasingly been challenged, revealing the large areas of overlap between the two. As Peter Thompson (2009: 283) argues, such apparently conflicting representations of the GDR should be viewed not as polar opposites, but rather as 'the conjoined twins of really-existing socialism'.

Recognition of this fact is increasingly finding its way into popular culture. As Chloe Paver notes in Chapter 8, for instance, museums which house narratives of both repression and the everyday are no longer so difficult to find; the DDR-Museum in Berlin underwent major renovation in 2010, as did the Dokumentationszentrum Alltagskultur der DDR in Eisenhüttenstadt in 2012, precisely in order to incorporate a greater focus on power structures. Just as such binaries are increasingly being challenged, so is the notion that the end of the GDR necessarily marked the end of an era. Although the close of the 'short twentieth century' is commonly marked by the end of the Cold War, the impact of this change on individual lives has varied hugely, and in some cases continuity is as prevalent as change. One need only mention, for example, the continuing gulf between *Ossis* and *Wessis* in unified Germany, or the notion of the 'wall in the head' – identified by Peter Schneider back in 1982 – which are still present today. Indeed, difficult financial circumstances and decisions in recent years may have had global causes but have often been understood as the product of local trends (see Hodgin and Pearce, 2011: 3). It is perhaps not surprising that the tradition of the 'Monday demonstration', originating in Leipzig in 1989, has seen a resurgence, and the desire to 'continue' the revolution of 1989 features in the manifestos of certain civic groups (see Chapter 11). Within the cultural sphere, this wider debate also relates to the question of how far the end of the GDR state necessarily also implies the end of GDR culture, and to what extent continuities exist between pre- and post-*Wende* cultural production (see Rechtien and Tate, 2011); it is clearly not possible to draw a neat line between the socialist past and the capitalist present in the cultural sphere any more than it is in the political arena.

'GDRs of the mind'

This volume seeks to shed further light on our understanding of the above discussions, while paying particular attention to ongoing debates within memory studies. Like many publications resulting from the twentieth anniversary, this volume has the advantage of being the work of an international group of scholars who can offer a somewhat distanced perspective on the often fraught internal debates. Central to this volume, however, is the fact that most of the contributors were members of the 'After the Wall' Network from its inception and therefore worked together over a period of two years, discussing key theoretical and methodological issues as they related to members' different disciplines. While those different disciplines and indeed our individual political and personal perspectives on the GDR precluded any (in any case undesirable) homogenising approach to the topic, the debates around those issues have both enriched our individual contributions and provided coherence to our overall approach. Underpinned by an interdisciplinary dialogue on memory and remembrance, this volume will thus be of interest not only to those engaged in GDR studies, but also to those working on such questions in different contexts.

The opening section, 'Theoretical Reflections', serves to outline a number of the theoretical and methodological issues that beset researchers of memory, with a focus on the GDR. The first chapter, by Silke Arnold-de Simine and Susannah Radstone, provides an overview of the theoretical concepts and debates which underpin the diverse contributions to this volume. The authors adopt a critical and self-reflexive stance, asking what a memory studies approach might contribute to our understanding, but also what it may serve to conceal, particularly in its frequent reliance on the neat binary of victim versus perpetrator.

The chapter situates the volume within the context of the so-called 'memory boom' (Huyssen, 1995), sets out the debates surrounding the key concept of 'collective memory' and suggests how a memory studies approach may throw light on the ways memories of the GDR are constructed and instrumentalised by diverse memory communities in the present and into the future. It also places the volume's concern with memory discourses within two wider contexts: first the often highly politicised debates within Germany about the 'historical accuracy' of representations of the GDR, and second a shifting global memory landscape that is increasingly concerned with recalling not just moments of national pride, but also more difficult aspects of the past. Patricia Hogwood's chapter follows by underlining the importance of theoretical and methodological frameworks. By examining the construction of key terms – such as *Ostalgie*, victimhood and normalisation – she shows how different disciplinary perspectives and research methods may influence the ways in which memories are reported and interpreted. In particular, Hogwood highlights the ways in which a political science approach may usefully complement other disciplinary perspectives, by seeking to capture not the integrity of memory, but rather its influence on the formation of social relations, political identities and institutional frameworks. Her emphasis on evidenced behaviour and a path-dependence approach highlight the unique position of east German society today, which has been framed by the institutions, legal frameworks and cultural influences of a western state like no other post-socialist transition society. With this in mind, she crucially asks what the benchmarks of 'normality' might be for contemporary east German society, and suggests that the route of 'normalisation' is unlikely to follow that envisaged by west German elites. As Hogwood stresses throughout, it is the selective nature of memory – in which remembering and forgetting are equal partners – which allows for the formation of new, forward-looking identities.

The second section, 'Narrative Frameworks of Memory', comprises three chapters which consider autobiographical and literary engagements with the GDR past, in particular the effect created by the use of different genre and media. Joanne Sayner's chapter addresses a topic which continues to be key to debates on the GDR past today: that of antifascism. In her analysis of the autobiographical writings of the communist resistance fighter Greta Kuckhoff, Sayner demonstrates that far from being merely a state-imposed doctrine alien to the GDR population, as is frequently suggested in contemporary debates, everyday antifascism had strong identificatory potential. She further shows that while Kuckhoff's message about antifascism remained broadly consistent throughout her life, she was able to use a range of different media to challenge its increasingly monolithic presentation in the GDR, and suggests that this plurality of sources may also help contemporary scholars achieve a more nuanced understanding of GDR antifascism. Sara Jones's chapter on autobiographical accounts of Stasi oppression also focuses on the importance of similar material being presented in different media, though in her analysis the different media are presented not as complementing but as reinforcing one another. Through her analysis of audio-visual recordings and transcripts of interviews with former political prisoners, an anthology of written accounts and a touring exhibition on the same topic, she demonstrates not only the distinctive features of these different media but also the way that a process of mediation and remediation constructs a 'staged' memory community. This enables the production of a coherent collective narrative of the GDR past which has clear relevance for present-day society. Elke Gilson's chapter, in contrast, focuses on the complexity which literary techniques can bring to debates about the GDR past, as it considers both the memory of the GDR *in* literature and the memory *of* GDR literature. Her analysis of Klaus Schlesinger's *Trug* (2000) sets its use of the doppelgänger motif in the context of both contemporary and former GDR writers' use of Romantic tropes, and she argues that while the simple opposition of western and eastern alter egos might suggest feelings of nostalgia for the simpler, more human life of the former east, in fact the uncanny aspects of the text warn against such a simplified reading; rather, they allow Schlesinger to explore the issue of how it is possible to integrate the (GDR) past fully into the present without becoming paralysed by it.

The following section, 'Beyond Nostalgia', brings together three chapters which examine questions typically related to nostalgia for the GDR. However, in examining the way in which notions of east Germanness are constructed, they resist simplistic notions of *Ostalgie*, and demonstrate the complex way in which post-*Wende* identities and attitudes are negotiated. Claire Hyland's chapter deals most directly with the notion of *Ostalgie*, and draws on the results of in-depth interviews carried out with east Germans born in the 1970s. She examines above all the question of agency in the construction of discourse around *Ostalgie*, and finds that although interviewees of this generation resisted any form of 'ostalgic' self-identity, they adopted dominant western narratives when talking about other (often older) easterners, whom they identified as 'ostalgic'. As such, Hyland highlights the complex maze of preconceptions and assumed knowledge which are negotiated on a daily basis.

Elaine Kelly examines an older generation with regard to concepts of nostalgia: east German composers who were born before or during the Second World War, for whom the end of the GDR brought with it much disappointment. In examining paradigms of diaspora and exile in their lives and works after 1990, she draws on Svetlana Boym's notion of 'reflective nostalgia', demonstrating how they expressed themes of loss and longing through ironic and cynical compositions. As Kelly highlights, not only did such works allow composers to engage critically with the post-*Wende* environment, but through them they also resisted unifying narratives of collective memory. Finally in this section, Chloe Paver examines east German museums of everyday life, and begins with the observation that most such museums now view *Ostalgie* from a certain distance. Indeed, this chapter transcends simple binaries by exploring the highly complex relationship of everyday objects from the GDR to the notions of colour and time. In uncovering common constructions of the GDR as variably drab or colourful – depending on the audience – or revealing the complex 'pastness' of many GDR objects, Paver demonstrates not only the multiple dimensions of museum displays but also the potentially diverse expression of post-*Wende* attitudes towards material culture.

The fourth section, 'Past Memories for Present Concerns', contains three chapters dealing with attempts to instrumentalise memories of the GDR and the *Wende* for present-day purposes. They consider top-down versus bottom-up constructions of memory and national versus local remembrance cultures to demonstrate the plurality of narratives that underlie any attempt at constructing a monolithic national memory culture. Anselma Gallinat's chapter considers official attempts by a local eastern German working group to establish a 'correct' memory of the GDR as a dictatorship in order to legitimise the democratic present and safeguard its future. She demonstrates that this narrowly pedagogical perspective makes it difficult for the group to grasp the finer nuances of former GDR citizens' political attitudes in the present, and that such a top-down construction of the past is not capable of embracing the complexity of the individual life stories and memories encountered in her second fieldwork location. Anna Saunders' chapter considers another example of an attempt to establish a political memory of the GDR and the events of 1989–90, in the controversial monument to freedom and unity to be unveiled in Berlin in 2014. Saunders provides an overview of the debates surrounding this memorial to demonstrate that despite considerable attempts to ensure a democratic design and selection process, the need to position the memorial within a wider German memory landscape of freedom and democracy has meant that complex historical details have inevitably been subordinated to the present need for a strong statement about democracy and unity. However, while the Berlin memorial may well be read as a predominantly western statement on democracy, it must also be understood within a wider context which highlights the surprisingly fragile and multi-layered nature of political memory. Part of that wider context is provided by Alexandra Kaiser's chapter, which deals with the city of Leipzig's attempts to establish its role in the peaceful revolution as part of the national narrative. Kaiser focuses on the 'festival of lights' in Leipzig on 9 October 2009 to suggest that such performative re-enactments allow for both a subversive reading (an attempt to restore a specifically east German perspective on the *Wende*) and a national reading which establishes the peaceful revolution in Leipzig as a foundational myth for the new FRG. However, she suggests that 9 October is unlikely to achieve the same emotional significance as 9 November in the national consciousness, and the second national memorial to this period, which is to be erected in Leipzig, is seen ironically as underscoring a still profoundly divided national memory culture.

The final three chapters examine the theme of 'Memories in Private and Public', and all highlight the way in which memories of private and public spheres of life in the GDR overlap and have often become indistinct – despite the popular paradigm of the private niche in public discourse on the GDR. This is the subject of Gabriele Mueller's chapter, which examines visual representations of the niche through pre- and post-*Wende* photography and recent television productions on the GDR. As she finds, the photography of Bernd Lasdin, who allows his subjects a high degree of individual agency, resists any unifying image of the GDR. In contrast, the makers of television films tend to fall back on well-established patterns of representation which correspond to audiences' visual knowledge and expectations. In doing so, they not only strip the niche of its complex and heterogeneous nature, but contribute to the musealisation of the GDR, creating an increasingly institutionally driven version of history. Owen Evans continues this theme by examining screen images, focusing on the case study of Christian Schwochow's film *Novemberkind* (*November Child*, 2008). In this chapter, he examines the psychological damage inflicted by the GDR on the private sphere of the film's main female protagonist – and, interestingly, the actress who plays this role – as she seeks to come to terms with both her personal past and that of the state which has shaped her family tragedy. In doing so, Evans not only demonstrates the need to revisit past and present perceptions of the GDR, but also highlights the impact of the GDR legacy beyond eastern Germany. In contrast, Mark Allinson turns to the public sphere in his examination of representations of the GDR military since 1990, yet finds that contrary to expectations, conflicting portrayals of the army are surprisingly absent from the public sphere, and both fictional and non-fictional depictions present largely similar experiences and memories on the part of soldiers. As he demonstrates, the relatively stable and uncontentious space accorded to the military in the memory landscape of the GDR results largely from the fact that the GDR military experience conformed to a well-established and non-politicised pattern found in other nations; in this sphere of activity, memory of the GDR proves to be far from exceptional.

Neither the chapters outlined above nor indeed the volume as a whole claim to present 'the' GDR; indeed, if there was one thing on which all members of the Network agreed, it might be summed up by the comment made by one of Anselma Gallinat's interviewees: 'There never was a "the" GDR' (Chapter 9: 156). However, we hope that the multiple perspectives – individual and disciplinary – presented here will provide some insights into the plural authenticities that we came to refer to as the 'GDRs of the mind'. Those who once called the GDR home may look back on it like Salman Rushdie (1992: 9) considering a photo of his childhood home in India, with a suspicion that their present is foreign whereas 'the past is home, albeit a lost home in a lost city in the mist of lost time'. This ostensibly lost past is certainly no less real to those who continue to inhabit, yearn for or oppose it, and no less influential in its effects on contemporary cultural and political debates. Yet as Rushdie suggests, that yearning, with its overtones of Boym's restorative nostalgia, is not enough, whether for the writer or the scholar. Few of the Network's members ever called the GDR home, and it was certainly never our aim to create what Rushdie (ibid.: 10) calls 'imaginary homelands'. However, like Rushdie's 'Indias of the mind', the 'GDRs of the mind' presented in this volume are both less and more than the physical reality of the past, the products of a broken glass which is 'not merely a mirror of nostalgia' but a 'useful tool with which to work in the present' (ibid.: 12).

Note on spellings and terminology

*Throughout the volume, East and West Germany are used to designate the pre-1990 GDR and FRG respectively, while east(ern) and west(ern) Germany are used to refer to present-day geographical regions.

Other common abbreviations and terms:

FRG – Federal Republic of Germany
GDR – German Democratic Republic
Ossi/Wessi – terms used to denote eastern and western Germans after unification (often derogatory)
Ostalgie – nostalgia for the former GDR
Stasi – Ministry for State Security
Wende – term used to refer to the period 1989–90 in East Germany (literally meaning 'change' or 'turnaround')
SED – Sozialistische Einheitspartei Deutschlands (Socialist Unity Party of Germany), the ruling party of the GDR.

Notes

1. Full details of the programme can be found at http://www.bstu.bund.de/SharedDocs/Veranstaltungen/Region-Berlin/0114_berlin_20-jahre-akteneinsicht.html. [date accessed 23 January 2012]
2. The title refers ironically to the practice of sending 'Westpakete' containing Western goods to friends and relatives in East Germany.
3. Information from a discussion between Debbie Pinfold and performers Christiane Günther, Sylvia Nitzsche and Fabian Bothe, 20 January 2012, Berlin.
4. The anniversary in 2009 was, for instance, marked in various ways by the UK's Germanist community other than through the 'After the Wall' Network: it formed the lead theme for that year's Conference for University Teachers of German in Belfast (March 2009) and gave rise to a seminar series at the University of Oxford; September 2009 also saw a major international conference at the University of Bath (in conjunction with the University of Reading), titled 'Twenty Years On: Remembering the GDR and Germany's Unification Process'. Further afield – and to name but two examples – October 2009 also saw themed conferences hosted in Dublin (University College Dublin and Goethe Institute Dublin) and Los Angeles (Wende Museum, UCLA and German Historical Institute, Washington DC).
5. See Clarke and Wölfel (2011) for further exploration of the broader debate concerning parallels between coming to terms with the GDR past and ongoing debates about memories of National Socialism.
6. The concept of *Eigen-Sinn* is used to encapsulate the idea of individual agency in negotiations between the private and public spheres.

References

Andrews, M. (2003) 'Grand National Narratives and the Project of Truth Commissions: A Comparative Analysis', *Media, Culture & Society*, 25, 45–65.

Balbier, U.A., C. Cuevas-Wolf and J. Segal (eds) (2011) 'East German Material Culture and the Power of Memory', *Bulletin of the German Historical Institute*, Supplement 7.

Boym, S. (2001) *The Future of Nostalgia* (New York: Basic).

Chansonwerkstatt homepage, http://www.chansonwerkstatt.de/ensemble [date accessed 23 January 2012].

Clarke, D. and U. Wölfel (eds) (2011) *Remembering the German Democratic Republic: Divided Memory in a United Germany* (Basingstoke: Palgrave Macmillan).

Erll, A. and A. Rigney (eds) (2009) *Mediation, Remediation, and the Dynamics of Cultural Memory* (Berlin: de Gruyter).

Fuchs, A., K. James-Chakraborty and L. Shortt (eds) (2011) *Debating German Cultural Identity since 1989* (Rochester, NY: Camden House).

Fuchs, C. (2012) 'Tausende kamen in Mielkes Büro', *Berliner Zeitung*, 14 January, http://www.berliner-zeitung.de/berlin/stasi-museum-tausende-kamen-in-mielkes-buero,10809148,11449646,item,1.html [date accessed 23 January 2012].

Geier, A. (2011) 'Mediating Immediacy: Historicizing the GDR by Bringing It Back to Life in Postmillenial Works of Fiction', in R. Rechtien and D. Tate (eds) *Twenty Years On: Competing Memories of the GDR in Postunification German Culture* (Rochester, NY: Camden House).

Hensel, J. (2002) *Zonenkinder* (Reinbek: Rowohlt).

Hodgin, N. and C. Pearce (eds) (2011) *The GDR Remembered: Representations of the East German State Since 1989* (Rochester, NY: Camden House).

Huyssen, A. (1995) *Twilight Memories: Marking Time in a Culture of Amnesia* (New York: Routledge).

Jones, S. (2011) 'At Home with the Stasi: Gedenkstätte Hohenschönhausen as Historic House', in D. Clarke and U. Wölfel (eds) *Remembering the German Democratic Republic: Divided Memory in a United Germany* (Basingstoke: Palgrave Macmillan).

Landsberg, A. (2004) *Prosthetic Memory: The Transformation of American Remembrance in the Age of Mass Culture* (Columbia: Columbia University Press).

Leeder, K. (ed.) (2009) 'From Stasiland to Ostalgie: The GDR Twenty Years After', *Oxford German Studies*, 38 (3).

Rechtien, R. and D. Tate (eds) (2011) *Twenty Years On: Competing Memories of the GDR in Postunification German Culture* (Rochester, NY: Camden House).

Rushdie, S. (1992) *Imaginary Homelands: Essays and Criticism 1981–1991* (London: Granta).

Sabrow, M. (ed.) (2009) *Erinnerungsorte der DDR* (Munich: Beck).

Sabrow, M., R. Eckert, M. Flacke, K.-D. Henke, R. Jahn, F. Klier, T. Krone, P. Maser, U. Poppe and H. Rudolph (eds) (2007) *Wohin treibt die DDR-Erinnerung? Dokumentation einer Debatte* (Göttingen: Vandenhoeck & Ruprecht).

Schlesinger, K. (2000) *Trug. Roman* (Berlin: Aufbau).

Schlußbericht der Enquete-Kommission (1998) 'Überwindung der Folgen der SED-Diktatur im Prozess der deutschen Einheit', 10 June, Drucksache 13/11000.

Thompson, P. (2009) ' "Die unheimliche Heimat": The GDR and the Dialectics of Home', in K. Leeder (ed.) 'From Stasiland to Ostalgie: The GDR Twenty Years After', *Oxford German Studies*, 38 (3), 278–287.

Williams, P. (2007) *Memorial Museums: The Global Rush to Commemorate Atrocities* (Oxford: Berg).

Part I

Theoretical Reflections

1
The GDR and the Memory Debate

Silke Arnold-de Simine and Susannah Radstone

This chapter will consider what it might mean to 'remember' the GDR after the fall of the Berlin Wall, setting out the theoretical concepts which have underpinned the discussions of the research network 'After the Wall: Reconstructing and Representing the GDR'. We will contextualise those theoretical concepts in a changing global landscape of remembrance in which understandings of what constitutes knowledge of the past and what it means to relate to the past in a meaningful way have shifted radically.

At face value the main concern in the fierce and often polemical debates surrounding the ways in which the GDR is remembered and represented in the public domain seems to be the question of 'historical accuracy': different memory communities accuse each other of not being able or prepared to face up to others', or indeed their own, past experiences of the GDR. This is paralleled in other debates that touch on the relations between history and memory, but for memory scholars interested in different practices, activities, forms and media of memory, it is only half the story: equally important is the question of why some aspects of the past are constantly revisited and discussed while others are purposefully repressed or involuntarily forgotten. Memory, in whichever form, is not a window onto the past; rather our vision of the past is constantly adapted to our needs in the present. Memory discourses mediate between our experience or knowledge of the past and the problems we face negotiating the present, and as such they are at the same time unreliable and yet significant (see Chapter 2). Memory research is therefore concerned with the analysis of memory narratives and debates with the aim of investigating the interpenetrative relationships between memory and identity, memory and social belonging, and memory and politics. Rather than being concerned with 'true history', memory research is interested in 'lived history' (Passerini, 1983, 1987; Portelli, 2003). To ask about 'memory' means to analyse how people experience, relate to and narrativise the past. This is one of the reasons why memory research opened up new directions in literary and film studies, approaching texts as 'memory texts' rather than as reflections, however mediated, of historical actuality. This does not imply that in studying memory, scholarship has given up on 'historical facts'; it means that in memory research, it is the processes by which individuals, communities and societies manufacture emotionally invested narratives of the past for themselves that are investigated and analysed.

Memory research does not focus exclusively either on the effects of the past on the present (determinist approach) or on the ways in which the present shapes understandings of the past (constructivist approach). Memory is understood to emerge through the mutual interactions of the past on the present *and* of the present on the past. Memory research does not simply complement more conventional historical approaches; it encourages reflection on our emotional and ideological investment in the past. Therefore it is inherently interdisciplinary, but at the same time concepts of memory cannot simply be translated or transferred either between disciplines or from one historical period to another: 'Memory has signified, and continues to signify, different phenomena in different historical situations, and within different theoretical or disciplinary paradigms' (Radstone and Schwarz, 2010: 7).

The so-called 'memory boom' (Huyssen, 1995) is more or less contemporaneous with the caesura on which this volume focuses: 'After the Wall' identifies a time before and a time after, and it suggests that special efforts are needed to bridge this particular temporal chasm. The 'memory boom' signifies a more general development in which, over recent decades, the prominence and significance of memory has risen across both the academy and culture. While western societies seem increasingly obsessed with relating to the past through the framework of memory, there is no shortage of criticism of what is seen by some as an excessive preoccupation with memory. For others the current concern with memory is best understood in relation to memory's increasing fragility. Following these analyses, recent history has been figured in relation to a series of losses, the corruption and decimation of memory (Terdiman, 1993). At the same time the engagement with memory also speculates on the possibilities for retrieval and redemption. Memory is seen by some as a redemptive force that can unlock a moment in the past. According to certain scholars, Walter Benjamin, whose work has had a profound influence on recent memory scholarship (Leslie, 2010), attributed a redemptive force to memory (Wolin, 1994), whereas others, such as Peter Osborne (1994: 87), refute this reading:

> Redemption itself, in the strict, absolute or Messianic sense, is not at stake. In this, Benjamin's later work remains steadfastly at one with his earlier writings, and with Scholem's nihilistic understanding of the Messianic idea. There is no redemption within historical time, only the redemption of history as a whole.

These divergent readings of Benjamin form part of a broader debate within which the alignment of memory with redemption is by no means unchallenged.

As the end of history has been proclaimed (through, for example, the concept of *posthistoire*; Baudrillard, 2001: 263) and the loss of historical consciousness deplored (Jameson, 1991), memory seems to have stepped into the breach and taken centre stage, both as a cultural preoccupation and, in consequence, as a theoretical concept in the humanities. However, according to critics such as Pierre Nora, 'we speak so much of memory because there is so little of it left' (1989: 7). This 'memory', which is the reaction to a perceived acceleration of time and to rapid change, is not even the genuine article (*milieux de memoire*). Rather, it is some kind of artificial substitute (*lieux de memoire*): modern society has become cut off from its past, and traditions are not 'organically' passed on but have to be 'artificially' recreated to be remembered, such as in museums or memorials.

Whatever the controversies around memory, there seems to be an agreement that the current academic preoccupation with memory emerges from an apparent paradox or contradiction: it is partly owing to the fear that memory is fragile and elusive, and therefore requires special efforts to be preserved, and partly to the sense that memory, rather than history, has become the dominant mode in which western societies relate to and frame the past *tout court* (Huyssen, 1995: 5). Pitting memory against history too absolutely risks setting up a false and oversimplified polarisation that sees history as striving for the ideals of analysis, criticism and intersubjective argumentation, and equates it with disinterested objectivity, detachedness and a clear distinction between past and present. From that point of view, relegating something completely to the realm of historical knowledge seems nothing short of shying away from an ethical responsibility towards the past. In addition, the memory boom is also linked to democratic renewal: by remembering their pasts, different groups, including minorities, are able to gain a voice, resulting in a plurality of memories in an expanded and possibly more democratic public sphere. But this development also creates different memory communities that promote their own narratives and fight for their recognition in the public realm.

The rise of memory in culture does not simply give voice to people's memories, provide exciting new projects in the memorial landscape or provoke new theories in memory research: it also presents scholars with a fresh set of questions. But instead of simply embracing the perspective of memory in academic work, scholars *of* the memory boom, and those deploying memory in diverse modes of theory and method, need to adopt a reflexive approach by questioning what the focus on memory reveals, while bearing in mind what it might screen. Thus, as suggested above, the tendency to pit memory *against* history, whether in action or in research, may come at the cost of screening areas of ambiguity.

In the second section of this chapter we move on to explore what memory research may contribute to studies of 'After the Wall'. We suggest that a memory studies perspective throws light, precisely, on the Wall's 'afterlife', understood as a dynamic process of remembering that can be grasped fully neither by a constructivist nor by a determinist analysis. We also suggest that, from the perspective of memory research, current disputes over memorialising the GDR find one context in the binarisms of memory discourses in general. Furthermore, we suggest that memory research enables an exploration of the instrumentalisation of memory, and sheds light on *Ostalgie*'s politics of desire. But before we can elaborate those arguments more fully, we need to address the question of memory beyond the personal.

Is there such a thing as 'collective memory'?

In everyday life as well as in scholarly approaches, the term 'memory' has more than one referent. Most commonly it stands for a neurophysiological capacity which resides with the individual and allows the recall of personal experiences which, if not preserved, will die along with the individual. But the term has also come to indicate a formation of social and cultural practices which extend individual memory beyond first-hand experiences (Cubitt, 2007: 1). At the beginning of the twentieth century, Maurice Halbwachs argued that there can be no neat separation between what he termed 'individual' and 'collective' memory: remembering is a social practice and individual memory can only be developed and fostered in a social context. In *Les Cadres sociaux de la mémoire* (1925), he explored the social construction and contextualisation of different forms of memory. Since the 1980s, when his theories were rediscovered, advocates, but also critics, have tried to build on and fine-tune his concept of 'collective memory'.[1] Some critics, such as Susan Sontag (2003) and Reinhard Koselleck (2004: 3), claim that only the individual neurophysiological capacity to remember should be called 'memory' and that it is misleading to talk about collective acts of 'remembering' when the term can at best only be used in a metaphorical sense and at worst creates a smoke screen for the political and ideological instrumentalisation of memory. Sontag suggests the term 'collective instruction' (Sontag, 2003: 76) rather than 'collective memory', which shifts the focus to questions about authority and ideology – that is, who is instructing, who is instructed and for what purpose? (Foucault, 1975). More recently, however, Olick *et al.* have defended the usefulness of the term 'collective memory'. Though they come close to replacing it with 'social memory' and though they argue that 'collective memory' may lack philosophical or operational precision (2011: 40), their retention of the term points back to the important insight bequeathed to us by Halbwachs that, given memory's social frameworks, 'the very distinction between the individual and social components of remembering ceases to make absolute sense.' (ibid.: 19).

Mediated representations constitute key dimensions of memory's social framework. Individual memories may refer to events witnessed – for example, on TV – which individuals did not live through, but to which they nevertheless relate in a personal and emotional way, treating them as meaningful stories which help them to define their identity, rather than as collectively constructed and acquired knowledge about the past. It seems that audiences are able to relate to certain representations, re-creations and re-enactments of the past in a way which creates not only knowledge but also a sense of belonging to a past which involves a strong emotional investment, sometimes to an extent that suggests the imaginative reliving of a past which was not even experienced first hand. In enabling individuals to transcend their life-span and feel a sense of attachment to the past, this kind of memory acquires an almost spiritual quality but has also been described as 'inauthentic' (Nora, 1989) or 'prosthetic' (Landsberg, 2004), depending on the theorist's more pessimistic or optimistic assessment of its function for the individual and for society.

Rather than being acquired through the first-hand experience of events, these memories are adopted and can therefore hardly grant the same sense of belonging as experiential, embodied memory – or can they? What happens when 'prosthetic memories' overwrite first-hand memories? Or is this simply an artificial division? Memory scholars are split between those who, having accepted the argument that there is a growing trend of memory acquisition, point to its potential to smooth out, or even erase, memories that might trouble a unified narrative of the nation (Burgoyne, 1997: 104–19) and those who think it provides a chance for empathic understanding and solidarity beyond one's own geographically and temporally limited communities (Landsberg, 2004). Public remembrance culture seems to be caught up in an ethical dilemma: to allow memories to fade away with their owners is deemed irresponsible and even a potential danger to democracy; but the decision to hang on to certain memories (and not to others) involves processes of identification, selection and mediation, which also pose ethical challenges.

The question of how we can legitimately lay claim to memories – our own or those of others – poses a problem for neuroscientists and psychologists, but it also has an ethical dimension. People who, for reasons of amnesia, trauma or repression, are dispossessed of their memories are faced with the problem of how they might recover and rightfully claim them. We can also be haunted by memories of events we did not live through: Marianne Hirsch (1997, 1999) introduced the term 'post-memory' for the second and third generations of Holocaust survivors who grew up with the legacy of the trauma, suggesting that post-memory can even extend beyond those who have familial links to the Holocaust. Like so many concepts in memory studies, this emerged in the context of Holocaust studies but soon gained a wider application. Individuals can be dispossessed of their family memories by a diasporic existence or by historical and ideological ruptures which stigmatise their memories as taboo. On the other side of the spectrum there is the issue of 'memory theft', a more or less conscious appropriation of memories that can include deceiving oneself or others about their genuineness. The issues around the ethics of memory appropriation have been explored in such diverse arenas as debates around false memory syndrome (e.g. Bruno Grosjean/Binjamin Wilkomirski's fictional memoir *Bruchstücke. Aus einer Kindheit 1939–1948*, 1995),[2] Hollywood films (e.g. Ridley Scott's *Blade Runner*, 1982/1992), and literary texts (e.g. W.G. Sebald's *Die Ausgewanderten*, 1992).[3] These examples have triggered discussions around questions of who has a right to certain memories, who is allowed to pass them on, and in which form they should, or can successfully, be passed on.

Memory scholars investigate very different things: how memories are generated on the level of individuals, groups, societies and nations, how they are constructed, transmitted and transformed by media and how, within all of these domains, they are reconstructed retrospectively according to present norms, aims, visions and projects. When analysing these social and cultural practices and texts by which a collectively shared sense of the past is being generated, negotiated and communicated, the concept of 'memory' that we are working with needs to be defined and the conceptual tools developed.

'Collective' or 'cultural memory' can only ever indicate memorial processes that pass through social formations. Some scholars navigate the grey zone between individual and collective memory by insisting on a clear separation between the two, locating the former firmly in the body and the latter in different kinds of media. We ought to distinguish between 'memory' as a capacity or activity on the one hand and as concrete practices or texts of memory, such as testimonies or memoirs, on the other (Radstone, 2005: 134). For Jan and Aleida Assmann, collective memory is constructed and passed on by social, political and cultural institutions and can therefore only exist in some kind of mediated form. According to Aleida Assmann (2008: 1), 'experiential memories are embodied and thus they cannot be transferred from one person to another'. But she also concedes that 'our personal memories include much more than what we, as individuals, have ourselves experienced' (Assmann, 2006: 211). For Assmann the terms 'collective' and 'cultural memory' denote ways in which human relationships with the past are actively constructed by social institutions 'with the aid of memorial signs such as symbols, texts, images, rites, ceremonies, places, and monuments' (Assmann, 2004: 26). She argues that we need to distinguish between

- the memories of an individual which are only shared with his/her immediate environment (communicative memory);
- collectively organised acts and public rites of commemoration (political memory);
- articulations and representations of memory which gain a wider forum in different cultural arenas in which they have different functions and are controversially discussed; and because they exist in material form, can be archived, 'rediscovered' and reinterpreted (cultural memory) (Assmann, 2006).

Although Assmann's terminology is useful for formulating research questions, these differentiations and classifications can at best function as heuristic tools.

Given that the contributions in this volume aim to explore how the political and the psychical, the public and the private, and individuals and society interact with and inform each other in processes of remembering the GDR, these heuristic distinctions might even stand in the way of such an approach. The phenomena studied do not usually fit into neat categories but instead occupy the interfaces between these clear distinctions. For example, personal memories are never strictly individual but are already shaped by internalised narrative patterns: according to Ansgar Nünning, autobiographical memory is as much an effect of 'genre memories' as it is a representation of past events (Nünning and Erll, 2006). Personal processes of remembering and medial representations of events and memories are intricately intertwined. There is a smooth transition between memories of events we witness in the flesh and experience first hand, and those we only see – for example, on television. This is complicated by the suggestion that the characteristically non-linear and condensed memory text already has an affinity with cinematic expression: 'Cinema, in other words, is peculiarly capable of enacting not only the very activity of remembering, but also ways of remembering that are commonly shared; it is therefore peculiarly capable of bringing together personal experiences and larger systems and processes of cultural memory' (Kuhn, 2010: 303). Whereas this blending together of things we hear, see and experience ourselves poses a problem for judges or indeed historians who are interested in accessing the genuine memories of witnesses and trying to confirm the veracity or indeed falsity of those memories, for others the capacity of media representations not only to mould memories but to create and generate them is seen as a chance to pass on memories to generations that have no first-hand experience of the events in question.

The differentiation between various media and the effect of their medial characteristics on the transmission of memory is central to a range of theories of cultural memory: Aleida Assmann's distinction between communicative, political and cultural memory, for example, is at least partly based on the different forms of mediation – that is, whether memories are transmitted orally or in written form through diaries and letters, film or literature, memorials or museums. Alison Landsberg's term 'prosthetic memory' (2004) suggests that cinema enables individuals to experience events through which they themselves did not live as if they were their own memories. Eric Santner's *Stranded Objects* (1993) describes how nations come to live with unassimilable pasts through the medium of cinema. Marianne Hirsch looks at how photographs transmit traumatic memories across generations and how this 'adoption' of memory is linked to 'locations' of memory, such as the family (1997). All of the issues raised so far – whether about the distinctions and overlap between personal and collective memory, the politics of memory transmission or the mediality of contemporary memory – are of direct relevance when we come to the question of remembering the GDR. Over the last two decades, indeed, questions concerning how the GDR is remembered, by whom, in what form, to what effect and in the service of which interests have, if anything, become increasingly fraught.

Remembering the GDR

Recent decades have seen major changes in the global landscape of remembrance: nations are increasingly required to remember not only times of glory or martyrdom but also difficult pasts which, though they do not inspire pride or positive identification, need to be worked through. With regard to Germany, unification has certainly contributed to complicating an already difficult situation: not only did East and West Germany have very different perceptions of the National Socialist past which needed to be negotiated, but the legacy of the GDR produced its own discourse of perpetrators and victims, a discourse which is also at times politically and ideologically instrumentalised to relativise National Socialist crimes and interpret the suffering of GDR citizens as a heroic sacrifice for unification.

In present-day Germany the state has a major investment in the way in which the GDR is remembered, not least because there is an understanding that people's political attitudes are based on the kind of memories which are fostered. According to Anselma Gallinat (Chapter 9), the assumption is that political education for democracy cannot simply rely on an official *Aufarbeitung* (reworking of the past) of the GDR by historians, but that the state has to make sure that the East German dictatorship is not downplayed in personal life-stories which portray the GDR through a nostalgic perspective. The split in GDR remembrance culture between what is considered everyday (n)ostalgia, on the one hand, and remembrance of the GDR as an *Unrechtsstaat* (illegitimate state) and dictatorship, on the other, tends to rely on the assumption that concern with everyday life in the GDR is at best a naïve sentimentalising and at worst an intentional banalising of the GDR past. The focus on the Wall, the Stasi and the repressive character of the state, however, is seen to form the basis for a critical and intellectually viable approach. This simplified distinction does not take into account the fact that both approaches have ideological implications, and it chooses to ignore the premise that 'the personal is always political'. In May 2006 a report with recommendations regarding the future of GDR remembrance culture and its institutions was published by an expert committee of enquiry, appointed by the Social Democratic Party (SPD/Sozialdemokratische Partei Deutschlands) – Green coalition (1998–2005). The committee was convened by the director of the Centre for Research on Contemporary History (Zentrum Für Zeithistorische Forschung) in Potsdam, Martin Sabrow, and consisted of scholars, experts in GDR history and members of the former GDR opposition movement. Among its recommendations the report suggested that there was a need for a stronger emphasis on memories of resistance and opposition (Sabrow, 2007: 9) – something the committee felt was underrepresented in the GDR memory landscape. It also criticised the 'trivialisation of the GDR' in the 'uncritical collection of GDR everyday culture' by the DDR-Museum (Berlin) and the Documentation Centre of Everyday Life in the GDR (Dokumentationszentrum Alltagskultur der DDR, Eisenhüttenstadt), advocating a new museum that would deal with everyday life in the GDR under the dictatorship (Sabrow, 2007: 20, 35). However, on publication, the committee was accused of '*Verniedlichung der DDR*' ('sentimentalising of the GDR') (Schwartz and Wentker, 2007: 373) and the new minister of culture under the Christian Democratic Union (CDU)–SPD grand coalition (2005–09), Bernd Neumann (CDU), distanced himself from the report. The inclusion of the very concept of everyday life in the so-called 'Sabrow Report' seemed to indicate to victims associations that an attempt was being made to trivialise life in the GDR.

Wherever one looks, GDR remembrance culture is framed in terms of neat polar opposites: *Alltag* versus *Unrechtsstaat*; consumer culture versus state oppression; *Ostalgie* versus political debate; *bunt* (colourful) versus *grau* (grey) (see Chapter 8); perpetrator versus victim; memory versus history. While these polarisations are partly driven by ideological and political interests, public funding strategies or the demands of tourism, and do not do justice to the multiple layers of memory at work in post-GDR society, they still form the dominant paradigm in public discourse. One can clearly see that state funding and media coverage both fuel this polarisation of the GDR memory debate.

However, this is not just evidence of a clash of interests between different memory communities or between a top-down official narrative (history) versus bottom-up personal stories (memory). We must ask ourselves whether modes of cultural/collective memory in general have the tendency to structure the past through such binaries. There are several indications that this might be the case: collective memory operates between the extremes of hyper-memory (*Hypermnesie*) on the one hand and amnesia on the other. Meanwhile, the centrality of the Holocaust within memory discourses *and* memory studies has meant that the dominant modes of memory are, or have been perceived as being, remembering that which has been 'done to', and remembering in order to come to terms with that 'doing'.[4] This bifurcation and binarism can stand in the way of thinking through the complexities and ambiguities of politics and can limit our capacity to grasp the grey areas between the 'done to' and the 'doing'. The fact that German as well as global memory culture is focused on perpetrator–victim narratives means that stories which conform to this narrative pattern are more likely to be heard. The problem is that this approach ignores what the Sabrow Report saw as the 'correlation between the regime and society ranging from acceptance to revolt, enthusiasm to disdain, discontented loyalty to "Nischenglück" (withdrawal from society into an environment of like minded people)' (Schwartz and Wentker, 2007: 373). The range of lived experience cannot be categorised in simple binaries: it proves to be much more complex and ambiguous.

To give a voice to the communicative memory of the people who experienced the GDR first hand seems to guarantee that marginalised and ambiguous memories as well as oppositional or counter-narratives can be heard and may even force revisions of larger historical narratives. But this also results in different *Erinnerungsgemeinschaften* (memory communities), which produce conflicting and at least partially incompatible memory narratives competing for public funding, for media attention and generally for endorsement in the public sphere. As a bottom-up discourse, communicative memory may appear preferable to an authoritative top-down version of the past, but the question of whose memories are validated is not only decided on the basis of historical authentication or ideological inclination but is also motivated by ethical criteria. According to Aleida Assmann, we should ask not only about the validity but also about the integrity of memories. What is their effect? Do they create and perpetuate hate and a desire for revenge or do they foster reconciliation and justice? Are they malign or benign?

> The issue is not only whether a collective memory construct is true or false, but also why it manages to convince [...] It is therefore no

longer the constructedness of a collective memory as such but the use to which it is put that has become the basis for investigation, evaluation, and critique.

(Assmann, 2008: 10)

And considering Sontag's critique of the concept of collective memory, we need to modify the question to: how are memories instrumentalised and whom do they benefit?

Some former GDR citizens who had suffered under the regime of the Socialist Unity Party of Germany (SED) want to make their memories of repression and opposition heard. To those memory communities, authentic places and objects serve to illustrate their stories and also – more importantly – to provide proof. The renaissance of certain GDR products, on the other hand, which started about ten years after unification, rested at least partly on their popularity with tourists (e.g. the *Ampelmännchen*, the green or red men on pedestrian traffic lights in the GDR) or with young Germans who had never experienced the GDR. Contrary to popular perceptions, *Ostalgie* is therefore by no means the equivalent of sentimental memories of everyday life in the GDR, and the term covers as much as it reveals (see Chapter 6).

With her notion of 'reflective nostalgia', Svetlana Boym challenges the assumption that nostalgia is necessarily an uncritical result of the failure to engage with one's history in a meaningful way. She argues that apart from a restorative function, in which a longing for something lost is expressed, nostalgia can also have a critical reflective function.[5] It is not simply a sentimental re-creation of the past but allows for a critical mediation between past and present in which multiple narratives can co-exist (see Chapter 7). As *Ostalgie* is also a phenomenon in western Germany, not only in the ex-GDR, this raises questions about what it might tell us about west German identity as well as about fears and hopes for reunified Germany. If reunification signifies on one level the triumph of the market and of global neo-liberalism, does *Ostalgie* indicate a yearning for a utopian third way, based on elements of a vanished past? Does its treasuring of threatened objects – the *Ampelmännchen,* for instance – betray a longing less for the 'security' fostered by an authoritarian state than for modes of identity less regulated by global capital? Perhaps, in fantasy, those *Ampelmännchen* walked more 'freely' than we do today, trapped in the (failing) market-place. Perhaps, too, it is their very 'non-belongingness' in the commodity world of the global market-place that renders *Ostalgie*'s objects – once the signifiers of deprivation and sameness – magical objects of desire. Nostalgia may speak of a desire, that is, not for the East German past but for modes of collectivity and politics whose *mise-en-scène*, strange as it may seem, is a memory landscape that once bespoke the negative of all that might be wished for, in and by the West: the once rejected becomes the apotheosis of desire.

Ostalgie is just one of several frameworks central to the way in which the GDR has been remembered, and in this chapter it has served as an example of how memory research allows us to question some established assumptions around GDR remembrance culture and to show the investments of West Germany and other countries in the memory of the GDR. The turbulent times being experienced in present-day Europe may remind those working in memory studies of Walter Benjamin's description of Klee's painting *Angelus Novus*, with its angel blown backwards by the storm of so-called progress as history's debris piles up (1968: 257–8). He suggests that it is in such stormy conditions that memory images might emerge anew: 'To articulate the past historically does not mean to recognize it "the way it really was" (Ranke). It means to seize hold of a memory as it flashes up at a moment of danger' (ibid.: 255). As we have suggested throughout this essay, to study memory is not to study the past. Rather, memory research seeks to trace the dynamics of lived past/present relations as they emerge and as they set terms for the future. If one thing is clear, it is surely that under the pressure of the European present, memories of the GDR will continue to be revised. In this account we hope we have offered some pointers towards understanding how memory research might begin to think about the meanings of such revisions and their import for the future. The questions we have raised will be revisited in the following chapters.

Notes

1. It is worth noting that Olick, Vinitzky-Seroussi and Levy (2011: 22) argue that an account of Halbwachs' influence should not be reduced to 'a simple forgetting followed by recovery'.
2. English translation: *Fragments* trans. John E. Woods, in Maechler (2001).
3. English translation: *The Emigrants*, trans. Michael Hulse (London: Harvill, 1996).
4. Antze and Lambek (1996: vii) comment on the 'central role that trauma and victimization have come to play within the politics of memory'. For example, the ritual of an apology indicating an admission of guilt, such as Bill Clinton's apology for slavery (1998) or, ten years later, Australia's prime minister Kevin Rudd's apology to the Aborigines, has become a recurring feature in world politics.

5. 'Restorative nostalgia puts emphasis on *nostos* and proposes to rebuild the lost home and patch up the memory gaps. Reflective nostalgia dwells in *algia*, in longing and loss, the imperfect process of remembrance [...] Restorative nostalgia manifests itself in total reconstruction of monuments of the past, while reflective nostalgia lingers on ruins, the patina of time and history, in the dreams of another place and another time' (Boym, 2001: 41).

References

Antze, P. and M. Lambek (1996) *Tense Past: Cultural Essays in Trauma and Memory* (London: Routledge).

Assmann, A. (2004) 'Four Formats of Memory: From Individual to Collective Constructions of the Past' in C. Emden and D. Midgley (eds) *Cultural Memory and Historical Consciousness in the German-Speaking World Since 1500* (Oxford: Lang), 19–37.

Assmann, A. (2006) 'Memory, Individual and Collective' in R. E. Goodin and C. Tilly (eds) *The Oxford Handbook of Contextual Political Analysis* (Oxford: Oxford University Press), 210–24.

Assmann, A. (2008) 'Transformations between History and Memory' in A. Mack (ed.) *Collective Memory and Collective Identity*, Special Issue of *Social Research*, 75 (1) (New York: The New School), 49–72.

Baudrillard, J. (2001) 'The Illusion of the End' in Mark Poster (ed.) *Jean Baudrillard: Selected Writings* (Stanford, CA: Stanford University Press), 254–65.

Benjamin, W. (1968) 'Theses on the Philosophy of History' in H. Arendt (ed.) *Illuminations* (New York: Schocken), 253–64.

Boym, S. (2001) *The Future of Nostalgia* (New York: Basic).

Burgoyne, R. (1997) *Film Nation: Hollywood Looks at US History* (Minneapolis, MN: Minnesota University Press).

Cubitt, G. (2007) *History and Memory* (Manchester: Manchester University Press).

Foucault, M. (1975) 'Film and Popular Memory': An Interview with Michel Foucault (trans. Martin Jordan), *Radical Philosophy*, 11, 24–9.

Hirsch, M. (1997) *Family Frames: Photography, Narrative and Postmemory* (Cambridge MA: Harvard University Press).

Hirsch, M. (1999) *The Familial Gaze* (Hanover: University Press of New England).

Huyssen, A. (1995) *Twilight Memories: Marking Time in a Culture of Amnesia* (New York: Routledge).

Jameson, F. (1991) *Postmodernism, or the Cultural Logic of Late Capitalism* (Durham: Duke University Press).

Koselleck, R. (2004) 'Gibt es ein kollektives Gedächtnis?', *Divinatio*, 19 (2), 1–6.

Kuhn, A. (2010) 'Memory Texts and Memory Work: Performances of Memory In and with Visual Media', *Memory Studies*, 3 (4), 298–313.

Landsberg, A. (2004) *Prosthetic Memory: The Transformation of American Remembrance in the Age of Mass Culture* (New York: Cambridge University Press).

Leslie, E. (2010) 'Siegfried Kracauer and Walter Benjamin: Memory from Weimar to Hitler' in S. Radstone and B. Schwarz (eds) *Memory: Histories, Theories, Debates* (New York: Fordham University Press), 123–35.

Maechler, S. (2001), *The Wilkomirski Affair: A Study in Biographical Truth* (New York: Schocken).

Nora, P. (1989) 'Between Memory and History: Les Lieux de Memoire', *Representations*, 26, 7–24.

Nünning, A. and A. Erll (2006) 'Concepts and Methods for the Study of Literature and/as Cultural Memory' in A. Nünning, M. Gymnich and R. Sommer (eds) *Literature and Memory: Theoretical Paradigms, Genres, Functions* (Tübingen: Narr), 11–28.

Olick, J.K., V. Vinitzky-Seroussi and D. Levy (eds) (2011) *The Collective Memory Reader* (Oxford: Oxford University Press).

Osborne, P. (1994) 'Small-scale Victories, Large-scale Defeats: Walter Benjamin's Politics of Time' in A. Benjamin and P. Osborne (eds) *Walter Benjamin's Philosophy: Destruction and Experience* (London: Routledge), 59–109.

Passerini, L. (1983) 'Memory', *History Workshop Journal*, 15 (Spring), 195–6.

Passerini, L. (1987) *Fascism in Popular Memory* (Cambridge: Cambridge University Press).

Portelli, A. (2003) *The Order Has Been Carried Out: History, Memory, and Meaning of a Nazi Massacre in Rome*. English translation (New York: Palgrave Macmillan).

Radstone, S. (2005) 'Reconceiving Binaries: The Limits of Memory', *History Workshop Journal*, 59 (Spring) (Special Feature: 'Rethinking Memory'), 134–50.

Radstone, S. and B. Schwarz (eds) (2010) *Memory. Histories, Theories, Debates* (New York: Fordham University Press).

Sabrow, M. (2007) 'Die Empfehlungen der Expertenkommission zur Schaffung eines Geschichtsverbundes "Aufarbeitung der SED-Diktatur"' in M. Sabrow, R. Eckert, M. Flacke, K.-D. Henke, R. Jahn, F. Klier, T. Krone, P. Maser, U. Poppe, and H. Rudolf (eds) *Wohin treibt die DDR-Erinnerung? Dokumentation einer Debatte* (Göttingen: Vandenhoeck & Ruprecht), 17–45.

Santner, E. (1993) *Stranded Objects* (Chicago: Chicago University Press).

Schwartz, M. and H. Wentker (2007) 'Erinnerungspolitik auf dem Holzweg. Zu den Empfehlungen der Expertenkommission für eine künftige "Aufarbeitung der SED-Diktatur"' in M. Sabrow, R. Eckert, M. Flacke, K.-D. Henke, R. Jahn, F. Klier, T. Krone, P. Maser, U. Poppe, and H. Rudolf (eds) *Wohin treibt die DDR-Erinnerung? Dokumentation einer Debatte* (Göttingen: Vandenhoeck & Ruprecht), 369–74.

Sontag, S. (2003) *Regarding the Pain of Others* (New York: Penguin).

Terdiman, R. (1993) *Present Past: Modernity and the Memory Crisis* (Ithaca, NY: Cornell University Press).

Wolin, R. (1994) *Walter Benjamin: An Aesthetic of Redemption* (Berkeley, CA: University of California Press).

2

Selective Memory: Channelling the Past in Post-GDR Society

Patricia Hogwood

Collective memory, comprising the ways in which the past is perceived, shared, and constructed through daily interactions, ceremonial, or negative manifestations such as taboo, has become a focus for scholarship that crosses disciplinary boundaries within the humanities and social sciences. This chapter points to some potential new avenues for memory research using insights from different disciplines. Specifically, it draws on political science approaches, together with those from cognate social science disciplines, to examine ways in which current memory research on the GDR might usefully be supplemented. Adopting an alternative perspective on some of the common assumptions and themes in GDR memory research helps us to reassess the analytical priorities of the field and to explore alternative research methodologies and agendas. It is well beyond the scope of this chapter to present a comprehensive catalogue of political science approaches to the challenge of remembering the GDR; themes have therefore been selected to highlight different ways in which a political science perspective may inform contemporary debates in GDR memory research. These include the temporal perspective of political science; the significance of memory for society; the construction of memory collectives; the contextualisation of memory in identity formation; and constructions of victimhood. The chapter suggests a path-dependence approach as one potential platform for the combination of memory studies approaches with insights from social science disciplines. It concludes with a contribution to the 'normalisation' debate, illustrated by 'evidenced behaviour' of the way memories of the GDR influence east German consumer behaviours.

Politics and memory in post-GDR society

While asking the same set of questions as other contributions in this volume, this chapter adopts assumptions and priorities typical of the discipline of political science. For example, the temporal perspective of the chapter lies firmly in the present and future. Rather than seeking to understand the GDR past in its own right, the aim here is to understand the construction and characteristics of memory collectives that draw on the GDR heritage, together with their implications for contemporary social identities and relations within united Germany. Memories of the GDR past may subconsciously influence individuals and collectives in their interactions with the present-day realities of the FRG. Alternatively, they may be consciously deployed as a resource in contemporary political agendas. Different memory collectives will construct alternative GDR histories to shore up their own identities and justify their political choices and aims for the future. As Anselma Gallinat stresses (see Chapter 9), since German unification political elites have given high priority to establishing an official history of the Socialist Unity Party (SED) regime in the GDR, because this forms a central plank in the democratisation project for the new Germany. The significance of establishing an official discourse is enhanced because of its role in legitimising the new 'Berlin' Republic. Political science's forward-looking perspective, together with its interest in strategies, projects and agendas, marries well with this volume's aim of applying lessons from memory research to current and future developments in east Germany.

One feature of memory research into the GDR past is its preoccupation with the reliability of memory, its validity and integrity. This owes much to the early development of memory studies by historians (e.g. Winter, 2000; Schulze, 2004). In using memory as methodology, a discipline grounded in a documentary research tradition may be expected to prioritise the verifiability of sources. While this preoccupation has led to some fruitful methodological developments, its tendency to produce fragmented and often conflicting findings can be frustrating for the researcher and slow the development of knowledge in the field. Seen from a political scientist's perspective, the significance of memory is quite different. Rather than looking to capture and represent the integrity of memory, political scientists look to the influences memory exerts on political identity, social values, modes of participation, and institutional and policy design. In the words of Confino and Fritzsche's seminal study, the essential question is 'how memory *forms* social relations – as opposed to the traditional way of asking how memory represents social relations' (2002: 5, italics in original).[1] From this perspective, the accuracy or otherwise of memory is less significant than its impact on individual and group behaviours and decision-making. In this way, memory can be perceived as mediating between historical experience and contemporary behaviours. Individual or shared memories exert an indirect or mediated impact on collective behaviours. This perspective allows the researcher to accept that memory can be simultaneously unreliable and potentially very significant in social and political development. We can acknowledge that it is not memory preserved intact that drives social and political development, but rather 'selective memory': a distillation of perceptions and constructs that might correspond to a greater or lesser extent to lived experience.

Accepting the flawed nature but potentially significant impact of memory on social identity and development opens memory research to bolder experimentation with methodologies and analytical approaches. For example, from a political scientist's perspective, the focus of enquiry in memory research shifts from recounted memories of 'experienced' life to what we can learn about what is remembered, treasured, tacitly avoided or openly rejected through 'evidenced' behaviour. Instead of working with what individuals can recall or what they choose to tell of their memories, the researcher can observe the way that memories of the past influence actual patterns of contemporary behaviour. In examining the decisions and actions of individuals within a collective context, a focus on evidenced behaviour combines two advantages. First, it helps to establish the relative importance of memory in influencing such behaviours compared with other contextual factors. Second, it tends to yield findings with potential for wider application than the immediate research context.

Moreover, political science adopts a particular perspective on the nature and construction of a 'collective'. It is perhaps self-evident and yet important to stress that, for political scientists, a collective is an inherently political phenomenon, defined and delineated around political values and the pursuit of political aims. Distinguishing political collectives is no straightforward matter, as within a political community many collectives may co-exist and interact with one another. Some may overlap; some may be nested within others. Some may cohabit quite comfortably while others conflict. This volume focuses on the problems and opportunities presented by remembering the GDR for the development of the 'new' political community of the post-1990 FRG. The FRG is a polity linked by common historical bonds and now by a common legal and institutional framework, but marked internally by the legacies of a 40-year ideological state division. The ideological, geopolitical and historical circumstances of German unification have essentially precluded a truly objective debate on the GDR past (Herbert, 1998: 387–8; Sa'adah, 1998: 107; Beattie, 2008: 2). Instead, these unique circumstances have given rise to a highly politicised and conflicted public memory discourse rooted in the east-west divide of the Cold War years.[2] This chapter simplifies the complex relationships involved by reducing the political 'memory collectives' under consideration to three. It considers how memories of the past are channelled in contemporary post-GDR society through the political communities of: post-GDR or east German citizens; west German citizens; and the post-1990 FRG state. In fact, two other 'silent' players are involved: the GDR state and the National Socialist state. Although now defunct, the varied forms of self-construction deployed by the GDR state during its lifetime are still drawn actively into the discourses and debates of the three 'active' memory collectives. In practice, this has enhanced an inherent asymmetry of power relations in the post-GDR memory debate. Although not identical in terms of their interests and strategies, the memory collectives of the post-1990 FRG state and of west German citizens tend to be mutually reinforcing. On the other hand, east Germans often experience, construct and evaluate memories of the GDR quite differently from west Germans and the FRG state. Since the demise of the GDR, these eastern popular discourses have lacked an equivalent state 'partner' to reinforce their political weight. This asymmetry is particularly significant given that not only the substantive memories of the GDR past are contested, but also the legitimacy of the key memory collectives' interpretations of that past. The ideological divisions of the Cold War years have superimposed on the contemporary memory debate the question of which of these three memory collectives has the right to interpret the GDR past. East German evaluations of the SED regime may be contested because of their presumed lack of objective distance; west German evaluations because of their presumed 'colonial' perspective and ideological triumphalism. Given the experience of National Socialism and the conflicts of 'negative remembrance' (Schulze, 2004: 640), some may still question any moral judgement German commentators make on other regimes. For its part, the FRG state has explicitly questioned the legality of the SED and remains preoccupied with the question of SED repression. In the 1990s, two successive parliamentary commissions of enquiry were launched to investigate the legacy of the SED state. Their titles alone signalled quite unambiguously the ideological bias of the investigations. The first (1992) was titled 'Working through the history and consequences of the SED dictatorship in Germany' and the second (1995) 'Overcoming the consequences of the SED dictatorship in the process of German unity'. While these were represented as institutional channels for transitional justice, they also provided a forum at state level for the renegotiation of inner German political power relations and identities (Sa'adah, 1998: 119–27; Ross, 2002: 176, 184–91; Beattie, 2008: 13). Inevitably, this institutionalisation of the post-GDR reconciliation debate has biased the resulting discourses in favour of western-oriented, state interpretations. Further, in the absence of an eastern state counterpart, the FRG state has been free to access the negative legacy of the National Socialist regime in order to delegitimise the memory of the GDR state, and frequently, by extension, popular memories of life in the GDR. Western discourses frequently assert a 'double burden' of collusion by east Germans, first with the National Socialist regime and secondly with the SED state. Another factor that entrenches asymmetric power relations between the western memory collectives on the one hand and the east German popular memory collective on the other is the fact that east Germans demonstrate a highly ambivalent relationship both to their GDR state heritage and to the west German 'reference culture' that frames the post-1990 FRG (Hogwood, 2002). These characteristics of asymmetry and ambivalence are central to memory discourses on the GDR. Although problematic in many ways, the highly politicised channelling of the post-GDR memory landscape offers some interesting insights into the construction of memory. In particular, it highlights the normative construction of collective memory; its mutability; and the selective nature of memory discourses at state level. This selectivity of collective memory is particularly interesting, as it reinforces the idea that it is not so much the objective and comprehensive documentation of memories that influences social identities and behaviours, but rather the dominant interpretations of memories.

A strength of social science perspectives more generally is a concern with the contextualisation and comparison of research findings. Memory research tends towards introspection and this can distract researchers' attention from very significant external constraints both on the construction of memory and on behaviours prompted by memory. One example is the commodification of memory through the phenomenon of so-called *Ostalgie* (see Chapter 6). Western discourses have a tendency to universalise this phenomenon, equating it with all things east German. However, this perception should not be carried over unquestioningly into research design (Neller, 2006: 16). It would be inappropriate to assume a priori that all recollections of everyday life in the GDR can be interpreted as manifestations of *Ostalgie*. This would almost certainly overstate the significance of *Ostalgie* in the lives of east Germans. Contextualisation and comparison help the researcher to make analytical distinctions between the phenomenon of *Ostalgie* as it is experienced in the post-GDR setting; similar phenomena experienced under conditions of post-socialist transition in other countries (e.g. Linz and Stepan, 1996; Plasser and Pribersky, 1996; Mischler and Rose, 2002; Todorova, 2010); and the quite general 'lifecycle' nostalgia widely manifested in post-industrial societies: a cross-cultural expression of individuals' relationships with consumer products and artefacts at formative stages of their lives. In this vein, the author Reinhard Ulbrich has contested interpretations of his post-GDR novel *Spur der Broiler* (*Trace of Broiled Chicken*, 1999) as an *Ostalgie* book. For him, it is simply a book about growing up (Twark, 2007: 143). What differentiates and intensifies the phenomenon of *Ostalgie* in the post-GDR setting is the very unusual political context in which it operates. The commodification of *Ostalgie*, particularly through consumer goods, embodies the ambivalence of the social and political relationship of the two Germanys (Hogwood, 2011). It is lent exaggerated significance and emotional resonance by the fact of the formal dissolution of the GDR, leaving *Ostalgie* items as relics of a past with a finite end point. It is *Ostalgie* in this specific sense that constitutes a unique influence in post-GDR identities.

Many researchers have noted the dominance of so-called 'trauma' studies in the field of memory research. Nowhere is this more evident than in German studies. Some of the key texts in memory research have been devoted to the remembrance of the Holocaust or of Germany's National Socialist past more generally (e.g. Maier, 1988; Danyel, 1995; Herf, 1997; Kattago, 2001). Trauma studies have made a major contribution to the way people remember the past as a community, particularly through the family and through institutional channels for the (re)construction of collective memory (e.g. Welzer, Moller and Tschuggnall, 2002). They have also been pivotal in the development of key concepts relating to the experience and construction of memory, such as 'victimhood' and 'normalisation'. It is not surprising, therefore, that researchers have turned to such studies in examining the liminal conditions brought about by the rapid dissolution of the normative, legal and economic structures of the GDR and the encapsulation of the post-GDR democracy project within an ideologically opposed west German 'reference culture'. However, it is important to consider the applicability to current contexts of some of the key concepts emerging from this classic literature. The concepts of victimhood and normalisation, while certainly relevant to understanding memories of the past in contemporary east German society, should first be analytically decoupled from the National Socialist period of history and recast for the contemporary context of post-socialist transition.

At an analytical level, rather than assuming victimhood almost as an inherent attribute of specific groups, a researcher should allow for more differentiated understandings. It is important to ask whether GDR citizens did or did not perceive themselves as victims of their state; and if so, who saw themselves as victims, to what degree, and in what contexts. In the literature of German studies, evidence abounds of the human rights abuses suffered by individuals and groups at the hands of the SED state. However, the majority of East Germans neither engaged strongly with the regime nor strongly opposed it, but were able to reconcile themselves to a life within the parameters of state ideology and rules (Ahbe, 2005: 44). In post-GDR society, then, perceived victimisation at the hands of the state cannot be assumed to have been a universal, nor even a majority experience. Among east Germans, both the experience and evaluation of victimhood may prove to be quite differentiated. Whereas those who suffered human rights abuses will be readily acknowledged as victims of the state, should those who, for example, experienced constraints on their freedom to travel or to choose a career also be seen as victims of a kind?

The issue of victimhood demonstrates how different disciplinary perspectives and research methods can influence the ways in which memories are reported and evaluated. This is significant, since different representations of past victimhood, if incorporated into official discourses, can carry different implications for the way in which the concept is used as a political resource in a post-transition regime. Methodologies favoured by memory research such as subject-led interviews and focus groups may have contributed to the dominant perception in the literature of victimhood as essentially a group phenomenon. This perception carries an implication of an enduring fragmentation of post-GDR identity. First, it risks perpetuating unbridgeable divisions between self- or state-designated victim groups in east Germany and those east Germans who, simply by their exclusion from these groups, may be deemed to have passively colluded with an oppressive GDR state. Secondly, with victim groups' social identity rooted in the past, individuals who perceive themselves as part of a group victimised by the SED state may experience greater difficulties in adapting to new social realities than those who do not categorise themselves in this way.

As such, a group-based perspective suggests that victimhood is a definitive influence on east German society and identity. Political science's preoccupation with regime change and democratic transition offers a contrasting perspective on victimhood in the GDR. Studies of regime transition perceive victimhood essentially as a temporal phenomenon linked to regime characteristics. Moreover, according to some interpretations at least, victimhood can be seen as a transitory phenomenon. In the FRG, a centre-right interpretation viewed German unification under FRG terms as a liberation of the east Germans, whereas an alternative leftist interpretation viewed it as a disgraceful 'colonisation' by an ideologically hostile FRG state. The former interpretation suggested that liberation from SED oppression would promote all-German social integration; the latter that the imposition of western hegemony in united Germany amounted to a new and universal form of state victimisation of east Germans, reflected in their status as 'second class citizens'. Either way, in contrast to group constructs of victimhood, concepts of victimhood as a temporal phenomenon linked to regime change do not carry the same implications for a future east German society divided by identities forged around resistance and de facto collusion.

A path-dependence approach offers one possible way in which future research on post-GDR normalisation might combine memory studies with cross-disciplinary insights. In analytical terms, path dependence has distinct advantages for a study of the adaptation of identities under the conditions of transition determined by German unification. It allows the researcher to distinguish between the entrenchment of individual and collective values and to analyse change in these values in response to new circumstances. The elaboration of path-dependence approaches, particularly within the disciplines of economics and psychology, has highlighted the cognitive processes by which individuals and groups engage with the selection and consolidation of alternatives. These insights enable a researcher to evaluate individual choices and responses within a wider context of collective identities. This potential for linkage of individual behaviour with developments in collective norms is essential, since the development of values and expressions of self-legitimation in society takes place in a collective context involving continuous self-reinforcement. Identities and interests are learned, sustained, contested and adapted through interaction (Blumer, 1969; Wendt, 1999: 184–9, 331; Ross, 2009: 140). Given the context of the radical social change experienced by east Germans, a further advantage of the approach is its overt consideration of the time context in which large-scale social changes occur relative to one another (Pierson,

2004: 12). Moreover, it can be applied to developments in the construct of ideational and knowledge frameworks (Ingrao and Israel, 1990; Hall, 1993; Jolink and Vromen, 2001).[3] Within the social sciences an emerging institutionalist literature, based on the work of economists, is seeking to construct analytically rigorous conceptual tools for explaining processes of path dependence in social settings (e.g. Pierson, 2004: 22; Levi, 2009: 119–21).

German memory collectives and post-GDR 'normalisation'

Through unification and the 'inner unity' project, west German elites and policymakers have consistently posited post-GDR normalisation as a trajectory that simply replicates the FRG's post-National Socialist democratisation and cultural development. The memory collective of the FRG state views normalisation as a learning experience with its end point in the seamless assimilation of east German popular culture into the west German paradigm. To this end it has established a range of 'command' structures (see John, Smith and Stoker, 2009: 368) which include the FRG's common legal framework and the parliamentary commissions of enquiry noted above. The manipulation of memories of the GDR can be seen as a policy tool which has been quite prominent in the state's pursuit of inner unity. The FRG state has adopted a dual approach combining the promotion of memories of the 'crimes' of the SED regime with what Connerton terms the 'prescriptive forgetting' of its norms and achievements (Connerton, 2008: 61–2). Combining the cultivation of negative memories of the GDR regime with the delegitimation of more positive memories will, it is hoped, encourage the development of an all-German identity grounded in western sociopolitical norms. However, even if this aim were uncontested, writers from a range of disciplines including politics, geography and sociology suggest that a linear developmental 'progression' to a western ideal may not be realisable. There is evidence to suggest that aspects of western models may be resisted or revised according to the needs of the community undergoing transition (Smith and Jehlička, 2007: 395). Certainly, no other post-socialist transition has been framed by direct incorporation into the legal and institutional framework of a western state. Nor has any post-transition community been as directly influenced by a western reference culture as the east Germans. These factors may point to a more successful transference of western norms than elsewhere in the former Soviet systems. Nevertheless, rather than anticipating that developments in post-GDR society will inevitably conform to a western paradigm of normality, the researcher should question what the benchmarks of normality might be for post-GDR society. To what extent is east German society learning from west German or other external reference cultures and to what extent is it setting its own goals and aspirations in accordance with its own civic memories and social norms? Also, questions of normalisation should be considered not only in relation to the past – notably the National Socialist and SED regimes – but also to the post-1990 adaptation to late-capitalist economic structures.

In the 20 years since German unification, east Germans have surprised observers with the speed and confidence with which they have adapted to the new economic structures and pressures that frame their lives. In particular, east Germans have enthusiastically embraced western consumer culture. This ready adaptation provides a unique opportunity for the researcher to observe, through the evidenced behaviour of consumer spending levels, patterns and preferences, ways in which cultural memory is informing individual and collective responses to the liminal experience of transition. This body of evidence offers a fascinating insight into the conflicts over unification experienced by east Germans.[4] In the east, German unification was initially greeted with elation and the celebration of all things western. This was reflected in a strong consumer preference for west German products, from the most basic daily food items to luxury goods that had not been easily available in the GDR. However, shortly after unification there was a sharp economic downturn, which brutally confronted east Germans with previously unexperienced disadvantages of a market economy. The impact of the rapid shift from a sense of liberation and unbounded opportunity to one of intense vulnerability and even betrayal by the FRG state has been described as a 'second *Wende*' (following the *Wende* or transition represented by German unification) (Mackat, 2007: 49). East Germans used their purchasing power to register a political protest: the mood of the people was reflected in the collective consumer response of a return to eastern products and, in particular, a new demand for *Ostalgie* products. This consumer revolt soon moderated, but the spending preferences of eastern consumers have since revealed an ambiguous relationship to west German consumer culture. At the level of aggregate spending and in terms of spending in specific market sectors (such as food and drink, household goods and maintenance, leisure, etc.) the current consumer profile of east Germans closely mirrors that of west Germans in almost every respect. It appears that east Germans are using consumer spending to approximate a west German lifestyle. At the same time, east Germans differ markedly from west Germans in their brand preferences and responses to advertising. They choose different brands from west German consumers. They respond more positively to advertising messages that convey traditional 'socialist' values or the functional value of the goods advertised, rather than the social status conferred by conspicuous consumption (Ahbe, 2005: 46–7; Mackat, 2007: 17–19, 111–12). These factors suggest the development of a consumer culture at once framed by the west German 'model' and differentiated from it in ways that suggest a conscious link with a past socialist heritage.

At the more general level of identity formation, these findings imply that the emerging east German memory collective actively relates positive memories of life under the GDR to the new realities of life under united Germany. Instead of accepting the specific combination of selective memories and 'prescriptive forgetting' disseminated by the FRG state, the east German memory collective selects its memories on its own terms. East Germans retain an emotional attachment to norms learned under the GDR, such as sociability and social interaction (McFalls, 1999: 11–13). They retain memories that recall such positive values because these help individuals to manage the cognitive dissonances of transition from socialism to capitalism. These selected memories contribute to a distinctive identity distinguished by ambivalence in relation to the west German 'norm'. At the same time, east Germans must 'forget' both that set of civic values inculcated by the GDR state and the ideological hostility once levelled at the former FRG, as these are incompatible with the life skills needed to flourish under the FRG's capitalist, liberal democratic system. With this, the east German memory collective embodies the type of forgetting 'that is constitutive in the formation of a new identity' (Connerton, 2008: 62–3). As Connerton explains, this type of 'forgetting' should not be understood as a loss. Instead, it represents an active and constructive choice to discard memories that no longer serve any useful purpose and that might even obstruct the development of new identities and aims. This combination of remembering and forgetting suggests that the emerging post-GDR identity is essentially forward-looking: that memories of the GDR are selected and reconstructed in order to secure survival under new social and economic conditions. Moreover, it suggests that 'normalisation' in the former GDR will not follow the path envisaged by western state elites. The learning process involved in normalisation will not be a top-down process directed by political elites, but will instead be constructed by the east Germans themselves through a continuous process of selection and rejection of memories supporting positive identities and life chances under conditions of late capitalism.

Conclusion

In conclusion, political science and cognate disciplines have much to contribute to the development of memory research into the GDR. They help to demonstrate the essential selectivity of memory transference, particularly under conditions of regime change. Memory collectives emerge as highly normative and mutable constructs, incorporating mutually reinforcing 'remembered' and 'forgotten' details of the past that serve to justify today's political priorities. Memory collectives embody differential selections of remembered and forgotten details that form a basis for different interpretations and future-oriented collective agendas. A balance between remembering – whether personal, social or institutionalised – and tacit silence around 'forgotten' details is essential in managing the cognitive dissonances in the transition from an old political rationale to a new one (Connerton, 2008: 63). In relation to the post-GDR context, a political science perspective highlights the significance of asymmetric power relations between the memory collectives of the FRG state and west German citizens on the one hand, and the east German citizens – who lack a state 'partner' – on the other. Moreover, the chapter has highlighted that the way in which key terms for debate are constructed – including *Ostalgie*, victimhood and normalisation – can have profound implications for research design and for the interpretation of research findings. Social science approaches suggest, as a supplement to traditional methods in memory research, the use of 'evidenced behaviours' to assess the impact of memory on contemporary society. A path-dependence approach offers one possible vehicle for combining memory research with insights from social science disciplines. With its conceptual potential for examining the impact of memory under conditions of large-scale social change and the transference of memory influences from the individual to the collective level, path dependence presents interesting opportunities for developing contemporary debates on GDR memory.

Notes

1. Confino and Fritzsche (2002: 5) supply a useful definition of memory as 'a symbolic representation of the past embodied in social action'.
2. For a good overview of the internal partisan divisions within these east-west camps, see Beattie (2008).
3. The notion of path dependence has more typically been applied to nuts-and-bolts studies of institutionalisation and technological innovation, or alternatively to processes of regime change. For applications to institutionalisation

processes, see, for example Stefes (2010). For applications to technological innovation see, for example, David (1985); Arthur (1989, 1994). For applications to processes of regime change see, for example, Collier and Collier (1991).
4. Here and following, see P. Hogwood (2012).

References

Ahbe, T. (2005) *Ostalgie. Zum Umgang mit der DDR-Vergangenheit in den 1990er Jahren* (Berlin: Bundeszentrale für politische Bildungsarbeit Berlin).
Arthur, W. B. (1989) 'Competing Technologies and Lock-In by Historical Small Events', *Economic Journal*, 99 (March), 116–31.
Arthur, W. B. (1994) *Increasing Returns and Path Dependence in the Economy* (Ann Arbor, MI: University of Michigan Press), 1–12.
Beattie, A. H. (2008) *Playing Politics with History. The Bundestag Enquiries into East Germany* (New York: Berghahn).
Blumer, H. [1969] (1986) *Symbolic Interactionism: Perspective and Method* (Berkeley, CA: University of California Press).
Collier, R. B. and D. Collier (1991) *Shaping the Political Agenda: Critical Junctures, the Labor Movement, and Regime Dynamics in Latin America* (Princeton, NJ: Princeton University Press).
Confino, A. and P. Fritzsche (eds) (2002) *Work of Memory: New Directions in the Study of German Memory and Culture* (Urbana, IL: University of Illinois Press).
Connerton, P. (2008) 'Seven Types of Forgetting', *Memory Studies*, 1 (1), 59–71.
Danyel, J. (ed.) (1995) *Die Geteilte Vergangenheit: Zum Umgang Mit Nationalsozialismus und Widerstand in Beiden Deutschen Staaten* (Berlin: Akademie).
David, P. A. (1985) 'Clio and the Economics of QWERTY', *American Economic Review*, 75 (2), 332–7.
Hall, P. (1993) 'Policy Paradigms, Social Learning, and the State: The Case of Economic Policymaking in Britain', *Comparative Politics*, 25 (3), 275–96.
Herbert, U. (1998) 'Drei deutsche Vergangenheiten: Über den Umgang mit der deutschen Zeitgeschichte' in A. Bauerkämper, M. Sabrow and B. Stöver (eds) *Doppelte Zeitgeschichte: Deutsch-deutsche Beziehungen 1945–1990* (Bonn: Dietz).
Herf, J. (1997) *Divided Memory: The Nazi Past in the Two Germanys* (Cambridge MA: Harvard University Press).
Hogwood, P. (2002) ' "Red is for Love . . . ": citizens as consumers in East Germany' in J. Grix and P. Cooke (eds) *East German Distinctiveness in a Unified Germany* (Edgbaston: University of Birmingham Press).
Hogwood, P. (2011) 'The 'Ostalgia' Trap? Ostalgia and the Ambivalence of Inner German Relations in East Germany's Path to 'Normality' ', Political Studies Association (PSA) Annual Conference, London, 19–21 April 2011.
Hogwood, P. (2012) 'Political (Re)Learning and Consumer Culture in Post-GDR Society', *German Politics*, 21 (1), 1–16.
Ingrao, B. and G. Israel (1990) *The Invisible Hand: Economic Equilibrium in the History of Science* (Cambridge, MA: MIT Press).

John, P., G. Smith and G. Stoker (2009) 'Nudge Nudge, Think Think. Two Strategies for Changing Civic Behaviour', *The Political Quarterly*, 80 (3), 361–70.
Jolink, A. and J. J. Vromen (2001) 'Path Dependence in Scientific Evolution' in P. Garrouste and S. Ioannides (eds) *Evolution and Path Dependence in Economic Ideas: Past and Present* (Cheltenham: Edward Elgar).
Kattago, S. (2001) *Ambiguous Memory: The Nazi Past and German National Identity* (Westport: Praeger).
Levi, M. (2009) 'Reconsiderations of Rational Choice in Comparative and Historical Analysis' in M. I. Lichbach and A. S. Zuckerman (eds) *Comparative Politics. Rationality, Culture and Structure*, 2nd edn (Cambridge: Cambridge University Press).
Linz, J. J. and A. Stepan (1996) *Problems of Democratic Transition and Consolidation. Southern Europe, South America and Post-Communist Europe* (Baltimore, MA: Johns Hopkins University Press).
Mackat, A. (2007) *Das Deutsch-Deutsche Geheimnis* (Berlin: Superillu).
Maier, C. S. (1988) *The Unmasterable Past: History, Holocaust and German National Identity* (Cambridge MA: Harvard University Press).
McFalls, L. (1999) 'Eastern Germany Transformed. From Postcommunist to Late Capitalist Political Culture', *German Politics and Society*, 17 (2), 1–24.
Mischler, W. and R. Rose (2002) 'Learning and Re-Learning Regime Support: the Dynamics of Post-Communist Regimes', *European Journal of Political Research*, 41, 5–6.
Neller, K. (2006) *DDR-Nostalgie. Dimensionen der Orientierungen der Ostdeutschen gegenüber der ehemaligen DDR, ihre Ursachen und politischen Konnonationen* (Wiesbaden: VS Verlag für Sozialwissenschaften).
Pierson, P. (2004) *Politics in Time. History, Institutions and Social Analysis* (Princeton: Princeton University Press).
Plasser, F. and A. Pribersky (eds) (1996) *Political Culture in East Central Europe* (Aldershot: Avebury).
Ross, C. (2002) *The East German Dictatorship: Problems and Perspectives in the Interpretation of the GDR* (London: Hodder Arnold).
Ross, M. H. (2009) 'Culture in Comparative Political Analysis' in M. I. Lichbach and A. S. Zuckerman (eds) *Comparative Politics. Rationality, Culture and Structure*, 2nd edn (Cambridge: Cambridge University Press).
Sa'adah, A. (1998) *Germany's Second Chance: Trust, Justice and Democratization* (Cambridge, MA: Harvard University Press).
Schulze, R. (2004) 'Review Article. Memory in German History: Fragmented Noises or Meaningful Voices of the Past?', *Journal of Contemporary History*, 39 (4), 637–48.
Smith, J. and P. Jehlička (2007) 'Stories Around Food, Politics and Change in Poland and the Czech Republic', *Transactions of the Institute of British Geographers*, 32, 395–410.
Stefes, C. (2010) 'Bypassing Germany's *Reformstau*: The Remarkable Rise of Renewable Energy', *German Politics*, 19 (2), 148–63.
Todorova, M. (2010) 'From Utopia to Propaganda and Back' in M. Todorova and Z. Gille (eds) *Post-Communist Nostalgia* (New York: Berghahn).
Twark, J. E. (2007) *Humor, Satire and Identity. Eastern German Literature in the 1990s* (Berlin: de Gruyter).

Welzer, H., S. Moller and K. Tschuggnall (2002) *'Opa war kein Nazi': Nationalsozialismus und Holocaust im Familengedächtnis* (Frankfurt/Main: Fischer).

Wendt, A. (1999) *Social Theory of International Politics* (Cambridge: Cambridge University Press).

Winter, J. (2000) 'The Generation of Memory. Reflections on the Memory Boom in Contemporary Historical Studies', *Bulletin of the German Historical Institute* (Washington, DC), 27, 69–92.

Part II
Narrative Frameworks of Memory

3
Reframing Antifascism: Greta Kuckhoff as Author, Commentator and Critic

Joanne Sayner

> I have just in the last few weeks received a number of already faded letters and greetings from dead friends. The senders died in 1942 and 1943 under the executioner's guillotine – it is only now that the messages carried by reliable friends and helpers have found their way to me.
>
> (BArch N2506/261)

Opening her radio broadcast titled 'Resistance Fighters' with these words, Greta Kuckhoff emotively conjures up those executed for anti-Nazi resistance. For her listeners in August 1947, this programme was a forthright confrontation with the memories of a survivor. For those currently interested in tracing how histories of resistance have been written, however, her words represent much more than that: they point to the delicate materiality of memory – to the contingency of last letters having been written, surviving the end of World War II, arriving with addressees both intended and unforeseen at the time of writing, and becoming the permitted subject of a programme in a radio station which was at that time under Soviet control. Both the letters and the transcript of the radio programmes are part of a fascinating history about the commemoration of resistance to Nazism which goes to the very heart of contemporary debates about remembering and rethinking the GDR: the subject of these sources is antifascism, one of the most contested terms in re-evaluations of East Germany's past.

Antifascism, as the cornerstone of ideology in the GDR, has been central to debates about whether the state was a dictatorship, and about differences between officially sanctioned antifascist memory and everyday antifascist experiences of GDR citizens (e.g. Groehler, 1990; Grunenberg, 1993; Rabinbach, 1996; Faller, 1997; Leo and Reif-Spirek, 2001; Agethen *et al.*, 2002; Ahbe, 2007; Sabrow *et al.*, 2007; Herf, 2008; Hähnel-Mesnard, 2009). The term antifascism has been used synonymously with totalitarianism and has been dismissed as an 'ideological lie' and 'a pervasive antifascist sham' (Diner, 1996: 123–4). More differentiated analyses have traced competing definitions of the concept in political, historical, cultural and academic contexts, and have aimed to reconstruct diachronically and synchronically the complexities and contradictions of the discourse (Erlinghagen, 1997; Barck, 2003; Beattie, 2008). Within these competing contexts, the 'identificatory potential of antifascism' has been particularly disputed. As Helmut Peitsch has shown, the relationship between personal and official memory has often been downplayed as part of an argument that antifascism was imposed upon, or external to, the GDR population (Peitsch, 2011).

This chapter engages with contemporary debates by examining the representation of memories of an antifascist past. It considers how Greta Kuckhoff told her story of antifascist resistance over four decades through different media and genres of memory, from radio programmes and letters to journal articles and autobiography. It suggests that Kuckhoff attempted to convey a consistent message about her antifascist past, while moving towards more overtly autobiographical genres, as traditionally understood. It argues that her corpus of life writing is significant in the context of contemporary representations of East German life histories due to its focus on individual agency and its challenges to official state narratives, people and institutions. Her texts, the chapter concludes, must be situated among those which represent both a 'positive, everyday taking-for-granted of antifascism' as well as a confrontation with 'problematic hackneyed clichés' within state-sanctioned discourse (Barck, 2003: 11). The chapter begins the analysis of these different representations of antifascism with a brief outline of understandings of genre. Before doing so, however, it introduces the resistance group to which Kuckhoff belonged.

'The Red Orchestra'

The nomenclature chosen by the Nazis, 'The Red Orchestra' ('Die Rote Kapelle'), was an umbrella term for what were in fact different resistance groups within Europe, often with little or no contact to each other (Coppi, 1996: 436). It served to emphasise a supposed communist connection, although those resisters working in Berlin with Greta Kuckhoff came from many different sociopolitical backgrounds. Beginning in 1933, the group concentrated on practical, pedagogical resistance, disseminating antifascist leaflets and information about the horrific reality of the Nazi regime and helping those persecuted by the state. During the war, some members of the group were involved in attempts to transmit information to the Soviet authorities and were therefore accused of spying. The Berlin circle was arrested in autumn 1942 and Kuckhoff's husband and friends were executed as traitors during the following months (Coppi, Danyel and Tuchel, 1994). Initially condemned to death, Kuckhoff survived the war after her sentence was commuted to ten years' imprisonment. From 1945 she worked in institutionally significant positions in the Soviet Zone and later the GDR, becoming the first head of the state bank in 1950 and later Vice President of the Council of Peace. Throughout her life she worked to get the members of the Berlin 'Red Orchestra' commemorated in a way that she thought properly reflected their actions and priorities. Beginning immediately on her release, she gave speeches, wrote letters, presented radio broadcasts and began writing essays conveying her memories. While no one way of transmitting the past occurred to the exclusion of the others, it is possible to detect various patterns in her life writing between 1945 and her death in 1981.[1]

Forms of memory and 'genres-for-them'

Contemporary literary, media and memory studies often have much in common when conceptualising form. Processual, performative aspects of genre, media and memory are frequently stressed, as is the role of the recipient(s) in constructing meaning (Dowd *et al.*, 2006). In line with this, rather than seeing genres as deterministic, formulaic, conventional or merely prescribing form, this chapter is based on an understanding of genre as shifting, unstable performance which 'creates effects of reality and truth, authority and plausibility'. It looks at 'how generically shaped knowledges are bound up with the exercise of power' (Frow, 2006: 1–2) and considers the effect of Kuckhoff's choosing to rely on certain forms of life writing (or life-representation) at particular times (Stanley, 2004: 224). As such, it draws on a conceptualisation of different genres as belonging to an 'economy: a set of interdependent positions that organize the universe of knowledge and value' (Frow, 2006: 4–5). Kuckhoff's repeated reinscription of antifascist histories in different genres prompts an examination of the relationship between these genres, so-called points of 'genre contact' (that is, 'the sharing of common "ways of seeing" between texts'), and the way they frame her story in different historical contexts (Olick citing Bahktin, 1999: 383). Drawing on Liz Stanley's work, it considers how an individual might use different genres to convey a message and what the meanings are of these 'genres-for-them'; that is, how people like Kuckhoff 'who produced a variety of "public" and "private" writings, [seem] to inscribe their *own* structural divisions between different kinds or forms of writing' (Jolly and Stanley, 2005: 100). In Kuckhoff's case, this concept is widened to account for the fact that her life writings did not just include different genres but also different media.

Parallel to discussions about genre in literary studies are those in media studies which view the media as constitutive and productive rather than merely reproductive. Theories about the mutual interdependence of genre in literary studies are mirrored by work on the processes of remediation in media studies (Bolter and Grusin, 1999). All media representations of the past are in some ways mediations of what has gone before. In Kuckhoff's case it is possible to speak of 'inter-medial reiteration of the story across different platforms' (Erll and Rigney, 2009: 2). This often happens quite explicitly when her radio broadcasts are reprinted in newspapers, her speeches in letters, and her journal articles in her autobiography. It is also, however, a less explicitly cumulative process, as her story is told and retold in different formats.

At the intersection of literary and media studies is memory studies. An emphasis on the dynamic processes of social memory construction draws attention to how different genres and media 'provide frameworks for shaping both experience and memory' (Erll and Rigney, 2009: 1–2). 'Memory' in this context refers both to 'a capacity or activity on the one hand *and* concrete practices or texts of memory [...] on the other' (Arnold-de Simine and Radstone, Chapter 1: 25, my italics). This chapter considers experience, individual memory as socially mediated, and the ways in which it is communicated to other individuals and collectives. In what follows selected examples from Kuckhoff's antifascist project will be examined, beginning with the radio broadcast from 1947.

Voicing antifascism

In the immediate post-war period approximately 50 per cent of households in Berlin owned a radio (Classen, 2004: 269). As Alexander Badenoch (2008: 1, 35) explains, it was a particularly important medium for the reshaping of German self-identity and self-worth after the end of the war. The quotidian regularity of the format and the relative predictability of programme times enabled listeners to rebuild routines, as well as being an important source of information. As with all cultural production, radio was subject to the control of the Allies. Between October 1946 and May 1947 Kuckhoff worked mainly for the Soviet-controlled station. She wrote and presented a 'Commentary of the Day' ('Kommentar des Tages') on a weekly basis. Her broadcasts covered a variety of issues, predominantly the economic situation, but also denazification and gender equality (BArch N2506/261). In the following, I consider a broadcast on antifascist resistance in order to show how her early representation of her resistance group included elements which were to remain consistent throughout the following decades.

Following the opening reference to the letters written by members of the 'Red Orchestra', Kuckhoff refers to 'two feelings' that that arise from them. Firstly: 'However much we did, it was not enough. We did not succeed in shaking the German people of all classes and defeating National Socialism by our own efforts' (BArch N2506/261). Secondly, 'after the devastating experiences that our fatherland had to go through, it will be the task of the few who remain from the ranks of the resistance fighters to complete where we did not succeed' (ibid.). Kuckhoff therefore insists that it was not Germans who freed themselves and that they still had to earn their victory. Kuckhoff portrays the surviving resisters as confronting the same problems as they had done during Nazism – that they now faced a lack of trust from the general population despite the fact that history had proved them right. She thus reflects on what Christoph Classen (2004: 239) has described as widespread resentment from the population, who did not want to know about resistance to Nazism in the early post-war period. She refers to the 'sometimes surly but often curt and mocking treatment' that the resisters encountered. In contrast, she argues, the population needs to be convinced to do 'the right thing'. This is characterised as 'peaceful co-operation' and a recognition that the survivors were right. For Kuckhoff, it is not supposed to be 'a form of heroic song' ('eine Art Heldenlied') but instead 'an awareness at long last and a comprehensive reorientation'. This reorientation involves 'clarity in economic, cultural and political questions' and a rebuilding that touches the 'roots' of Germany's Nazi past (BArch N2506/261).

Kuckhoff then turns in her broadcast to the way in which anti-Nazi resistance is being commemorated. She refers to Allen Dulles's book which had just been published in New York, titled *Germany's Underground*. Elsewhere she writes that it was in fact this text that prompted her to produce the radio programme because it was the first book published in North America on inner-German resistance (BArch N2506/35).

Her criticisms of Dulles's account are based on his attribution of responsibility for Germany's future purely to those who had resisted due to 'moral and religious reasons'. She points out that Dulles names only members of the group known as '20th July' and church groups as deserving of the status of builders of Germany's new democracy (see Dulles, 1947: 198). In contrast, she claims, he dismisses the 'Red Orchestra' in the same words as their Nazi accusers had, as 'idealists who senselessly fell victim to betrayal'.[2]

The radio broadcast contains a variety of narrating perspectives which are illustrative of Kuckhoff's attempted negotiations with her audience. It begins by asserting her first person authority, that is, her positioning as one who survived ('I have just received [...]'). It places her within the resistance group ('However much we did, it was not enough'), but at the same time distances her from them ('the task that the survivors have been set by the dead has not yet been completed by us'). The broadcast is, on the one hand, critical of the wider German population who, freed from 'the pressure of the fear of the concentration camp and scaffold', are still failing to confront the reality of the situation; on the other, it firmly and repeatedly situates Kuckhoff within the collective of 'our nation'. These shifting perspectives embody the delicate position of the speaker – aware that she is saying something the audience may well not want to hear but nevertheless determined to say it anyway. The broadcast was therefore not part of a narrative of antifascist victory and liberation which the listeners could unproblematically buy into. Yet her archived papers show appreciative letters from listeners to her programmes, suggesting that she was able to form an emotional bond with at least some of her addressees. She herself later reflected: 'I learned to express my thoughts so that people really listened to me.' (BArch N2506/31).

Challenging correspondence

If Kuckhoff challenged the general population through her radio broadcasts, it was in her letters that she most directly confronted representatives of the GDR state. Her archived papers contain thousands of texts to private and public addressees, and many of these deal with her understanding of antifascism. Particularly during the 1950s and 60s she addressed high profile figures, including Ulbricht and Honecker, about the representation of the group in GDR historiography (Sayner, forthcoming). In addition, several letters in particular take issue with another form of memory, that is, the depiction of resistance in the Museum for German History in Berlin. A letter from 25 June 1963, sent to the SED and addressed only to 'Comrades', is unambiguous in its opening criticism of what Kuckhoff sees on display there:

> I do not like the portrayal of the resistance in the GDR. It seems to me that the diverse methods of the resistance work are not being shown sufficiently, rather the struggle of the different groups is being represented in an undifferentiated way – even though different names and places are mentioned. The group to which my husband and I belonged is, in my opinion, being represented completely inadequately, in parts even incorrectly.
>
> (BArch N2506/37)

The letter continues with a recognition that while there are always space restrictions in museums, the '20th July' group has been given more room than the 'Red Orchestra'. She describes her group as significant for two reasons: first, because it comprises a diverse group of 'allies' and embodies the idea of the 'People's Front'; and second, because they act as 'an example worth imitating' ('ein nachahmenswertes Exempel') from the antifascist struggle of the past which is important for present attempts to solve 'the German question'. In contrast, the letter claims, the exhibition is characterised according to the schemata of the Gestapo, which merely served to strengthen claims being made at that time that this group was a spy ring.[3] Rather than recognising the group as members of the anti-Hitler coalition, Kuckhoff continues, the representation at the museum suggests that the group is considered 'with a slight feeling of shame'. The letter closes by advocating that resistance either needs to be portrayed in its historical context, with a recognition of all the problems that reconstruction entails, or not at all.

The letter's impersonal, collective recipients are not addressed directly within the main body of the letter. Instead, passive and third person constructions convey the harshest verdicts. The voice of the first person singular does convey the anger of the writer, but this is mitigated by a strategic change to the first person plural when reference is made to serving 'our cause' ('unsere Sache') the GDR. Political allegiance is reinforced by reference to key terms of GDR state rhetoric: 'If it was right to stand up for liberation with your whole being against Fascism in order to build a genuine democracy, to build socialism – then one can't be ashamed of the strength of the resistance work (even when success was denied it)'. If, following Margaretta Jolly and Liz Stanley (2005: 93) we agree that in a letter 'the "truth" of the writing is in the relationship [between the writer and addressee] rather than in its subject', such negotiations of authorial perspective are significant; they are markers of Kuckhoff's positioning in support of the GDR but against these actions of its representatives.

It is clear from the volume of letters in her archive that Kuckhoff consistently used this form of writing to engage with different representations of antifascism. As noted above, through her letters she reflected not only on museum exhibitions but also on historiography and the success of her own radio broadcasts. They were also the form she repeatedly employed in negotiations with journal editors and publishers in relation to her most conventional forms of life writing, that is, journal articles and autobiography. As such, within Kuckhoff's life writings, this genre is particularly marked by its 'quotidian present' (Stanley, 2004: 208).

While Kuckhoff continued with multiple forms of remembering throughout her life, there is a distinct shift towards first-person narrative prose towards the end of the 1960s as a result, her correspondence suggests, of her continued dissatisfaction with the official, state representation of antifascist resistance. In a letter to her colleague Josef Stadler in November 1968, she writes:

> I am going to take the necessary steps to relinquish my state functions with immediate effect and to consider it my last social duty, in so far as it is at all possible in accordance with the task that our comrades set us, to write down my memories. No, I'm not thinking about a publication which could not anyway appear without the approval of the Party. But perhaps in the future, if not in the present, one will need such material that has not been thinned out or moulded, which certainly does not lay claim to historically valid representation, but to absolute honesty.
>
> (BArch N2506/199)

That she believes her written memories will provide a forum to communicate this 'absolute honesty' in a way her previous work has not, obviously reflects the expectations she has of this kind of life writing. She proceeded to publish first journal articles and then her autobiography.

Journalistic representation of resistance

Kuckhoff wrote many articles for newspapers and journals. In terms of her representation of antifascist resistance, however, it is a series of articles for *Die Weltbühne* from 1969 and 1970 that is most illustrative. Some of these were pre-publications of the text that was to appear as her autobiography in 1972. They include portraits of key figures in the 'Red Orchestra' as well as several first-person narratives which describe pivotal moments in Kuckhoff's life; from her return to Germany after studying in the USA during the late 1920s, to her experience of the aftermath of the pogrom against the Jewish population on 9 November 1938. One of the more directly autobiographical articles from 1970 was called 'Der Widerstand der letzten Tage' ('The Resistance of the Final Days'). Rather than describing the resistance of the underground group before their arrest, it refers to the activities of Kuckhoff and her fellow prisoners and their activities in the final days of the war as the prison system was collapsing.

Although many of Kuckhoff's other journal articles focus on individuals who did not have political beliefs, 'Der Widerstand der letzten Tage' begins with a description of the bravery and quick thinking of Hannah Melzer, the so-called 'Iron Johanna', who, the narrator asserts, maintained the 'dignity of a Communist' during a decade of imprisonment (Kuckhoff, 1970: 549). Discussions between Melzer and the narrator-protagonist about the future, on the 'first measures that would be necessary' after the end of the war, pre-empt the protagonist's involvement in the new economic structures of the state: 'Hannah thought particularly about the Party, I thought about the economy' (ibid.: 550). The format of the journal article speeds the reader through the precariousness of the events during the final days of the war and the transportation of prisoners from one place to the next:

> We ended up in Waldheim: packed like sardines into the cells, most of us with shaved heads, all skin and bone, and preoccupied by the question as to whether liberation or an entry into the local register of deaths was more likely.
>
> (ibid.: 551)

At the same time, prolepses encapsulate a hopefulness and impatience for the end of fighting and links are made to events in the narrative future, to contacts made with other foreign and German prisoners 'for later' (ibid.: 551). The memories in this journal article are structured in such a way as to allow for repeated emphasis on continuities between the past and present. Hyperbole of the narrative present is merged with the need for personal contact and memories which bridge the traumas of the past:

> Every hope, the love which had been broken since the execution of my husband and our close friends, shot like a current to the sea of

> the future: the party! I would come to know it, to feel its strength and warmth – of which my husband had often spoken when I was on the point of breaking down. The love for my son was also embedded within this. I didn't know when or how I would find him.
>
> (ibid.: 551)

When a 'young Red Army soldier' finally liberates Waldheim, the prisoners organise the distribution of clothes, food and medication, embroiled for a while in 'a lot of daily, painstaking work, on which the brightness of liberation hardly fell' (ibid.: 551). This emphasis on the practical work that needed to be accomplished continues in the closing comments of the article, which accord most clearly with dominant state discourse at the time:

> But we wanted to go home. Certainly, the Nazis and their army had been defeated. But now it was essential to dispossess their employers and to begin the enormous work of political education [Überzeugungsarbeit]. It was our task now, to make *our* victory out of the liberation, for which we had the nations of the anti-Hitler coalition, and especially our Soviet comrades, to thank – the victory which led to socialism!
>
> (ibid.: 552)

The collective of those imprisoned becomes the collective that builds socialism. At the same time, the narrative ends by reminding the reader that neither Germany nor its antifascist fighters liberated themselves; the article thus problematises a simple recuperation of the resistance narrative as a victory narrative. Both of these elements can be read as challenging the dominant state narrative of antifascism at that time: Kuckhoff is describing the roles of those who remained in Germany, not the leaders of the KPD who returned from exile after the war and often promoted a narrative of KPD-led victory (Danyel, 1995: 33).

Beatrice Vierneisel (1997: 134) suggests that Kuckhoff used *Die Weltbühne* to publish aspects of her life story that the Party reviewers of her autobiography found problematic. Former journal editor Helmut Reinhardt characterises *Die Weltbühne* as a place where the authors had more freedom than in other publications because of the relatively low circulation figures (Geserick, 1999: 124). While the episodes were reworked and repeated in her autobiography, the format of this journal article gave Kuckhoff the space for an immediate, powerful and personal snapshot at a time when the memories of the 'Red Orchestra' were being recuperated by the state in a reductive, homogenising narrative of KPD-led triumph (Sayner, forthcoming).

Autobiographical reports

The relevance of past resistance activities to current political action is subsequently seen most clearly in the structure of Kuckhoff's text *Vom Rosenkranz zur roten Kapelle: ein Lebensbericht* (*From the Rosary to the Red Orchestra: A Life Story*, 1972). As I have argued elsewhere, this text describes her childhood, her student days in the USA, and her political development during the resistance to Nazism (Sayner, 2007). Despite being subtitled 'A Life Story', the narrative ends in 1945. It achieved seven print runs between 1972 and 1979, was translated into Hungarian and Czech, and sold several hundred thousand copies. It reiterates many of the aspects of Kuckhoff's antifascist understanding which had been present since her earliest speeches in the immediate post-war period, and it explicitly tackles West German historiography and those who still condemned the group as spies and traitors. Through details of the resistance work the narrative describes the diversity of the Berlin group, including the many women involved, and it makes clear that Kuckhoff's antifascism was based on anti-racism. The publication and subsequent reception led to hundreds of requests to speak about her story in interviews, at schools, youth groups and other socialist state institutions, where, as the transcripts of her speeches and published interviews show, she was able to reiterate her beliefs that present-day antifascism should be based on dialogue, that it benefits from confrontation with people who think otherwise, and that it must not remain static but respond to societal changes and challenges.

The overwhelmingly positive reception of *From the Rosary to the Red Orchestra* encouraged Kuckhoff to begin work immediately on the second volume of her autobiography, which was to cover the period from 1945. However, representing the antifascism of the GDR was to prove more difficult than portraying the resistance to Nazism. As her archived papers show, she was to begin recounting her memories many different times with at least three very different approaches. All were titled either 'The Metal Nightingale' or 'The Brass Nightingale', referring to a toy made for Kuckhoff by her father and which she finds on her return to her otherwise empty flat in 1945 (BArch N2506/131).

One version of approximately 60 pages covers her return to Berlin following her release from Waldheim and to her home that had been confiscated in 1942. It describes the practical and social difficulties she encountered as someone unknown in political circles and resented by her former neighbours. With incredulity, it confronts her fellow Germans with their supposed ignorance of the events of the Holocaust. It explains how she slowly began to do political work, first making speeches and then beginning her radio broadcasts. It covers the difficult search for her son and the emotion of his return. It includes a visit to Nuremberg, where she attempts to testify against the judge who had ordered the torture of the members of the 'Red Orchestra' group and had insisted on death sentences for many. It is a compelling text which is forthright in the way it confronts her mistakes and portrays the confusions and contradictions of the post-war period.

Draft outlines of a second text, presumably summaries for a publisher, show that she intended to begin the post-war narrative in 1957, with a trip to Columbo and her role in the GDR Council of Peace serving as the catalyst for her memories. The difficulties Kuckhoff had in writing the post-war autobiography are encapsulated in the way she justifies this starting point: 'I'm choosing 1957 because soon after that my professional work came to an end. I suffered a lot from that but I don't want to let in any of the bitterness that I felt in 1958 – and for a long time afterwards – when the farewell came without reason' (BArch N2506/131). It was in 1958 that she was forced to resign from her position as head of the state bank due, she writes, to doubts being cast on her political beliefs. There are only a few archived papers of this version of the text. In contrast, there is a lengthy draft of a fictional portrayal of the immediate post war period also titled 'The Metal Nightingale'. Annotations on the top of the manuscript state that it was sent to the editor of Kuckhoff's first autobiography, Erika Lewerenz. The narrative describes the situation of two youngsters without their parents, their various encounters with Russian soldiers, the black market and refugees, and their daily struggles for survival in bombed-out cities. Apart from the general historical backdrop, there is little direct autobiographical content in this narrative.

Despite numerous undated drafts for all of these versions in the archives, none ever came to fruition. A letter to her publisher in 1976 somewhat belies the extent of these sources but points to the difficulties she was having:

> I haven't written anything. It almost seems to me as if the path is so strewn with collapses, ambushes and confused thoughts that I could just as well say: leave it [...]. But the post-war period is just as important as the struggle before it. But here there are more taboos which

> seem insurmountable. Just cross me off your list [...] and don't wait any longer.
>
> (BArch N2506/264)

Apart from the brief description of the trip to Columbo in 1957, Kuckhoff's post-war narrative thus ends in autobiographical prose only a few years after the end of the war.

Conclusions

When an author creates a narrative in the present about the past, she or he does so within the framework of pre-existing expectations about form, truth and reality. As such, an examination of genre and media provides a useful theoretical positioning within determinist and constructivist memory debates (Olick, 1999: 384). It emphasises that memory is always 'a dimension of political practice' (Popular Memory Group, 1982). Although Kuckhoff used different genres and media to structure and convey her experiences, her overriding message remained consistent throughout: that memories of antifascism were being homogenised and, as a result, their political potential for the present was being lost. In the post-Wall context where conceptualisations of antifascism are contested, these life writings are no less significant: her texts demonstrate a deeply felt personal engagement with antifascist discourses that has little in common with contemporary narratives about externally imposed monolithic official antifascism in the GDR, and may thus provide a point of identification for some former East German citizens who are left feeling alienated from reductive understandings of the role of antifascism in their lives (Leo, 2009: 30). At the same time, however, they remind us of the very real tensions and problems of GDR antifascism and prevent a contemporary nostalgic recourse to an uncritical, 'untainted' post-war antifascist past (Leo, 2009: 42).

Through her numerous interventions, Kuckhoff wanted to challenge the prevailing representation of her resistance group. Her attempts at writing her second prose autobiography failed and the draft versions, along with her correspondence, suggest that they did so because of the inconsistencies she saw between her antifascism of the present (built as it was on her antifascist resistance of the past) and the representations the political system would have allowed at that time. Yet, despite this failure, antifascist understandings and a 'second' autobiography are undoubtedly present in Kuckhoff's life representations since 1945. Her antifascism is incremental, uses different genres and media, and reflects and constructs an iterative, everyday antifascist practice. The memories of this negotiated antifascism thus provide a mediating position in contemporary debates about antifascism. Kuckhoff took a positive antifascism for granted and identified with its prominence within the GDR, but her ultimate inability to complete her autobiographical project simultaneously reminds us of the limits of that identification.

It may be that Kuckhoff's unique position (as one of the few surviving females of the 'Red Orchestra' resistance group and a key figure within the economic system of the GDR) made her negotiated antifascism individual and unrepresentative. However, while the 'mosaic of the cultural history of antifascism' is still being written on the basis of emerging archival sources, it is arguably too soon to tell (Barck, 2003: 19). It is, however, possible to read all of Kuckhoff's dialogical life representations as 'presuming a response and thus an "after" ' (Stanley, 2004: 221). One such response, as Arnold-de Simine and Radstone remind us, can be to question the integrity of the memories already recovered. In her radio broadcasts, letters, journal articles and published autobiography, Kuckhoff advocated a diversity of memories and refuted monolithic and monocausal explanations. She consistently drew attention to the ways in which antifascist resistance was being remembered. She repeatedly challenged her addressees to engage in critical and constructive dialogue. In a context where memories of the past are significant for contemporary self-understandings, there are certainly worse things that could be used to inform German identities of the present and of the future.

Notes

1. Greta Kuckhoff's 'Nachlass' is held in the Federal Archives, Lichterfelde-Berlin at BArch N2506. Thanks to archivist Ulf Rathje for his continued support during the course of this research.
2. At this time there was controversy as to why the 'Red Orchestra' group in Berlin was captured and whether it was due to information obtained by the Gestapo after arrests had been made. Kuckhoff maintains it was because Soviet authorities transmitted a barely disguised message which contained not only their names but also their addresses (Kuckhoff, 1972).
3. This narrative was originally most dominant in the West but East Germany later recuperated it in order to emphasise links to the Soviet Union (Sayner, forthcoming).

References

Agethen, M., E. Jesse and E. Neubert (eds) (2002) *Der missbrauchte Antifaschismus. DDR-Staatsdoktrin und Lebenslüge der deutschen Linken* (Freiburg: Herder).

Ahbe, T. (2007) *Der DDR-Antifaschismus: Diskurse, Generationen, Kontexte und Identitäten* (Leipzig: Rosa-Luxemburg-Stiftung).
Badenoch, A. (2008) *Voices in the Ruins: West German Radio Across the 1945 Divide* (Basingstoke: Palgrave Macmillan).
Bahktin, M. (1963) *Problems of Dostoevsky's Poetics*. Edited and translated by C. Emerson. (Minneapolis, MN: University of Minnesota Press).
Barck, S. (2003) *Antifa-Geschichte(n). Eine literarische Spurensuche in der DDR der 1950er und 1960er Jahre* (Cologne: Böhlau).
Beattie, A. H. (2008) *Playing Politics with History: The Bundestag Inquiries into East Germany* (New York: Berghahn).
Bolter, J. D. and Grusin, R. (1999) *Remediation: Understanding New Media* (Cambridge: MIT Press).
Classen, C. (2004) *Faschismus und Antifaschismus. Die nationalsozialistische Vergangenheit im ostdeutschen Hörfunk (1945–1953)* (Cologne: Böhlau).
Coppi, H. (1996) 'Die "Rote Kapelle" im Spannungsfeld von Widerstand und nachrichtendienstlicher Tätigkeit. Der Trepper-Report vom Juni 1943', *Vierteljahreshefte für Zeitgeschichte*, 44 (3), 431–58.
Coppi, H., J. Danyel and J. Tuchel (eds) (1994) *Die Rote Kapelle im Widerstand gegen den Nationalsozialismus* (Berlin: Hentrich).
Danyel, J. (1995) 'Die Opfer- und Verfolgtenperspektive als Gründungskonsens? Zum Umgang mit der Widerstandstradition und der Schuldfrage in der DDR' in J. Danyel (ed.) *Die geteilte Vergangenheit: Zum Umgang mit Nationalsozialismus und Widerstand in beiden deutschen Staaten* (Berlin: Akademischer Verlag), pp. 31–46.
Diner, D. (1996) 'On the Ideology of Antifascism', trans. Christian Bundermann, *New German Critique*, 67, 123–32.
Dowd, G., L. Stevenson and J. Strong (2006) *Genre Matters. Essays in Theory and Criticism* (Bristol: Intellect).
Dulles, A.W. (1947) *Germany's Underground* (New York: Macmillan).
Erlinghagen, R. (1997) *Die Diskussion um den Begriff des Antifaschismus seit 1989/90* (Berlin: Argument).
Erll, A. and A. Rigney (2009) 'Introduction: Cultural Memory and its Dynamics' in A. Erll and A. Rigney (eds) *Mediation, Remediation, and the Dynamics of Cultural Memory* (Berlin: de Gruyter), pp. 1–14.
Faller, K. (1997) *Abschied vom Antifaschismus* (Frankfurt/Oder: Editionen).
Frow, J. (2006) *Genre* (London: Routledge).
Geserick, R. (1999) '"Man brauchte nur ich zu sagen..." Chef-Redakteure und eine Leserin im Gespräch: Klaus Polkehn (*Wochenpost*), Hartmut Berlin (*Eulenspiegel*), Helmut Reinhardt (*Die Weltbühne*) und Brigitte Struzyk' in S. Barck, M. Langermann and S. Lokatis (eds) *Zwischen 'Mosaik' und 'Einheit'. Zeitschriften in der DDR* (Berlin: Links), pp. 116–28.
Groehler, O. (1990) 'Zelebrierter Antifaschismus', *Journal Geschichte*, 5, 46–55.
Grunenberg, A. (1993) *Antifaschismus: Ein deutsches Mythos* (Hamburg: Rowohlt).
Hähnel-Mesnard, C. (ed.) (2009) *Antifaschismus Revisited: Geschichte – Ideologie – Erinnerung* Special Issue *Zeitschrift der Auschwitz Stiftung Brüssel*, 104 (Paris: Kimé).
Herf, J. (2008) 'Post-Totalitarian Narratives in Germany: Reflections on Two Dictatorships after 1945 and 1989', *Totalitarian Movements and Political Religions*, 9 (2–3), 161–86.
Jolly, M. and L. Stanley (2005) 'Letters as/not a Genre', *Life Writing*, 1 (2), 91–118.

Kuckhoff, G. (1970) 'Der Widerstand der letzten Tage', *Die Weltbühne*, 25, 549–52.
Kuckhoff, G. (1972) *Vom Rosenkranz zur Roten Kapelle: Ein Lebensbericht* (Berlin: Neues L.
Leo, A. (2009) 'Antifaschismus' in M. Sabrow (ed.) *Erinnerungsorte der DDR* (Munich: Beck), pp. 30–42.
Leo, A. and P. Reif-Spirek (eds) (2001) *Vielstimmiges Schweigen. Neue Studien zum DDR-Antifaschismus* (Berlin: Metropol).
Olick, J. K. (1999) 'Genre Memories and Memory Genres: A Dialogical Analysis of May 8, 1945 Commemorations in the Federal Republic of Germany', *American Sociological Review*, 63, 381–402.
Peitsch, H. (2011) 'How Memory is Remembered: The Potsdam Memory Archive 1995–96' in D. Clarke and U. Wölfel (eds) *Remembering the German Democratic Republic: Divided Memory in a United Germany* (Basingstoke: Palgrave Macmillan), pp. 249–65.
Popular Memory Group (1982) 'Popular Memory: Theory, Politics, Method' in R. Johnson (ed.) *Making Histories: Studies in History Writing and Politics* (London: Hutchinson), pp. 205–52.
Rabinbach, A. (1996) 'Introduction: Legacies of Antifascism', *New German Critique*, 67, 3–17.
Sabrow, M., R. Eckert, M. Flacke (eds) (2007) *Wohin treibt die DDR-Erinnerung?: Dokumentation einer Debatte* (Göttingen: Vandenhoeck & Ruprecht).
Sayner, J. (2007) *Women without a Past? German Autobiographical Writings and Fascism* (Amsterdam: Rodopi).
Sayner, J. (forthcoming) 'Communicating History: The Archived Letters of Greta Kuckhoff and Memories of the "Red Orchestra"' in M. Fulbrook and A. Port (eds) *Becoming East Germans: Socialist Structures and Sensibilities after Hitler* (Oxford: Berghahn).
Stanley, L. (2004) 'The Epistolarium: On Theorizing Letters and Correspondences', *Auto/Biography*, 12, 201–35.
Vierneisel, B. (1997) 'Das Erinnerungsarchiv. Lebenszeugnisse als Quellengruppe im Institut für Marxismus-Leninismus beim ZK der SED' in M. Sabrow (ed) *Verwaltete Vergangenheit. Geschichtskultur und Herrschaftslegitimation in der DDR* (Leipzig: Akademischer Verlagsanstalt), pp. 117–44.

4
Community and Genre: Autobiographical Rememberings of Stasi Oppression[1]

Sara Jones

When an individual writes about his or her life, he or she produces a narrative that offers not only an insight into broader historical processes, but also a particularly subjective interpretation of these events and their impact on the individual and the group. Among efforts to come to terms with the past, life writing offers the reader a sense of authenticity that is difficult to replicate in other genres. Where these narratives are produced by the victims of state violence, they gain the status of testimony; these individuals may be viewed as eyewitnesses ('Zeitzeugen'), whose past suffering serves to legitimate both their memories and their right to be heard. As Christian Heuer (2010: 76) argues, particularly in the case of traumatic histories, the narration of experience in ego-documents seems to become proof of the authenticity of the biography: 'These documents are thereby more than simply narrated life history. They appear as documents of fact.'[2]

The significance of autobiographical memories in the process of remembering the GDR in general, and the East German State Security Service (Stasi) in particular, can be seen in the vast number of different autobiographical accounts that have emerged since 1989. Traditional autobiographies by victims, informants and Stasi officials are complemented by collections of victim memoirs, often structured around a particular theme or site of suffering. Documentary films, internet forums and museum exhibitions provide further spaces for the narration of autobiographical memories. These published memories, in turn, are selected from the vast number of narratives that have not been mediated or are communicated only orally. Somewhere in between the published and the unmediated lie memories that have been given media form, but whose audience is limited to a closed group of specialists or family members: for example, the large collection of interviews contained in the eyewitness archive ('Zeitzeugenarchiv') at the Stasi prison memorial, Gedenkstätte Hohenschönhausen, and private letters or diaries.

These representations of the past have in common the assertion of an identity between narrator and protagonist and a claim of referentiality to past events. However, the media forms in which they are produced and reproduced are extremely varied. Astrid Erll (2011: 114) highlights the importance of the medium in the production of memory: 'Media are not simply neutral carriers of information about the past. What they appear to encode – versions of past events and persons, cultural values and norms, concepts of collective identity – they are in fact first creating.' Sibylle Krämer (1998: 79) describes the effect of the medium on the message it encodes as an unintentionally produced, pre-discursive and pre-semantic trace. This chapter aims to identify this medial trace for three sets of autobiographical accounts of state oppression in the GDR: unpublished interviews recorded by the eyewitness archive at Gedenkstätte Hohenschonhausen; the 2007 anthology, *Gefangen in Hohenschönhausen* (*Imprisoned in Hohenschönhausen*); and the touring exhibition, *Gewalt hinter Gittern* (*Violence behind Bars*), displayed from June to August 2010 at the prison memorial. The selected accounts are produced in a variety of media, but share a link to Gedenkstätte Hohenschönhausen – a controversial site that has played a significant role in memory-political debates relating to the GDR past. Analysis of these different media forms can contribute to an understanding of the interaction between communication, community and the mediation of memory, and the particular impact of this institution on the political framing and reframing of the past.

Interviews

The eyewitness archive in Hohenschönhausen is responsible for collecting and storing interviews with former inmates of the prison. The interviews are conducted by an archivist, transcribed and saved both in written form and as an audio-visual recording. The eyewitness project is intended both to archive for the purposes of future research the experiences of those incarcerated here and to serve the more immediate needs of the memorial, including the construction of a permanent exhibition planned for early 2013. In the context of the archive, the same interview is thus mediated in two different forms: written and audio-visual. Although the narrative is largely identical (allowing for errors, omissions and misunderstandings on the part of the transcriber), the medium that produces the narrative is not. In this way, this material offers an excellent basis for analysis of the impact of different media forms on memory and the identification of a medial trace on the messages produced.

A notable feature of the audio-visual recordings of the interviews, in this regard, is that they allow the viewer actually to see an image of the eyewitness, rather than simply reading his or her words. The camera records not only the narrative of the individual, but also the individual him- or herself. The gaze of the visitor becomes that of the interviewer behind the camera: the visitor is invited to see, apparently first hand, the emotional response of the victim to the narration of his or her past. In the words of Carl R. Plantinga (1997: 70), 'the filmed interview allows us to *see* and *hear* the interviewee, giving us information about spatial context, gesture, facial expression, tone of voice, and inflection that could not come across in a written interview'. This reduces the sense of distance between the narrative, speaker and viewer and suggests greater immediacy, as the medium has greater transparency. This is not to imply that the audio-visual testimonies offer a window on the past, or direct access to the testifying victim. These recordings, in common with all cultural representations, offer 'mediated immediacy' (Pirker and Rüdiger, 2010: 18); however, this particular form of representation is likely to be *experienced* as more authentic by the recipient. Following Krämer (1998: 74), the more transparent medium fulfils its function more effectively, because it stays below the threshold of our perception; nonetheless, it may still leave its trace on the message.

The impression of transparency and the impact of the visual medium are further highlighted through comparison with the written versions of the exchanges. The transcription of the interview cannot reflect the flow of the conversation: aspects such as participants speaking over each other, or silences and hesitation. Moreover, certain passages are difficult to comprehend without the audio-visual recording, as they are reliant on the gestures of the participants. In the interview with Klaus-Dieter S., for example, S. attempts to explain the body language of the Stasi officers in the room:

> *S.*: And these people, they had thick bundles of keys in one hand and constantly did this...
>
> *Interviewer*: They banged the bundle of keys on the table...
>
> *S.*: No, not on the table, just like this, they just played with it, like this... and...
>
> (Zeitzeugenarchiv, 2008b: 20)

In the audio-visual recording, S. demonstrates the way in which the officers swung their bundle of keys to and fro, but the reader of the transcript alone would not have this visual image to aid understanding and is thereby made aware of the limitations of the written medium. This can be viewed as an example of what Krämer (1998: 74) describes as the 'murmur' of the medium as it (temporarily) loses its transparency: 'Only in the murmur, but that is in the disturbance or even in the breakdown of its trouble-free service, does the medium remind us of its existence.' A similar effect is seen when the flow of the interview is interrupted by problems with the technology or the need to change the tape (e.g. Zeitzeugenarchiv, 2006: 11–12, 2009a, 2009d: 19). The transcript also frequently blends out the 'live' features of the conversation, notably non-relevant discussion and asides that do not relate to the interview: for example, in an interview with Michael B. on 5 December 2007, the camera records the interviewer asking B. to change his glasses due to the reflection of the light, and B. commenting on her collection of books at the start of the conversation. The transcriber does not include these aspects of interpersonal exchange in the written account (Zeitzeugenarchiv, 2007b), and the presence of them on the audio-visual recording again gives the viewer the impression of being witness to a live conversation.

A second impact of the interview form is the necessary presence of the interviewer as interlocutor. In the eyewitness archive at Hohenschönhausen, two quite different styles of interview can be observed, resulting from the development and professionalisation of the work of the memorial. Where several of the interviews, particularly from the period 2007–08, were conducted by the head of the archive, herself a former political prisoner, later interviews were more frequently carried out by individuals with a background in historical research and no immediate link to the history of political persecution in the GDR.[3] The difference in style is quite striking and is determined not only by different understandings of the nature of the exchange, but also by the subject positions of the interviewer and interviewee. The transcripts where the interviewer is also a former political prisoner frequently read as conversations between two eyewitnesses, with each putting forward his or her view of the past. While the interviewers who do not have personal memories of political persecution allow the eyewitness to speak relatively freely and without interruption, when the interviewer is also a former political prisoner she more obviously directs the conversation towards those elements she considers important. An example of this can be seen in the interview with Peter W. conducted on 4 December 2007.

The interviewer asks W. to speak of his experiences in the GDR after his exmatriculation from university, particularly with regard to the infiltration of the Stasi into his everyday life. W. responds: 'Okay, I was in two different case files, once in OV Revisionist. That was a collective term in Leipzig....' Slightly irritated, the interviewer interrupts: 'Please don't recite the Stasi files to me now; I would prefer to learn from you how you lived back then. What your attitude to life was.' (Zeitzeugenarchiv, 2007a: 12).

The interviewer also tends to mix her memories into the conversation and is willing to contradict W., as is seen in the following exchange regarding the division between political and criminal prisoners in his place of incarceration:

> *Interviewer*: In terms of the ratio, the numerical ratio – what would you guess? Mostly political?
>
> *W.*: At least three quarters political, at least.
>
> *Interviewer*: So there weren't any situations where you felt threatened.
>
> *W.:* Not at all, no.
>
> *Interviewer*: By majority criminals – or such networks. You see for the women in Hoheneck it was –
>
> *W.*: Not at all. I know that has often been described. Cottbus quite different, no. It was a network of cooperativeness that I experienced, which continued to exist in part after the imprisonment.
>
> (Zeitzeugenarchiv, 2007a: 44)

This combination of interruption, mixing and overlapping of memories, and the seemingly equal status of the interlocutors in the process of remembering make these exchanges appear strikingly similar to the conversational remembering that occurs in intimate memory communities, including victim support groups and associations.[4]

However, a key difference between the exchanges recorded by the archive and interactions between individuals in other remembering communities is that these exchanges are mediated. This is particularly important when we consider the position of the viewer or reader. In contrast to a personal confrontation with the eyewitness, the viewer's response is not part of the original exchange and he/she is dependent on the interviewer to direct the conversation. As a result of the medium, the spoken language of the eyewitness loses its ephemeral nature – the viewer can rewind and replay the testimony as often as he/she likes – but it also loses its interactivity as far as the recipient of the memorial medium is concerned.

Furthermore, the structure of the interview indicates that the exchanges are in fact directed at an implied viewer or reader; that is, intended for a wider audience. For example, in the interview with S. on 10 June 2008, the interviewee states that his father was not included by name in the intercessions at the Evangelical church. The interviewer interrupts:

> Now, we have to explain that: intercession is the inclusion of individuals, who have been arrested and politically prosecuted in the GDR, as part of the Evangelical church, as part of the great prayer on Sundays.
>
> (Zeitzeugenarchiv, 2008b: 7)

This insertion of explanatory sections into the conversation indicates that these exchanges are not solely for the benefit of interviewer and interviewee, but that a future audience is anticipated. This again marks this form apart from other types of conversational remembering. In the interviews, the recording, or mediation, of the memory is the principal aim, not, as in other intimate remembering communities, the process of remembering itself.

Anthologies

A second form of mediation of victim memories can be seen in the 2007 anthology of eyewitness testimony, *Gefangen in Hohenschönhausen*, edited by Hubertus Knabe, the director of the memorial. This is a disparate collection of texts, written in different styles and for different purposes. Read as individual pieces, it is in particular the contributions written before the *Wende* that vary in terms of their form, purpose or implied addressee. The letters by the actor Heinrich George, for example, written during his incarceration in the Soviet special camp ('Speziallager'), are marked by a sense of immediacy, emphasised by the use of the present tense, and by the intimacy and familiarity that characterise these letters between husband and wife. Where the majority of contributions appear to serve the purpose of giving testimony, these letters are primarily a means of communication with loved ones. Familial and social concerns and interests intermingle with George's description of life as a Soviet prisoner (George, 2007). Similarly, the contribution by Kurt Müller, erstwhile Vice President of the West German Communist Party, also takes the form of a letter, written by Müller in 1956 and addressed to Otto Grotewohl, then Minister President of the GDR.

The purpose of the letter is demonstrated clearly by its emphasis on proving that Müller could not possibly have been guilty of the crimes he was accused of and that his interrogators, including Erich Mielke, had broken laws enshrined in the GDR constitution. Where the terrible conditions of the 'submarine' prison are the focus of the majority of contributions describing this period, only three of the 28 pages of Müller's letter discuss this aspect of his experience (Müller, 2007).

The majority of texts included in the anthology are written in simple prose form, employing a first-person narrator and focaliser; however, the accounts by the professional writers, Jürgen Fuchs and Klaus Kordon, both extracted from longer literary works, contrast with the other contributions through their use of different narrative perspectives and voices. Kordon's piece, taken from *Krokodil im Nacken* (*Plagued by a Crocodile*, 2002), is written entirely in the third person and the protagonist is identified as the fictional Manfred Lenz (Kordon, 2007). In this respect, and in contrast to the other pieces in the volume, Kordon does not enter into an autobiographical pact with the reader. Fuchs's text, an extract from *Vernehmungsprotokolle* (*Protocols of an Interrogation*, 1978), is composed of shifting narrative perspectives and styles, marked by different typefaces or layouts: the 'inner voice' of the protagonist is intermingled with the more composed reflections on his imprisonment and with paragraphs from GDR law (Fuchs, 2007).

How should we view this incorporation into one volume of such varied texts, written at different times and for different purposes? We might view this as an example of what Astrid Erll and Ann Rigney (2009: 5), following Jay David Bolter and Richard Grusin, have described as '"repurposing" [...] taking a "property" [...] from one medium and re-using it in another. In this process, memorial media borrow from, incorporate, absorb, critique and refashion earlier memorial media.' Erll and Rigney (ibid.: 8) also describe the phenomenon as 'remediation', a process 'in which the same story is recalled in new media at a later point in time and hence given a new lease of cultural life'. How then does Knabe remediate these disparate accounts to form a new cultural product, and what is the effect of this remediation? Here the paratextual features of the volume and Knabe's introduction are significant. The title and subtitle of the collection, *Gefangen in Hohenschönhausen: Stasi-Häftlinge berichten* (*Imprisoned in Hohenschönhausen: Stasi Prisoners Report*), indicate to the reader the common heading under which the various accounts should be read – the experience of Stasi imprisonment in Hohenschönhausen – even if the texts themselves focus on spaces that are quite diverse, from the Soviet special camp of the 1940s to the

Ministry for State Security (MfS) work camp attached to the prison. The chronological ordering of the contributions, based on when the author was imprisoned, rather than when the text was written, places emphasis on the events remembered, rather than on the form this narrative takes. In this respect, the ordering also helps to draw the reader's attention away from the different contexts in which the pieces were produced and to focus it on the commonalities in their description of life in the camp or prison. Moreover, Knabe has given the original texts new titles which, in turn, have a structuring effect through suggesting an emphasis or key feature: 'In the Quarantine Barrack', 'The Cellar Prison', 'The Informer Network'.

Knabe's introduction to the volume, which gives a history of the prison and a description of the conditions experienced there over the 44 years of its existence, provides the context in which the accounts are to be read. Here Knabe references the contributions to the volume in support of statements in his chronological summary; he thereby brings the texts together in an overarching historical account and suggests that they are to be viewed as evidence underpinning this narrative. Moreover, Knabe goes beyond the victim testimonies to comment on the nature of the GDR in general and thereby contributes explicitly to contemporary debates among politicians and historians. He makes clear that, in his view, there could be no 'normal life' in the GDR away from the instruments of oppression:

> In the system of repression in the GDR, the prisons were only the tip of the iceberg. Even more important than the arrest and sentencing of would-be escapees or those who thought differently was the deterrent effect of these measures on the rest of society. [...] They [the citizens of the GDR] knew that the MfS possessed a level of power only possible in totalitarian states.
>
> (Knabe, 2007: 15)

He thereby extends the significance of descriptions of the misery of internment and suggests that these accounts should be read as relevant for the experience of the GDR population as a whole.

Knabe not only indicates his view of the value of these accounts for our understanding of the past and the nature of the GDR, but also points towards their political meaning for the present. The power of the Stasi is set in direct opposition to the intelligence agencies of the FRG: Knabe notes that, in united Germany, domestic and foreign secret services are separated and the activities of the intelligence agencies are controlled by parliament (2007: 15). The democratic systems of the FRG are thus given legitimacy through comparison with the dictatorship. However, Knabe also points towards the failure of this democracy to punish the vast majority of those who were guilty of human rights abuses under the dictatorship of the Socialist Unity Party (SED) (ibid.: 17). The contributions to the anthology are evidence, for Knabe, that those Stasi officers who maintain that Hohenschönhausen was a site of law and justice are lying and he sets this in direct opposition to Florian Henckel von Donnersmarck's film *Das Leben der Anderen* (*The Lives of Others*, 2006): according to Knabe, no Stasi officer secretly helped those incarcerated in Hohenschönhausen and it is these victims who are the real heroes of history, not 'the fictional perpetrators in the cinema, who are tormented by scruples' (2007: 19). Knabe thus suggests that the anthology offers a corrective 'truth' that aims to counter the 'lies' of the perpetrators and the historical inaccuracies of fiction. In this respect, he frames the pieces as a contribution not only to the collective understanding of the GDR, but also to the political debates of the present. These communicative and literary accounts are brought together to form a new cultural artefact that, it is intended, will offer a dissonant, authentic, and, in this framing, 'more truthful' version of the past. In this way, Knabe blurs the distinction usually drawn between fictional and autobiographical texts, suggesting that the fictional pieces in the volume can also be read as mimetic representations of individual experience. He notes that Fuchs and Kordon have 'processed' their experiences in 'literary' rather than 'documentary' form (ibid.: 18–19); however, their ordering in the volume according to when the author was imprisoned, rather than when the piece was written, and Knabe's description of the texts in the volume as 'reports' (Berichte) (ibid.: 18–19), construct these pieces as having a quite different relationship to historical 'truth' from that of Donnersmarck's blockbuster.

The framework that Knabe provides, particularly the generalisation of individual experience into an overarching historical account, contrasts with the atomisation of victim experience in the eyewitness archive. The memories in the archive are structured by the interview form and the questions posed; however, the narrative of the witness is not explicitly given any representative function – each interview stands only for itself. The viewer or reader may draw conclusions about the GDR past from this material, but he/she is not directed by a particular narrative. This also means that the interviews record dissonant pasts: for example, the testimony of Bruno S., a former Stasi officer who was incarcerated in the mid-1970s. Bruno S. expresses controversial political views regarding, for example, the motivations of West and East German informants (IMs). He states that the majority of West Germans collaborated for financial gain, whereas those in the East informed out of political conviction: 'In the GDR there was still the ideal, perhaps stultified, unfortunately stultified, we are finding that out now, but in the West it was in principle only done for dosh.' (Zeitzeugenarchiv, 2008a: 22) This narrative of an idealistic East against a purely capitalistic West jars with the expectation of complete condemnation of state socialism by this individual who also suffered at the hands of the MfS, and with the narrative of Knabe's introduction to the anthology. Similarly, in contrast to Knabe's valorisation of liberal democracy through juxtaposition with the oppressive aspects of the GDR, Bruno S. uses his experiences at Hohenschönhausen to highlight problems in contemporary capitalist regimes: 'There's a Guantanamo, which I don't welcome; there's interrogations by our FRG, we can happily include that here, where they fly people abroad, to Arab states, where they are allowed to be interrogated with torture [...]' (Zeitzeugenarchiv, 2008a: 19).

The touring exhibition

The absence of an overarching framework in the eyewitness archive is in many respects due to the fact that these memories are not part of the public face of the memorial, and therefore do not require interpretation for the benefit of the reader or visitor. However, mediated eyewitness accounts, such as these, are intended to form a key element of the memorial's permanent exhibition, due to be opened early in 2013 (see König, 2007: 279). We cannot say definitively what form the public mediation of these memories might take. However, an analysis of the touring exhibition *Gewalt hinter Gittern*, displayed at the memorial from 16 June to 30 August 2010, can give an indication of the potential impact of this presentation. The exhibition was a joint initiative by Gedenkstätte Hohenschönhausen and Gedenkstätte Bautzen. It consisted of a series of display cases that had the appearance of the stacks of an archive. The visitor could walk between the stacks and view the material displayed on both sides. At the end of each stack, the theme of that particular row was printed: 'Violence behind Bars'; 'I Confess'; 'Red Terror'; 'Perpetrators without Punishment'. The presentation was multimedia and included: objects from prison life; authentic documents pertaining to GDR law, conditions in the prisons and the arrest and punishment of individuals; television screens; and information boards giving biographical details of prisoners and of Stasi personnel. In the context of autobiographical memories, the most significant element of the exhibition was the focus on individualised accounts; as stated on the introductory board: 'The exhibition documents by means of example the scarcely known level of violence in GDR prisons.' The individual narratives contained in the exhibition are thus selected from the large number available and intended to be seen as representative of the experience of incarceration in the GDR.

These 'exemplary' biographies were displayed in a number of different formats. The first row contained television screens with a continuous loop of pictures of the prison, interspersed with quotations from the accounts of former inmates, for example:

> No heating in the arrest cell and then damp walls and then you constantly had to use the bucket.
>
> (Siegmar Faust)

> Sleep deprivation – what a form of torture! I can no longer think, I'm dizzy and feel sick.
>
> (Elizabeth Graul)

The third and fifth rows expanded on these extracts with fuller biographical details about the individuals, including copies of authentic documents relating to their arrest and imprisonment, and photographs taken at the time of their incarceration. In addition, headphones allowed the visitor either to listen to a spoken extract from a written autobiographical account (for example, in the cases of Fritz Sperling, Elizabeth Graul and Rudolf Wehrstedt), or to view an excerpt from an audio-visual interview with the eyewitness recorded by the memorial (for example, Tatjana Sterneberg, Birgit Willschütz, Siegmar Faust, Stefan Lauter). The quotations from the first row, taken from these autobiographical narratives, were redisplayed in the context of the other biographical material.

In that the audio-visual testimony and much of the written material are taken from the eyewitness archive or from other autobiographical accounts, we can view the exhibition as a form of remediation. Drawing on the work of Bolter and Grusin, Erll and Rigney (2009: 4) describe the 'double logic of remediation':

> On the one hand, most memorial media strive for ever greater 'immediacy'. The goal is to provide a seemingly transparent window on the past, to make us forget the presence of the medium and instead present us with an 'unmediated memory'. On the other hand, this effect is usually achieved by the recycling and multiplication of media.

This concept of the 'double logic of remediation' would seem particularly pertinent to an analysis of this exhibition. The auto/biographical dimension of the display offers a greater sense of immediacy and authenticity. In the audio-visual accounts the visitor feels him- or herself confronted directly with the eyewitness, who offers a seemingly unmediated narrative of their past. The documents linked to the trial and imprisonment of the individual are either originals or copies of originals and thus build on this sense of direct contact with the past. The photographs of GDR prisons as they appeared before or shortly after the *Wende* offer the visitor, following Roland Barthes (1993: 80), 'certainty that such a thing had existed', a certainty consolidated by the situation of the exhibition on the site of one of these prisons.

Nonetheless, according to the 'double logic of remediation', this sense of immediacy is, in fact, created by the use of a wide range of media forms and by their arrangement in the context of the exhibition. The authentic documents would mean little to the average visitor were they not placed alongside the biographical details of the individual to whom they pertain. In this respect, they undergo a form of remediation, in that they are taken out of their original context and function in the archives of the Stasi and justice system, and placed in this memorial exhibit. The recorded audio testimony, where written autobiographical accounts are read aloud, is a repurposing of the written material designed to give the visitor a greater sense of immediacy. The audio-visual interviews perhaps appear to offer the most unadulterated view of the past, but here the past is first recreated in narrative form by the eyewitness, and then mediated – not only by the impact of the audio-visual form, as discussed above, and the editing process of the curator, but also by its contextualisation in the exhibition space.

Part of this context is, once again, the selection and editing of the eyewitness accounts, and the political narrative accompanying the auto/biographical displays. This is provided by the information framing the eyewitness stories, notably the introductory placard, the text of which has been recorded and is played aloud as the visitor walks around the exhibition. The text emphasises that the GDR was an 'unjust state', that violence in prisons was 'a matter of course', and that more than 200,000 imprisonments in the GDR were for political reasons (*Gewalt hinter Gittern*, 2010). The rows dedicated to the general presentation of the nature of violence in GDR prisons and its sanctioning by the regime, as well as the stack 'Perpetrators without Punishment', which documented the apparent failure to prosecute those responsible in united Germany, reinforce this message and expand its relevance for contemporary society. If the visitor views the exhibition in sequence, the narrative he or she reads is highly suggestive: the prisons of the GDR were violent; the violence was supported by the dictatorial regime; the violence had an immense emotional and physical impact on victims, who continue to suffer; those responsible for this suffering have escaped justice. In this regard, the framing of the exhibition is comparable in both substance and effect to Knabe's remediation of the written accounts in *Gefangen in Hohenschönhausen*. Here too, memory matter has been selected from the 'archive', brought into an overarching political and historical narrative, and given new media form with the potential to impact on collective understandings of the GDR past.

Mediated remembering communities

Do these victims of the Stasi, whose autobiographical memories are mediated alongside each other in these different forms, and who share the experience of incarceration at this site, build a remembering community? Do they, following Aleida Assmann (2006: 24), constitute a network of memories that lend one another coherence and credibility? It can certainly be argued that the interviews, contributions to the anthology and eyewitness narratives displayed in *Gewalt hinter Gittern* repeat particular themes and share several details and emphases in their accounts of life in Hohenschönhausen, especially in the case of individuals who focus their remembering on the same period. Although the narratives are, in many cases, markedly different in form and style, the presence of these motifs across the texts and audio-visual recordings does mean that the memories produced and reproduced in the context of the memorial appear to cross and overlap, strengthen and support each other.

Nonetheless, for Assmann (2006: 28), memory constitutes community in this sense not through cultural media, but through conversational or social remembering, and therefore must be made up of synchronous memories, rather than the diachronic collection of texts found in Knabe's volume and remediated in the exhibition, or the disembodied narratives of the eyewitness interviews. The individual eyewitnesses do not, in any physical sense, remember together. Earlier narratives might be incorporated into later testimony; however, the memories mediated at a later point in time cannot modify the earlier versions in terms of their content in the same way that individual memories have been shown to change in conversational remembering (Welzer, 2002, 2010). The framing of the anthology and the exhibition may influence the way these narratives are received, but it does not change their substance. In this respect, the memorial media are not originally produced in a remembering community; however, in the case of the anthology and exhibition, they are presented as a cohesive whole and, if the reader perceives the common themes and motifs running throughout, they might be received as such. In this sense they are what I will term a 'staged' or 'mediated' remembering community that is produced by the remediation of the original memory documents. As discussed above, the interviews in the archive lack an overarching ideological framework, and the reader or viewer is free to make meaning from the accounts for themselves. Nonetheless, here too we can observe a mediated remembering community. The archive groups and orders these memories in their mediated form, and with free access to the material, the recipient of these memorial media can view simultaneously narratives that have been produced years apart.

The Hohenschönhausen memorial in its function as an institution promotes a specific narrative of the GDR past and its relevance for contemporary society. This is seen not only to a large extent in the tours themselves, but also in the secondary media linked to or directly produced by the memorial. A feature shared by many of these media is that they remediate the stories told in earlier memory matter, be they letters, literary works, individual autobiographical texts or interviews with eyewitnesses. In this way, these media forms reproduce and reframe the same autobiographical narratives in multiple genres. The remediation of these stories alongside each other gives them the appearance of supporting and overlapping with one another to form a coherent collective narrative about this aspect of the GDR past. In this respect, the construction of mediated remembering communities also has an important political dimension, for it plays a critical role in ensuring that particular versions of the past become salient.

Notes

1. This research was carried out as part of the project 'Reconstructing the Stasi', generously supported by The Leverhulme Trust.
2. Unless otherwise stated, all translations from German are my own.
3. I was given access to five interviews in this style (Zeitzeugenarchiv, 2009a–2009e).
4. See Welzer (2002) for a detailed examination of the processes of communicative memory within families, and Gallinat (2006) for an exploration of the role of memories of persecution in the construction of identity in victim groups.

References

Assmann, A. (2006) *Der lange Schatten der Vergangenheit: Erinnerungskultur und Geschichtspolitik* (Munich: Beck).

Barthes, R. (1993) *Camera Lucida*, trans. R. Howard (London: Vintage). First published in French as *La Chambre Claire* by Editions du Seuil in 1980.

Erll, A. and A. Rigney (2009) 'Introduction: Cultural Memory and its Dynamics' in A. Erll and A. Rigney (eds) *Mediation, Remediation, and the Dynamics of Cultural Memory* (Berlin: de Gruyter), pp. 1–11.

Erll A. (2011) *Memory in Culture*, trans. S. B. Young (Basingstoke: Palgrave Macmillan).

Fuchs, J. (2007) 'Dann kommt die Angst' in H. Knabe (ed.) *Gefangen in Hohenschönhausen* (Berlin: List), pp. 268–300.

Gallinat, A. (2006) 'Difficult Stories: Public Discourse and Narrative Identity in Eastern Germany', *Ethnos*, 71.3, 343–66.

George, H. (2007) 'Briefe aus dem Lager' in H. Knabe (ed.) *Gefangen in Hohenschönhausen* (Berlin: List), pp. 37–49.

Gewalt hinter Gittern (2010), joint initiative by Gedenkstätte Hohenschönhausen and Gedenkstätte Bautzen, supported by the Stiftung Aufarbeitung der SED-Diktatur. Project led by H. Knabe, S. Klewin and C. Liebold, and displayed at Gedenkstätte Hohenschönhausen from 16 June to 30 August.

Heuer, C. (2010) '"... authentischer als alle vorherigen": Zum Umgang mit Ego-Dokumenten in der populären Geschichtskultur' in E. U. Pirker, M. Rüdiger, C. Klein, T. Leiendecker, C. Oesterle, M. Sénécheau and M. Uike-Bormann (eds) *Echte Geschichte: Authentizitätsfiktionen in populären Geschichtskulturen* (Bielefeld: Transcript), pp. 75–91.

Knabe, H. (2007) 'Einführung' in H. Knabe (ed.) *Gefangen in Hohenschönhausen* (Berlin: List), pp. 7–19.

König, F. (2007) *Die Gestaltung der Vergangenheit: Zeithistorische Orte und Geschichtspolitik im vereinten Deutschland* (Marburg: Tectum).

Kordon, K. (2007) 'Das Totenhaus' in H. Knabe (ed.) *Gefangen in Hohenschönhausen* (Berlin: List), pp. 251–67.

Krämer, S. (1998) 'Das Medium als Spur und als Apparat' in S. Krämer (ed.) *Medien, Computer, Realität: Wirklichkeitsvorstellungen und Neue Medien* (Frankfurt/Main: Suhrkamp), pp. 73–94.

Müller, K. (2007) 'Der geplante Schauprozeß' in H. Knabe (ed.) *Gefangen in Hohenschönhausen* (Berlin: List), pp. 101–29.

Pirker, E. U. and M. Rüdiger (2010) 'Authentizitätsfiktionen in populären Geschichtskulturen: Annäherungen' in E.U. Pirker, M. Rüdiger, C. Klein, T. Leiendecker, C. Oesterle, M. Sénécheau and M. Uike-Bormann (eds) *Echte Geschichte: Authentizitätsfiktionen in populären Geschichtskulturen* (Bielefeld: Transcript), pp. 11–30.

C. R. Plantinga (1997) *Rhetoric and Representation in Nonfiction Film* (Cambridge: Cambridge University Press).

H. Welzer (2002) *Das kommunikative Gedächtnis: Eine Theorie der Erinnerung* (Munich: Beck).

H. Welzer (2010) 'Re-Narrations: How Pasts Change in Conversational Remembering', *Memory Studies*, 3 (5), 4–17.

Zeitzeugenarchiv Hohenschönhausen (2006) 'Zeitzeugeninterview mit Carl-Wolfgang H., 18 September 2006'.
Zeitzeugenarchiv Hohenschönhausen (2007a) 'Zeitzeugeninterview mit Peter W., 4 December 2007'.
Zeitzeugenarchiv Hohenschönhausen (2007b) 'Zeitzeugeninterview mit Michael B., 5 December 2007'.
Zeitzeugenarchiv Hohenschönhausen (2008a) 'Zeitzeugeninterview mit Bruno S., 14 May 2008'.
Zeitzeugenarchiv Hohenschönhausen (2008b) 'Zeitzeugeninterview mit Klaus-Dieter S., 10 June 2008'.
Zeitzeugenarchiv Hohenschönhausen (2009a) 'Zeitzeugeninterview mit Wolfgang W., 16 March 2009'.
Zeitzeugenarchiv Hohenschönhausen (2009b) 'Zeitzeugeninterview mit Monika B., 26 May 2009'.
Zeitzeugenarchiv Hohenschönhausen (2009c) 'Zeitzeugeninterview mit Hartmut S., 4 June 2009'.
Zeitzeugenarchiv Hohenschönhausen (2009d) 'Zeitzeugeninterview mit Lutz L., 11 June 2009'.
Zeitzeugenarchiv Hohenschönhausen (2009e) 'Zeitzeugeninterview mit Torsten R., 16 June 2009'.

5
Doppelgänger in Post-*Wende* Literature: Klaus Schlesinger's *Trug* and Beyond

Elke Gilson

This chapter reflects on the 'memory of GDR literature' in a twofold way. It focuses on Klaus Schlesinger's *Trug* (2000) and analyses the Romantic, uncanny make-up of the doppelgänger relationship it depicts in order to discuss the novel's (thematic) treatment of the GDR past (i.e. memory of the GDR *in* literature). By situating the text within the author's *oeuvre* and relating it to other exemplary Berlin novels published around the turn of the millennium it also demonstrates the afterlife of narrative techniques which may be described as 'typical of the GDR' in post-*Wende* Berlin literature (i.e. memory *of* GDR literature today).

Drawing on both Niklas Luhmann's interpretation of the appearance and popularity of the doppelgänger figure in literature around 1800, and Freud's reflections a century later, this chapter will argue that the re-emergence of the doppelgänger in texts written by authors of different generations and origins around 2000 can be read as symptomatic of a broader social crisis of reflection and memory instigated by both the *Wende* and the turn of the millennium. Following the argument expounded by Laurie Ruth Johnson in her study *Aesthetic Anxiety: Uncanny Symptoms in German Literature and Culture* (2010), the final section of this chapter will examine the 'uncanny', which is brought to the fore primarily (though not solely) through the figure of the doppelgänger, and assess its value as a 'model for a modern embodied memory' (2010: 18). The resulting analysis will highlight the complexity that literary texts can bring to debates concerning appropriate ways to deal with the past.

Self-encounters in the city

Set in the mid-1980s, *Trug* tells the story of a Düsseldorfer, Strehlow, whose business trip to West Berlin is interrupted when he unexpectedly finds himself lost in the Eastern part of the city due to a U-Bahn breakdown. Strehlow's border crossing on the U-Bahn demonstrates striking similarities to that of Erwin Racholl, the eponymous hero of the story from Schlesinger's volume *Berliner Traum* (*Berlin Dream*, 1977). Strehlow, while travelling in the opposite direction to Racholl, shares his reluctance: 'unintended and against his will' (Schlesinger, 1980a: 15).[1] Again, like Racholl, Strehlow encounters his doppelgänger on the other side of the Wall – in Goethe's terminology, an 'incredible occurrence', which leads Peter Böthig (2000) to suggest that the subtitle should bear the genre designation 'novella', rather than 'novel'.

On the other side of the Wall, Strehlow suddenly finds himself staring at a reflection of his younger self in the window of a café, a reflection which changes into a living figure as soon as he enters the place. The protagonist proceeds to make the acquaintance of one of the regular customers, who dresses in a manner which Strehlow has not dared do since his youth; nevertheless, he is otherwise very similar in appearance to Strehlow. This similarity is confirmed by the waitress, who asks whether the two men are perhaps related (Schlesinger, 2000: 100). Their independent existence, as two individual characters, is thus authenticated by a third party. The 'other', as he is mostly referred to in the rest of the text, is called Skolud; his expression is mocking and challenging, and he seems mysteriously well informed about his baffled counterpart's past (e.g. 69).

Despite his initial reluctance, the protagonist allows himself to be engaged in conversation with the 'other', from which the reader learns that Strehlow also grew up in the East, although he fled 22 years ago, and that both characters had read the same subject, architecture, many years previously at university. While Skolud no longer profits professionally from his architectural degree, because the expectations of the communist state could not be reconciled with his own principles, Strehlow, in the West, has transformed into a cunning property broker who does not even baulk at corrupt practices. When confronted with the moral superiority of his opposite number, Strehlow feels that his high-handed approach to business is called into question. He gradually realises that he is fundamentally 'not so very different from his counterpart at all' (42), and that a long time ago he had even 'shared similar thoughts' (52).

The fact that Strehlow's doppelgänger, who reminds him of his own former ideals, represents a forgotten, or even repressed half of the protagonist's self, is suggested throughout the text by his pervasive sense of incompleteness and lack of harmony, for example, immediately before the encounter (Schlesinger, 2000: 9). Later in the text, while studying a painting which portrays, of all things, the 'Expulsion from Paradise', Strehlow conjectures that we 'have all, at some point and without noticing, lost something' (90). In the same way, a later chapter in *Trug* refers to Strehlow's 'poor equilibrium' (125) and a 'pervasive sense of imbalance' (129). The initial hallucination caused by the reflection in the windowpane had even led Strehlow to pose the following highly allusive question: 'Had he become a kind of Schlemihl and had he lost his reflection instead of his shadow?' (10). The reference to the Faustian pact made by Chamisso's Schlemihl fits perfectly with the suggestion throughout the rest of the novel that anything which no longer fitted Strehlow's new West German personality was split off and discarded following his flight to the West.

The East-West German dimension of the narrative provides the first and most obvious explanation for the fascination that the doppelgänger figure held for Schlesinger. Before *Trug* he had already made frequent use of self-encounters and cases of autoscopy, most explicitly in the aforementioned 'Die Spaltung des Erwin Racholl' ('The Splitting of Erwin Racholl'): at the end of the narrative, upon finding himself in 'the part of the city that was forbidden to him' (Schlesinger, 1980a: 15), Racholl is 'not surprised *to see himself*' (ibid.: 101, my italics) sitting on the U-Bahn seat opposite. The border-hopping of Schlesinger's protagonists was, for a long time, an integral part of the author's own existence, given that after his departure from the GDR in 1980 (which followed his expulsion from the East German Authors' Association in 1979) he remained in possession of a visa which allowed him to continue to commute between the Western and Eastern halves of the divided city of Berlin.

Schlesinger's Berlin-based narratives complement a number of post-war texts in which the Wall appears as an East-West German mirror. In a bar conversation that Strehlow overhears (Schlesinger, 2000: 127), the division of Germany is compared to a case of twins who have grown up separately. Other Berlin authors and contemporaries of Schlesinger have also examined divisions in Germany through reference to similar pairings, such as Monika Maron, in the column 'Tücken der Freiheit' ('Pitfalls of Freedom', 1995) for the *Spiegel* (later 'Zwei Brüder' ('Two Brothers', 2010)) and Reinhard Jirgl in *Abtrünnig* (*Renegade,* 2005), his Berlin novel 'from the time of trepidation'. Twins and the theme of doubling are also the subject of works by Helga Königsdorf and Brigitte Burmeister; even Fonty and his 'constant shadow', Tallhover, characters from Grass' *Ein Weites Feld* (*Too Far Afield,* 1995),[2] come to mind in this context; Kurt Drawert uses both the imagery of the shadow and the mirror in *Spiegelland* (*Mirror Land,* 1992) and *Ich hielt meinen Schatten für einen anderen und grüßte* (*I Mistook My Shadow for Someone Else and Said Hello,* 2008); in Peter Schneider's 'Berlin-Trilogy' doppelgänger and pairs of brothers reconnoitre the streets of the 'Siamese city' (1982: 7).

Schneider's 1982 dictum that the 'wall in the mind' would take far longer to destroy than the real Wall, which has been incessantly referred to since the *Wende,* already implied that the division of Germany would not only affect society as a whole, but have an equally powerful effect on individual biographies. In particular, many who were 'behind the Wall' as long as it existed felt themselves to be faced with an imminent decision: to stay or to go. This internal struggle with what Schlesinger (1980b: 174) called 'alternatives between which a person should not have to choose', led to a variety of self-divisions and self-encounters in prose by East German authors such as Christa Wolf (for instance, in 'Unter den Linden' ('Under the Linden Trees', 1974)), Wolfgang Hilbig (for example, in 'Er nicht ich' ('He not I', 1992)) and Monika Maron (as in *Flugasche* (*Flight of Ashes,* 1981)).[3]

Whether it represented the possibility of dramatising internal contradictions within the individual, or the confrontation of socio-ideological alternatives, the imagery of the doppelgänger has proven to be especially productive in portraying the divisions in Europe caused by the Cold War, the reality of which was particularly imprinted on everyday life in Berlin. In this respect the motif has, in other contexts, a rich history: Dostoyevsky, author of *The Double: A Petersburg Poem* (1846), a variation of whose plot appears at the conclusion of *Trug,* similarly came from a city regarded as a crossroads between the East and the West. The same applies to the contemporary Nobel Prize winner Orhan Pamuk, creator of doppelgänger narratives and author of *The White Castle* (1985/1991), in which inhabitants of the Turkish capital are confronted with the choice between the Occident and the Orient.

The doppelgänger relationship, rationalised in *Trug* as a crisis of personal memory, quite evidently invites an allegorical reading of the text, based not solely on the way the two doppelgänger characters are positioned in East and West Germany respectively, but also on the clichéd characterisation of Strehlow and Skolud as prototype representatives of their home countries. The narrative, moreover, undeniably uses the figure of the doppelgänger to integrate performatively two separate time periods: set in the mid-1980s, the story's use of doppelgänger imagery to deal with questions of perception and memory at the same time allows it to be regarded as a reflection of its time of publication (2000), when discussions about the memory politics of the Berlin Republic were more prominent than ever. In order to comprehend fully the complexities of the manner in which Schlesinger's prose responds to the challenges facing German cultural memory after the *Wende*, this chapter will proceed to examine the literary techniques which Schlesinger employed to construct the doppelgänger relationship in *Trug*.

'Memorial vision', epistemological doubt and the uncanny

From the outset, *Trug* contains all the characteristic attributes of a doppelgänger relationship cast in the (dark) Romantic mould, which is, for reader and protagonist alike, uncanny. In contrast to research on other authors with GDR backgrounds, like Christa Wolf, Franz Fühmann, Fritz Rudolph Fries, Günter de Bruyn or Wolfgang Hilbig, that on Schlesinger has touched on his references to authors such as E.T.A. Hoffmann, A. von Chamisso and Jean Paul only in passing, if at all.[4] This is surprising because their influence had already coloured Schlesinger's earlier texts, even if less obviously than in *Trug*. Reading this particular novel, one can recognise the first hints at a variation of the central autoscopic experience in E.T.A. Hoffmann's Nachtstück (Night Piece) *Das steinerne Herz* (*The Stone Heart*, 1817) in the detail of the youthful doppelgänger dressed in old-fashioned clothes. The title is programmatic as well, since *trugebilde* in Middle High German means 'ghost' (Schmitt, 2000).

In the first subchapter, which, with its richly connoted title ('Optical Interferences', Schlesinger, 2000: 9), alludes to potentially distorted perceptions, a fragment of a melody is used to trigger a recollection of Strehlow's childhood, and the narrator allows this to flow smoothly into the description of the protagonist's perception of the outside world. The urban walks and visits to pubs that Schlesinger's other heroes undertake are all permeated with similar moments in which their vision is filtered through memories which pave the way for the autoscopic experience. Their evocative force is indicated by a formula which is also used in *Trug*: 'he saw himself' (9, 131, 162, 169 among others). During his expeditions in the streets of East Berlin, which had been familiar to him for such a long time, Strehlow's memories overlay his perceptions, so that he often 'stares' at something 'without actually seeing it' (73).

Whether Strehlow's mysterious experiences in the East are the result of real events, or – in reference to the (sensorial) deception of the title – simply 'a short-term disturbance of his ability to perceive' (22), is problematised in particular during the conversations with his West Berlin friend Strack: 'Do you think I am suffering from hallucinations?' (87) The uncertain nature of the situation and the reader's confusion are exacerbated not only by the fact that Strehlow himself frequently and explicitly poses the question of whether his senses might be deceiving him, but also by the fact that his encounters with Skolud repeatedly take place during daydreams and in scenes clearly characterised as such. The central chapter, 'Conversations, Meditations', contains a meeting of a clearly hallucinatory nature with both Skolud and Ilka – the woman whom Strehlow had left behind in the East following his flight to the West (104). Strehlow's former beloved appears in a daydream, in which she walks silently alongside the protagonist (107). As a pure figment of his imagination, Ilka is the literary sister of either Olimpia from Hoffmann's *Sandmann* (*The Sandman*, 1816), or the female figure who is assumed to be present behind the window in *Das öde Haus* (*The Abandoned House*, 1817, by the same author), whose status as a real woman rather than a painting is never fully explained. Ilka's affinity with the female fantasy figures from Hoffmann's *Night Pieces* is intensified when Strehlow sees her a few hours later through a window using one of the earlier author's favoured optical devices, opera glasses:

> Having to crouch down to look through the low-set window, Strehlow saw what he initially thought to be a *shadow*, which seemed to be making gentle, almost swaying movements; however, the longer he looked, the clearer the figure became. [H]e held the *lenses* pointing at where she had vanished into the background [...] and as she walked into the glow of a *lamp*, which seemed to be hanging over a table, [...] she was so clearly there and so close that Strehlow felt he could simply stretch out his hand and touch her. He *stared and stared* at this figure. [...] For a long time [he] could not tear his eyes away, until the figure stood up and disappeared into the background, *turned off the light* and, in the *glow of a candle*, became a floating *shadow* once again.
>
> (Schlesinger, 2000: 138–9, my italics)

In a similar way to the initial encounter with Skolud in the first chapter, Strehlow's real encounter with the love of his youth, which takes place the day after the opera glasses experience, is introduced by a piece of music, 'which seemed familiar to him' (ibid.: 170), and which thereby seems capable of activating the imaginative force of memory (for a discussion of the same technique in the later works by Hoffmann, see Pelgrims, 2003). Like Skolud before her, Ilka also seems to walk out of a mirror towards Strehlow in a brief moment of hallucination (Schlesinger, 2000: 155).

Not only does the text employ optical instruments as a leitmotif, but the narrator also stresses all other factors contributing to the distortion of perceptions. Apart from alcohol and Strehlow's weariness (which, among other things, triggers his 'meditative state of semi-consciousness' (14), his 'heavy eyelids', and the 'acoustic twilight' (61) which surrounds him), the use of lighting comes to mind (unsurprising considering the frequency of allusions to Hoffmann): the darkness of the 'dimly-lit' pub; the gloomy streets; the flickering candles and the subsequent garish illumination of people and objects in 'the blazing glare of a light bulb' (131).

Ultimately, in the skilfully prepared but nonetheless perplexing conclusion to *Trug*, Strehlow's two East German acquaintances – two living and breathing shadows – turn his well ordered life upside down. Through subtle hints, marking mutual changes for each of the adversaries, Schlesinger fashions an exchange of roles between the two figures: Strehlow drinks increasingly heavily, while the 'other' drinks less and less; Skolud, who had previously paid little attention to sensible business practice, suddenly thinks only of 'deadlines'; Strehlow, on the other hand, forgets his. The formulae by which the two characters bid farewell also demonstrate narrative reversals (66 in comparison with 166). The exchange is complete when Skolud explicitly chooses the 'risks of freedom' over 'quiet servitude' (161), whereas the businessman from Düsseldorf is reminded increasingly of his student days in East Berlin by his wanderings through the city. On the night in which Strehlow finds long-lost happiness in the arms of the love of his youth, the 'other' uses Strehlow's passport to cross the border into West Berlin. The felonious finale of the narrative recalls once more Hoffmann's doppelgänger stories and lends a seemingly logical foundation to the impossible. The end of the narrative does, however, retain a degree of mystery: perhaps Strehlow has simply been living a 'dream-like version of reality' (173).

The recognition of the way certain literary texts trigger epistemological uncertainty, which writers create by, 'surely not unintentionally, preventing the reader from knowing whether he is being led into the real world or the author's own imaginary one', was the starting point for Freud's analysis of Ernst Jentsch's 1906 essay, 'Über die Zur Psychologie des Unheimlichen' ('On the Psychology of the Uncanny'). Freud's essay, 'Das Unheimliche' ('The Uncanny', 1919), contains his famous analysis of Hoffmann's *Sandmann*, and admittedly emphasises that in such cases the reader's uncertainty diminishes over the course of the reading, so that by the end he is in a position 'to recognise the facts of the matter by considering them rationally' (Freud, 1970: 254). However, the epistemological uncertainty (present initially, at least) remains a central component in later attempts to define the literary uncanny (see Todorov, 1975).

Many theorists have established a connection between a literary preference for uncanny stories, and contemporary needs in certain epochs (e.g. Johnson, 2010; Masschelein, 2011). The genre, together with its characteristic motifs, is then judged as a response to specific historical, cultural or social sensitivities. An interesting variation on this way of thinking is provided by the sociologist Niklas Luhmann's observations on *Die Kunst der Gesellschaft* (*Art as a Social System*, 1995).[5] In this work and even more explicitly in the essay 'Eine Redeskription romantischer Kunst' ('A Redescription of Romantic Art', 1996) the emergence of the uncanny doppelgänger in literature around 1800 is considered symptomatic of the epistemological doubt triggered by Kant with his so-called 'Copernican revolution' in the theory of knowledge.

Since Kant we know that the structures of knowledge established in the subject determine the apparent form of reality. According to Luhmann, when Jean Paul (1999: 66) classifies the doppelgänger in *Siebenkäs* (1796–97) as 'people who see themselves', he portrays them as 'modern' people who are no longer able to simply perceive the world for itself ('an sich'). Observing the outside world, they are compelled to reflect the conditions of their own perception, and are, therefore, paradoxically confronted with the world and themselves simultaneously (Luhmann, 1996: 336). This self-reflection materialises in the encounter with the doppelgänger; in this figure the individual comes face-to-face with his/her own past and the perspectives he/she has held up to this point.

Doppelgänger in post-*Wende* Berlin literature

The functional versatility of the doppelgänger in the portrayal of epistemological crises explains not only the fascination which this figure held for such authors as Jean Paul, Kleist and Hoffmann (among others), but it also enables us to understand the revival of this phenomenon in literature around the turn of the twentieth century, as psychoanalysis made the acknowledgement of 'the Other in the self' inescapable. That '[a]t the millennium the doppelgänger may yet prove to be a chosen figure for a mirroring of the mirroring of Romantic agony at the last fin de siècle' had already been predicted by Andrew Webber in 1996 (357), and is confirmed not only by Schlesinger's Berlin novel, written around the most recent turn of the century, but equally by the texts of many of his contemporaries, as well as those of his juniors. This section will demonstrate this observation, by drawing on two exemplary novels by Inka Parei and Norman Ohler.

The title of Parei's debut, *Die Schattenboxerin* (*The Shadow Boxer*, 1999) can be interpreted as equally programmatic as that of *Trug*. Like many of Schlesinger's texts, Parei's novel treats the subject of an unacknowledged past which lives on in the present and explores the effect memory has on perception. *Die Schattenboxerin* depicts a process of comprehension which takes place over several days, accompanied by wanderings through the city. From the outset the protagonist's susceptibility to hallucinatory experiences is obvious. As is so often the case in Schlesinger's texts, images drawn from memory merge with perceived objects to form at times oppressive hallucinations (Parei, 1999: 15). Ultimately, Parei's work also transforms Berlin's city centre into a site of confrontation with a section of the individual's past which has split off, been lost or perhaps even repressed. Her doppelgänger story concerns two women, Hell and Dunkel (meaning 'light' and 'dark'), whose physical likeness to one another is, as in *Trug*, confirmed by a third party, in this case a mutual friend. As in the case of Strehlow, Hell's sense of loss leads to a feeling of 'disturbed balance' (Schlesinger, 2000: 125), which 'breaks her sense of equilibrium' (Parei, 1999: 10). In Parei's text too, the central autoscopic experience (ibid.: 14) is introduced by the idea of looking into a mirror, a similarity also shared by Schlesinger's *Alte Filme* (*Old Films*, 1976), in which Kotte first becomes a stranger to himself in the mirror (1979: 26), then begins 'to see himself' (ibid.: 48–9) and, ultimately, sees increasing numbers of imaginary creatures in front of him (60).

Atmospheric circumstances, such as smoke, snowflakes, flickering light, darkness (all sources of distortion), which call into question the realism of Hell's perception in *Die Schattenboxerin* are highlighted just as strongly as Hell's exhaustion, which puts her in a similarly sleepy, vague state to that occupied by Schlesinger's daydreaming heroes. The fact that the heroine's shadow-boxing in Parei's novel begins with a journey on the U-Bahn through the city's 'ghost stations' – a consequence of the Wall – constitutes another conspicuous correspondence between Schlesinger's and Parei's narratives. Finally, in both *Trug* and *Die Schattenboxerin*, reversals in the characters' behaviour patterns prepare for the culmination of their reflexive mirror relationship in the open conclusion to the novel, in which they are mistaken for one another by the publican.

Norman Ohler's *Mitte* (*Centre,* 2001) provides a second example of a Berlin novel from the turn of the millennium which deals with 'spectral' themes similar to *Trug*. Once again programmatic, the title of the novel refers not only to the geographical location of the story, the eponymous district in Berlin, which in the wake of the *Wende* was the subject of multiple ideological contests and debates, but also to the internal struggle within the protagonist. In Ohler's ghost story, the hero, Klinger, is haunted by the ghost of the previous tenant of his dilapidated flat. There are hints that Igor, a 'sound artist', who is vocal in his criticism of society, is a previously known, more radical and more idealistic version of Klinger himself. The uncanny flatmate only casually comes to represent a doppelgänger of the protagonist through the rendering of Klinger's feeling that 'between him and Igor a flowing film had been stretched, the surface of a mirror' (Ohler, 2001: 197). He reminds the protagonist, however, that 'there is always the past to steal our solitude – *astonishingly*' (ibid.: 94). One of the two epigraphs to Ohler's novel tends towards this same insight: Ohler takes from Michel de Montaigne's reflections 'On Solitude' the idea that 'Our soul can revolve upon its own axis; it is company in itself, it has the wherewithal to attack and defend, to receive and give.' In the light of this motto the chorus of voices around Klinger may be seen as 'self dialogue'. Many of the urban encounters experienced by Schlesinger's protagonists Michael, Racholl, Kotte and Strehlow may also be considered in this way.

Ohler's novel similarly toys with hallucination-inducing factors, such as lack of sleep (2001: 61); experimenting with drugs (62); or optical instruments, such as Klinger's orange-coloured sunglasses.[6] It describes a 'town under peculiar illumination', using another motto at the beginning to refer to the city's special light conditions: 'At dusk the sense of terror can turn a signpost into a giant spectre' (7). With this quotation from Kant's *Versuch über die Krankheiten des Kopfes* (*Essay on the Illness of the Head,* 1764) Ohler establishes an explicit connection between his ghost story, which takes place in the period following the *Wende,* and the aforementioned initiator of the so-called 'Copernican revolution in the theory of knowledge', which had provoked a host of authors around 1800 to articulate their ensuing epistemological doubts in stories of ghosts, doppelgänger and mistaken identities. The fact that Igor exists solely as a result of Klinger's own delusion is confirmed by Igor's comic and, paradoxically, self-exposing answer to the question, 'what is he, anyway': Igor calls himself 'a chimera, like all phenomena' (Ohler, 2001: 166).

In order to intensify the eerie atmosphere of the story, Ohler's novel, in a similar way to *Trug*, makes use of machines which apparently act autonomously and which in both cases seem to defend the interests of the dead. While in *Mitte* a tape recorder recalls long-forgotten adages, Schlesinger's Strehlow discovers that his PC retaliates whenever he tries to type a sarcastic report about an encounter with a modern 'radio spiritualist' who 'believed herself capable of deciphering voices and messages of long-deceased people from the shortwave radio static' (Schlesinger, 2000: 71). As soon as Strehlow tries to reproduce the woman's declaration that 'the deceased are alive' in his mocking report, the writing on his screen vanishes and in its place a series of 'mysterious hieroglyphs appears' (ibid.). This suggestion of a 'revival of the inanimate' in the service of a past which refuses to be repressed, allows for a reading of the PC incident in *Trug* as a perfect example of a present-day uncanny experience which in the novel functions as an ironic comment on the self-righteous way the West German protagonist has done away with his East German past.

Trug, the uncanny and cultural memory in the twenty-first century

This chapter has hitherto examined two trends inherent in Schlesinger's use of uncanny motifs in *Trug*: on the one hand they bear witness to the development of a number of characteristic tendencies within his own work; on the other hand they can be understood as a conscious attempt to connect with existing literary traditions through intertextual references. Johnson (2010: 10) evaluates the uncanny as a thoroughly 'modern' phenomenon, with both progressive and regressive potential, which becomes manifest when reactionary and modern forces clash:

> I argue that the revolutionary possibilities inherent in anxious, frightening, uncanny experiences are clearest when traditionalist, nostalgic impulses meet modernity [...] when the forces of cultural change inspire a melancholic, nostalgia-driven desire to slow down to an earlier era's pace.

According to Johnson's reading, the uncanny develops over the course of the 'long nineteenth century' from Kleist to Schnitzler into a 'key component of a highly modern memory model' (ibid.: 17), whereby 'uncanny figures, whether they appear as traditional doppelgänger, [...] as strange but familiar portraits, or as hallucinations' (ibid.: 240) are understood as symptoms of a particularly modern problem, one of an 'excess of memory' (ibid.: 186–7).

This chapter has examined two other exemplary novels in order to demonstrate that in *Trug*, with its use of the doppelgänger motif, Schlesinger reflects the pulse of contemporary cultural debate, at a time when not only the turn of the twenty-first century, but also, and above all, the historical event of German reunification were provoking questions about the appropriate way to deal with memory and the past. While the sparkling windows of the rapidly rebuilt city have, often enough, been taken as a demonstration of the desire to hide the past behind their shiny panes, their mirror surface is used in texts by Schlesinger and many other contemporary Berlin-based authors to provide constant confrontations with memory, materialising in the form of the doppelgänger. The connection shown here between the works of Schlesinger, Parei and Ohler could be expanded to include many other Berlin narratives from the turn of the century, by authors of both the older and the younger generation: as Catherine Smale (2011, 2012) explains, even Christa Wolf and Irina Liebmann can be described as representatives of a 'Post-Wende Gothic'. Others who fall into this category include Cees Nooteboom (1999), Reinhard Jirgl and Kurt Drawert, as well as Antje Rávic-Strubel with *Fremd Gehen: Ein Nachtstück* (*To Foreign Lands: A Night Piece*, 2002) and Ricarda Junge with her ghost story *Die komische Frau* (*The Strange Lady*, 2010). In these and other narratives, spectres conduct a constant battle against forgetting the past.

Contrary to first impressions, however, Schlesinger's novel, in which the 'new' West German Strehlow is catapulted back into his East German past, cannot simply be interpreted as a narrative full of nostalgia, homesickness and retrospective longing for a time when society was characterised by greater humanity and solidarity and had not yet been corrupted by the vicious logic of profit. While the basic plot-line may suggest simply a 'book of yesterday' (Rietzschel, 2000 and others), an analysis of the narrative strategies reveals a much more complex evaluation of the afterlife of the (GDR) past. The way Schlesinger embeds the doppelgänger relationship in the literary tradition of the uncanny highlights the questions *Trug* raises about the (uncontrollable) perpetuation of the past and the fear that it evokes by its intimation of the burden of eternal recurrence. Strehlow's memorial wanderings through Berlin are often described in negatively connoted terms: the protagonist experiences 'discomfort' (Schlesinger, 2000: 109–10), terror, shuddering and fear; he is 'almost inundated with torrents of images' (ibid.: 33), and finds that his memories arise 'senselessly' (121).[7] Strehlow refuses to allow his 'perspective on the new to be predetermined' (96); he tries to fight his tendency to 'look without perceiving', and feels a 'longing for something unexpected' (97). Scepticism about treating the past with exaggerated reverence is ultimately articulated most clearly by Strehlow's West German friend, Strack. In response to the protagonist's East German adventures Strack observes that everything in life 'is permitted [...], except one thing: a remake' (92).

On the one hand, Schlesinger's novel, especially on the thematic level, reflects a case of problematic memory loss. The fact that in his confrontation with Skolud, Strehlow is obliged to reconsider the value of his doppelgänger's way of life can easily be interpreted allegorically as a comment on the arguably one-sided memory politics of the Berlin Republic ten years after the *Wende*. On the other hand, the novel simultaneously employs narrative and rhetorical techniques (such as the small lexical clues, the opinions of characters other than the protagonist and the many uncanny, und thus inherently unsettling, motifs) to approach the 'Use and Abuse of History for Life' ('Nutzen und Nachteil der Historie für das Leben') in an overtly critical manner, in accordance with Nietzsche's (1988) insights. *Trug* explores possible ways of living alongside the past in the present, but addresses just as much the need not to allow oneself to be paralysed by the past, in order to make life in the present possible. In this manner the uncanny in Schlesinger's story functions, indeed, as a 'model for modern memory', in line with Johnson's definition, because it 'involves a conception of repetition as a form of freedom, of acknowledging that we must go in and go back in order to go out and go forward' (2010: 240). In this respect it is noteworthy that younger contemporary authors are reacting to and commenting on questions concerning cultural memory in the new German capital in a similar, not necessarily direct or thematic way: their stories explicitly draw on the uncanny imagery so frequently used in GDR literature – which had been trying to come to terms with problematic pasts long before the unification of Germany.

Translated by Matthew Linehan

Notes

1. All translations from the German are by Matthew Linehan.
2. English translation: *Too Far Afield*, trans. Krishna Winston (London: Faber and Faber, 2001).
3. English translation: *Flight of Ashes*, trans. David Newton Marinelli (London: Readers International, 1985).
4. On the significance of romanticism for GDR-based authors, see for example: Gaskill, McPherson and Barker (1990), Köhler (2006) on Wolf, Corkhill (2008) on Hilbig and Decker (2009) on Fühmann.

5. English translation: *Art as a Social System*, trans. Eva M. Knodt (Stanford, CA: Stanford University Press, 2000).
6. These orange glasses can be understood as a playful reference to the 'green glasses' mentioned by Kleist in his letter to his fiancée during his 'Kant-crisis'. (Kleist, 2001: 634).
7. Kotte, the protagonist of *Alte Filme*, used the same adverb to characterise his hallucinations (Schlesinger, 1979: 76). The recognition of an 'eternal recurrence of the same' was the trigger for his crisis as well. The fear of being unable to break out of a never-ending cycle of repetition can generally be said to be one of the most important reasons for the popularity of uncanny figures in GDR literature, especially in the 1970s and 1980s.

References

Böthig, P. (2000) 'Ost und West und Teufelspakt. Klaus Schlesingers "Trug" – eine Novelle in Hoffmannscher Manier', *Frankfurter Rundschau*, 22 April.

Corkhill, A. (2008) 'Wolfgang Hilbig's Appropriation of Romantic Discourse', *Neophilologus*, 92 (1), 93–107.

Decker, G. (2009) 'Der Stachel Romantik. Franz Fühmann und das Unheimliche in der DDR', *Sinn und Form*, 61(1), 5–25.

Drawert, K. (1992) *Spiegelland. Ein deutscher Monolog* (Frankfurt/Main: Suhrkamp).

Drawert, K. (2008) *Ich hielt meinen Schatten für einen anderen und grüßte* (Munich: Beck).

Freud, S. (1970) *'Das Unheimliche (1919)' Studienausgabe. Band IV: Psychologische Schriften* (Frankfurt/Main: Fischer), 241–74.

Gaskill, H., K. McPherson and A. Barker (eds) (1990) *Neue Ansichten. The Reception of Romanticism in the Literature of the GDR* (Amsterdam: Rodopi).

Grass, G. (1995) *Ein weites Feld. Roman* (Göttingen: Steidl).

Hilbig, W. (1992) *Er, nicht ich* (Leipzig: Reclam).

Hoffmann, E. T. A. (1990) *Nachtstücke* (Stuttgart: Reclam).

Jentsch, E. (1906) 'Zur Psychologie des Unheimlichen', *Psychiatrisch-neurologische Wochenschrift*, 22, 203–5.

Jirgl, R. (2005) *Abtrünnig. Roman aus der nervösen Zeit* (Munich: Hanser).

Johnson, L. R. (2010) *Aesthetic Anxiety. Uncanny Symptoms in German Literature and Culture* (Amsterdam: Rodopi).

Junge, R. (2010) *Die komische Frau. Roman* (Frankfurt/Main: Fischer).

Kleist, H. von (2001) 'An Wilhelmine von Zenge, Berlin, den 22. März 1801', in Sämtliche Werke und Briefe (ed.) *Helmut Sembdner*, vol. 2 (Munich: DTV).

Köhler, A. (2006) 'Begegnung unter den Linden: der etwa tausendste Versuch zum Thema Christa Wolf und die Romantik', *Weimarer Beiträge*, 52 (4), 587–601.

Loest, E. (1974) *Schattenboxen* (Berlin: Neues Leben).

Luhmann, N. (1995) *Die Kunst der Gesellschaft* (Frankfurt/Main: Suhrkamp).

Luhmann, N. (1996) 'Eine Redeskription "romantischer" Kunst', in J. Fohrmann and H. Müller (eds) *Systemtheorie der Literatur* (Munich: Fink), 325–44.

Maron, M. (1981) *Flugasche. Roman* (Frankfurt/Main: Fischer).

Maron, M. (1995) 'Tücken der Freiheit', *Der Spiegel*, 13 March.

Maron, M. (2010) *Zwei Brüder. Gedanken zur Einheit 1989 – 2009. Mit Fotografien von Jonas Maron* (Frankfurt/Main: Fischer).

Masschelein, A. (2011) *The Unconcept. The Freudian Uncanny in Late-Twentieth-Century Theory* (Albany: SUNY).
Nietzsche, F. (1988) 'Unzeitgemäße Betrachtungen. Zweites Stück: Vom Nutzen und Nachtheil der Historie für das Leben', in G. Colli and M. Montinari (eds) *Sämtliche Werke. Kritische Studienausgabe*, vol. 1 (Munich: DTV), 243–334.
Nooteboom, C. (1999) *Allerseelen*, trans. H. von Beuningen (Frankfurt/Main: Suhrkamp).
Ohler, N. (2001) *Mitte. Roman* (Berlin: Rowohlt).
Pamuk, O. (1991) *The White Castle. A Novel*, trans. V. Holbrook (New York: Braziller).
Parei, I. (1999) *Die Schattenboxerin. Roman* (Frankfurt/Main: Schöffling).
Paul, J. (1999) 'Siebenkäs', in N. Miller (ed.) *Sämtliche Werke*, pt. I, vol. 2, 5th edn. (Munich: Hanser).
Pelgrims, M. (2003) ' "Die Fantasie erscheint Hoffmann zum Troste." Die Begegnungen in E.T.A. Hoffmanns Doppelerzählung *Die Irrungen* und *Die Geheimnisse* im Spannungsfeld zwischen Entdeckung und Erfindung' (unpublished dissertation, Ghent University).
Rávic-Strubel, A. (2002) *Fremd Gehen. Ein Nachtstück* (Munich: DTV).
Rietzschel, T. (2000) ' "Weißt du noch, die Kreppschuhe?" Schöne Endzeit: Klaus Schlesinger und die DDR der siebziger Jahre', *Frankfurter Allgemeine Zeitung*, 13 July.
Schlesinger, K. (1971) *Michael* (Rostock: Hinstorff).
Schlesinger, K. (1979) *Alte Filme. Eine Berliner Geschichte* (Frankfurt/Main: Fischer Taschenbuch).
Schlesinger, K. (1980a) 'Die Spaltung des Erwin Racholl', in *Berliner Traum: Fünf Geschichten* (Frankfurt/Main: Fischer Taschenbuch), 7–101.
Schlesinger, K. (1980b) 'Am Ende der Jugend', in *Berliner Traum. Fünf Geschichten* (Frankfurt/Main: Fischer Taschenbuch), 159–76.
Schlesinger, K. (2000) *Trug. Roman* (Berlin: Aufbau).
Schmitt, H. J. (2000) 'Die Sache mit Strehlow und Skolud: Doppelgängerschaft Ost/West. Klaus Schlesingers neuer Roman "Trug" ', *Süddeutsche Zeitung*, 23 März.
Schneider, P. (1982) *Der Mauerspringer. Erzählung* (Darmstadt: Luchterhand).
Schneider, P. (1999) *Eduards Heimkehr* (Berlin: Rowohlt).
Smale, C. (2012) ' "Ein Gespenst geht um": Christa Wolf, Irina Liebmann and the post-Wall Gothic', in A. Cusack and B. Murnane (eds) *Popular Revenants: German Gothic and its International Contexts* (Rochester, NY: Camden House), 242–58).
Smale, C. (2011) ' "Wir sind wie Spiegel": Irina Liebmann und der Doppelgänger', in R. Gaderer and M. Doll (eds) *Phantasmata. Techniken des Unheimlichen* (Vienna: Turia und Kant), 203–20.
Todorov, T. (1975) *The Fantastic. A Structural Approach to a Literary Genre* (Ithaca, NY: Cornell University Press).
Webber, A.J. (1996) *The Doppelgänger. Double Visions in German Literature* (Oxford: Clarendon Press).
Wolf, C. (1974) *Unter den Linden. 3 unwahrscheinliche Geschichten* (Darmstadt: Luchterhand).

Part III

Beyond Nostalgia

6

'*Ostalgie* doesn't fit!': Individual Interpretations of and Interaction with *Ostalgie*

Claire Hyland

Since the Berlin Wall fell in 1989, processes of remembering the GDR have been widely discussed in unified Germany and the idea of *Ostalgie* has become a key strand in these debates. Broadly understood as a form of nostalgia for the GDR, the idea has often been interpreted as a romanticisation of the socialist past and an attempt to underplay, or even overlook, the oppressive nature of the authoritarian state. The importance of these memory debates in understanding post-unification eastern identities should not be underestimated; as Patricia Hogwood explains in Chapter 2, exploring memories of the past helps to make sense of patterns of contemporary behaviour. This chapter explores how easterners interact with and negotiate the term *Ostalgie* when constructing east German identities. It draws on a series of in-depth interviews which were carried out between November 2009 and December 2010 with easterners who were born in the GDR in the 1970s and now live in Berlin. The findings are part of a doctoral project which explored how these individuals constructed their own and others' eastern identities, and how they engaged with and negotiated dominant discourses in this process. The interviews were designed to be largely participant-led, which ensured that participants expressed their own perceptions, as well as their understandings of the discourse about *Ostalgie*, without any prompting. *Ostalgie* emerged as a key idea in the ways that they made sense of themselves and of other easterners.

The first section discusses the concept of *Ostalgie*, outlining how it is commonly understood in the German public sphere and how it has been interpreted in academic literature in the field. The focus of the chapter then turns to the findings of the interviews. This analysis has been divided into two sections: the first addresses how the participants interacted with *Ostalgie* when discussing other easterners and the second explores how they engaged with the idea when presenting themselves. These sections explore interaction with *Ostalgie* on two levels: first with the term itself and second with the meanings associated with the term. The analysis demonstrates that, although participants do not identify with *Ostalgie* when constructing their own eastern identities, it is significant in their understanding of other easterners as well as in the way that they present their identities to others.

Perceptions of *Ostalgie* in unified Germany

Since its creation by cabaret artist Uwe Steimle in the 1990s, the term *Ostalgie* has become commonplace in conversations about the GDR in unified Germany. It acts as a dominant idea when it comes to remembering the GDR past, essentially describing sentiments of nostalgia for GDR life. Jonathan Bach (2002: 546), who works in the field of institutional memory and national identity, explains the expression as 'a household word for the perceived nostalgia for the east that presents itself in the form of theme parties, newly revived products and a general flowering of all things eastern'. The idea fits neatly into the concept of popular memory, coined by the Birmingham Centre's Popular Memory Group (BCPMG) to refer to 'knowledge of the past and present [...] produced in the course of everyday life'. When this concept first emerged in the late 1970s, it framed primarily the study of 'personal comparisons and narratives' and 'intimate cultural forms', such as photographs, objects and diaries (Popular Memory Group, 1998: 77). In her more recent work on popular memory, however, Tara Brabazon (2005: 70) widened its remit to include film, television and popular music, which, she claims, also provide 'a way to assemble a sense of how the past is produced outside of historical disciplinary borders'. In line with this concept, *Ostalgie* has manifested itself primarily within popular culture; it can be seen in the commodification of east German products and childhood characters, such as the *Sandmann*, and in TV shows, including ZDF's *Ostalgie Show*, MDR's *Ein Kessel DDR* (*A Pot of GDR*) and RTL's *DDR Show*.[1] In his extensive work on the subject, Paul Cooke (2003b: 135) has likened these programmes to the wider European television genre of nostalgia shows, comparing them to RTL's *Die 80er Show* and the BBC's *I love the 1970s*. In this sense, the renewed popularity of GDR confectionery, such as *Knusperflocken, Halloren Kugeln* and *Liebesperlen*, is similar to the comeback of British products like sherbet dabs and rhubarb and custards.

From this perspective, then, it appears that the commodification of the GDR past actually fits neatly into forms of popular memory which have spread across Europe as a whole.

Ostalgie differs from other European forms of popular memory, however, because it links to a socialist past, yet exists in the context of unified Germany; a paradox which makes it more contentious than other forms of post-socialist memory. *Ostalgie* appears, therefore, to be more at odds with what the Popular Memory Group (1998: 76) labels 'dominant memory', referring to 'the power and pervasiveness of historical representations, their connections with dominant institutions and the part they play in winning consent and building alliances in the processes of formal politics'. In unified Germany, dominant memory of the GDR tends to focus on the oppressive nature of the state, in particular 'the way in which the regime controlled the borders and on the activities of the "Stasi" ' (Knischewski and Spittler, 2006: 281). As Silke Arnold-de Simine and Susannah Radstone point out in Chapter 1, *Ostalgie* is frequently understood as a sentimentalisation or trivialisation of the GDR past, which goes against the norms of dominant memory. A large proportion of scholars on east Germany agree that, in the most extreme cases, *Ostalgie* is even read as a desire to return to GDR socialism. Cooke (2005: 104) claims, for example, that *Ostalgie* is said to be responsible for 'helping to keep alive anti-democratic principles' and is a sign that easterners wish 'to return to the values of the past' (2003a: 166). The idea of *Ostalgie* thus holds far stronger political connotations than other types of European popular memory, as anthropologist Daphne Berdahl (1999, 193) emphasises, claiming that it is 'readily dismissed in popular, political and academic discourses [...] as the questionable products of "GDR romantics," former Communist Party loyalists, now represented by the Party of Democratic Socialism (PDS)'.[2] Berdahl's claim is borne out by the vast majority of academic work carried out on the subject by political scientists who often link the rise of PDS voters in the eastern states during the 1990s to the increase in the popularity of *Ostalgie* (see, for example, Buchstein, 1995; Schroeder, 2008).

The controversy surrounding *Ostalgie* is perhaps better understood in the context of the way that the east is perceived more generally in the public sphere. The rapid unification process which, in short, saw the implementation of the west German social, economic and political systems in the former GDR in the space of ten months, left very little trace of the socialist GDR. This process appears to have set the tone for perceptions of the east in unified Germany. A recent publication by the Bundeszentrale für politische Bildung (Federal Office for

Political Education) reports that, even two decades after unification, eastern identity continues to be depicted as an 'alterity'. It is represented as a divergence from the contemporary German norm, which is almost always presented as being synonymous with the west German system (Ahbe and Gries, 2009: 12). Julia Belke's contribution to the publication (2009: 135–79), which draws on a longitudinal discourse analytical study of the political magazine *KONTRASTE*, demonstrates that representations of the east are conceived against the idea of a west German norm, and that in this conception easterners are presented as the inferior group. She claims that reports on the east commonly suggest

> that east Germans cannot get on with the market economy, that east Germans cannot manage money, that east Germans are ungrateful, that east Germans cannot get to grips with democracy and also that east Germans are too attached to *Heimat* and not prepared to step over the 'border'.
>
> (ibid.: 175)

Given that the dominant trend in unified Germany is to problematise the east, it is not surprising that *Ostalgie* is often looked upon as a romanticised view of the past which may threaten unity in Germany. The postcolonial scholars in the field (who, together with political scientists, make up the vast majority of researchers) tend to take this viewpoint as their starting point and can be separated into two groups according to their conclusions. The first group raises concerns about the impact of disparaging perceptions of the east on eastern identity construction, as shown for example, by John Theobald (2000: 131) in his work on post-unification perceptions of the east:

> The overwhelming consensual trend since 1990 has been to discredit the memory of the GDR and to diminish respect for all that it – and that includes its people – set out to realize in its 40 years of existence. When alternatives to this approach are advanced, they are – 'on message' with hegemonic discourse – generally dismissed as *Ostalgie* or as irrelevant and unrealistic speculation.

Theobald agrees that since the fall of the Wall, hegemonic discourse has tended to paint the GDR in a negative light. The influence of this discourse is claimed to be such that any attempts to counter these negative perceptions are met with exasperation and interpreted as wistful and backward-looking, or as 'ostalgic'. In short, *Ostalgie* is said to restrict, trivialise and undermine positive perceptions of the GDR; because it exists as a part of hegemonic discourse, it leaves little room for forms of eastern identity which challenge these problematic connotations to emerge in the public sphere.

The prevalence of the term in popular perceptions of the east, together with its rather dismissive and derogative connotations, explains why it is often problematised in academic work about eastern identities. In his work on *Ostalgie*, for example, social scientist Thomas Ahbe (1999: 87) highlights the range of meanings associated with the term, but points out that stigmatisation is a common thread which runs through all of the definitions. He claims '[the] stigmatising meaning of *Ostalgie* is one of the few consistencies in the use of the term'. Elaborating on the nature of this stigmatisation, he suggests that *Ostalgie* is associated with ideas of degradation, outdatedness and futility. For Ahbe, its kitsch manifestations in the form of GDR memorabilia and associations with a backward-looking longing for the GDR influenced mainstream perceptions of the east in unified Germany.

The second group of postcolonial scholars who take *Ostalgie* as their focus tend to adopt a more positive stance, claiming that it in fact signifies easterners' empowerment in the face of apparent western superiority. In her anthropological study of eastern objects, Berdahl (1999: 206) concludes that:

> this framing of eastern German identities and resistance to western German dominance in terms of product choices and mass merchandising entails a sort of *Ostalgie* for the present [. . .]: practices that both contest and affirm the new order of a consumer market economy.

Berdahl suggests not only that *Ostalgie* actually fits into the capitalist context of unified Germany, but also that easterners have ownership of it; it is not a part of the hegemonic discourse which dismisses positive perceptions of the GDR, but a sign that easterners are actively resisting western superiority. Cooke takes the idea of ownership a step further in his work on Leander Haußmann's hit film *Sonnenallee* (*Sun Alley*, 1999), a humorous portrayal of a group of adolescent boys contending with conventional rites of passage, such as sex and relationships, as well as issues specific to the GDR relating to the authorities and the black market. The 'ostalgic' nature of the film sparked criticism in the German press, in which it was even likened to National Socialist propagandistic comedies (Cooke, 2003a: 157). In his interpretation of the film, however, Cooke (ibid.: 167) offers a different perspective, claiming it:

> demands that the West German tradition should not be prioritised over the East, but that the full diversity of German experience should be embraced on the nation's quest for unity.

For Cooke, then, this form of *Ostalgie* is not only a sign of eastern resistance to western superiority, but a critical appraisal of both eastern and western views of German history. The key difference between this second group of postcolonial scholars and those outlined above is perhaps where they place the agency in their analyses of *Ostalgie*. For the first group, it seems that the west has taken ownership of the idea; *Ostalgie* cannot act as an outlet for positive memories of the GDR because it has been undermined by negative discourse about the east, and is therefore simply dismissed or read as a problematic attachment to the GDR. For the second group, however, easterners have maintained ownership of *Ostalgie*, and use it not only to express their preference for some aspects of the GDR, but also to resist western superiority.

The remainder of this chapter draws on the findings of in-depth interviews with easterners to explore the question of agency within the idea of *Ostalgie*. It distinguishes between perceptions of the self and others to reveal the tensions between popular memory and dominant memory in different forms of perceptions. The analysis discusses whether *Ostalgie* can serve as a popular memory discourse for positive perceptions of the GDR, or whether its potential to fulfil this role is overshadowed by more dominant memory. It addresses how the participants negotiate first the term itself, and second the idea that positive memories of the GDR are akin to frivolous idealisation of the socialist state or even a problematic politicised identification with the socialist state. As well as shedding light on the power relations between positive memories of the GDR and the dominant ideas which put the east in a more negative light, this approach reveals how the influence of dominant memory shifts in different social contexts.

Ostalgie in eastern identity construction

It was clear from participants' narratives that *Ostalgie* played a formative role in their identity construction, that is to say the way in which they constructed an understanding of east Germanness for themselves and for others. Of the 20 participants, 17 used the term without any prompting, usually with reference to GDR objects or products. The point where the term was most commonly used was without doubt when participants were given *Knusperflocken* and *Ampelmann* sweets, which overwhelmingly elicited an animated response, encouraging them to talk warmly about familiar objects from their past.[3] However, although almost all of the participants reacted enthusiastically to the sweets, all but two of them engaged with the term *Ostalgie* defensively. Furthermore, the participants distanced themselves from the image conjured up by *Ostalgie,* which depicts easterners as stuck in the socialist past and thus unable to accept fully the norms of unified Germany.

Ostalgie and other easterners

Mainstream stereotypes about the east resonated in most of the participants' narratives about others; all 20 were convinced that an 'ostalgic' group of easterners exists, and that this 'positive' attachment to the past was problematic.[4] The following extract, which is taken from Christian's interview, is typical of the participants' descriptions of 'ostalgic' easterners:

> There are also lots of people who are 'ostalgic', and it's really obstructive for their lives because they simply ... still, I mean, kind of live in a backward mentality.

Christian's use of the terms 'obstructive' and 'backward mentality' relates directly to the common perception that *Ostalgie* signifies being stuck in the past and implies that such attachment to the past is something which should be remedied. Also striking is the lack of empathy that Christian shows towards apparently 'ostalgic' easterners. He expressed a considerable lack of understanding and profound frustration at their apparent inability to move on from the past. This sentiment comes through even more clearly in the following extract, where he explains how he believes that *Ossis* are:

> Whiney somehow and the good old times and mmm and you see and it's not fair ... like that. [...] Sort of fixated on the past. That's something, where I'd say, that's an *Ossi*. I mean, now we have a new situation that he isn't getting to grips with. And if we're unhappy with this new situation, then we have to look at it, and what we are unhappy with, then we have to do something to make the situation better.

Christian's frustration is immediately clear from the mocking tone that he uses to parody 'ostalgic' easterners, suggesting that they mistakenly view the GDR as 'the good old times'. His use of the phrase, 'it's not fair', which is generally associated with childish complaining, emphasises that he considers *Ostalgie* to be a puerile mentality. Christian does not take into account any difficulties with which easterners were confronted during the turbulent transition into unified Germany. Instead, he appears to hold them responsible for apparently failing to come to terms with unification.

As well as showing little understanding for allegedly 'ostalgic' easterners, participants consistently claimed that this group tends to glorify the past. Like the idea that *Ostalgie* is akin to being stuck in the past, the perception that some easterners glorify the GDR was viewed as a problem in the context of unified Germany:

> *Ostalgie*, well I associate this term with a lot of negatives. You see, there are an awful lot of people, who also come from the former GDR, who say, yeah in the GDR, it wasn't all bad and there were lots of things, back then we all had work and there was always something to eat and social togetherness was easier, and then everything is, the positives are pushed to the forefront and the negatives are completely brushed aside... it's like a glorification, this *Ostalgie*.

Like all of the participants who discussed the glorification of the GDR, Daniel became increasingly infuriated in his narrative. When he imitated the easterners who he claimed glorified the past, he adopted a sarcastic tone of voice and rolled his eyes, suggesting that he had little patience for what he considered to be a rather ignorant view of the GDR. His claim that 'ostalgic' easterners fail to see the negative side of the GDR implies that they overlook the advantages that have come with the end of socialism.

The parallels between the participants' understandings of 'ostalgic' easterners and the dominant perceptions of the east are not the only striking features of these extracts. Importantly, they also shed light on where the participants locate themselves in relation to this apparently 'ostalgic' group, and therefore to *Ostalgie*. The consistent use of the third person suggests that while they believe that there are easterners who fit into this stereotype, they do not include themselves in this bracket. Their distance from *Ostalgie* is emphasised further by the profound degree of frustration and criticism that they target at this group, which makes it clear that they do not identify with it. The greatest indicator of the participants' distance from this group, however, was that they constructed a subgroup of easterners from which they were automatically excluded, and then ascribed the 'ostalgic' mentality to this group. For example, when I asked Jens if he could explain why some easterners were 'ostalgic', he said: 'I mean, *Ostalgie* obviously still has an effect on my parents' generation because there are certain GDR standards, which they still keep holding onto.' With this comment, Jens uses the social category of generation to construct a subgroup comprising only those born in the 1950s, which means that he, as someone born in the 1970s, is not a member. His exasperated tone then further emphasises his distance when he explains that this generation 'still keeps holding onto' GDR standards.

It seems, then, that the dominant memory of the east, which tends to present it in a negative light, undermines the positive attachment to the past which may be expressed through the popular memory of *Ostalgie* in participants' perceptions of easterners whom they had never met. The concerns raised by postcolonial scholars such as Theobald are borne out here; in line with hegemonic discourse, participants understood 'ostalgic' easterners as being stuck in the past and claimed that they glorified the GDR. When it came to perceptions of others, there was no evidence of participants taking ownership of the term to assert positive aspects of the past in the face of western superiority.

Ostalgie and perceptions of the self

The participants' desire to distance themselves from *Ostalgie* was also echoed in their narratives about themselves. When discussing their own memories of the GDR past, all of the participants consistently normalised their sentiments, thus distancing them from *Ostalgie*. This process manifested itself in two ways: the participants emphasised the importance of depoliticised memories relating to childhood and personal experiences, and likened their sentiments to western nostalgia. When explaining the importance of their pasts, they independently made direct reference to the 'ostalgic' stereotype so as to make it clear that their sentiments were not to be confused with it. Christian, for instance, claimed: 'My east German past is certainly important for me, but then on the other hand, it is not so important that I would lapse into some kind of *Ostalgie*.'

Christian's reference to *Ostalgie* without any prompting indicates that the term is one of the first to come to mind when the GDR past is the subject of discussion, despite the fact that it does not accurately describe the form of attachment that he is explaining. The vocabulary he uses also makes clear that he is keen not to be viewed as 'ostalgic'. The verb *verfallen* (translated as 'lapse') holds negative connotations, conjuring up images of moving backwards or deterioration. For Christian then, *Ostalgie* does not fit his understandings, and what is more, it threatens to distort his east Germanness, portraying it as a backward-looking and problematic identification.

Other participants did not explicitly distance themselves from the term *Ostalgie*, but instead altered its connotations by likening it to western nostalgia. This discursive process is exemplified in Lina's account of her attachment to the past:

> It has a link with my childhood. My childhood was in the GDR and I think many people are in some way nostalgically minded. I mean, I notice it extremely with my west German friends and colleagues when they say, hey, do you remember those sherbet sweets from such and such or something. And then... um... I think that's it, that's childhood. [...] But this *Ostalgie*, this aahh, the east, and there used to be this, it's simply nostalgia, because it was childhood and youth, and everyone in the world has that if they had a nice childhood.

Lina was keen to point out that, although she identified with *Ostalgie*, her own memories were not unusual, but a 'normal' form of remembering. She demonstrated this by stressing the intensity of west German nostalgia in her use of the word 'extremely'. As with the other understandings of *Ostalgie* relating to the self among this group, Lina redefined *Ostalgie* to relate only to private or personal memories, rather than to socialism or the state. This was illustrated by the repetitive use of 'childhood' and also 'personal memories', both of which appeared frequently throughout all of the interviews.

Further reading of how participants engaged with *Ostalgie* when discussing their own memories of the GDR sheds light on some of the possible reasons that they were so keen to distance themselves from it, or at least from its connotations. The following extract is taken from a section of Stefan's interview when *Ostalgie* was being discussed, specifically with reference to east German products:

> It's a kind of nut-nougat spread like *Nutella*, yeah, it used to be in the shops, I still have this memory from the GDR and I liked it back then and it's simply an example of a carefree childhood that evokes something up here [points to head]. From back then... it also tastes a bit different to *Nutella*... I also eat *Nutella*. [...] No politics.

From the outset, Stefan constructed his narrative to ensure that his decision to purchase east German chocolate spread was not misinterpreted as an 'ostalgic' attachment to the past. By linking it to childhood memories, he firmly separated his sentiments from those of the 'ostalgic' subgroup, which, as demonstrated above, was considered to hold a politicised attachment to the GDR. His rather long-winded clarification that his fond memories of a chocolate spread should not be misconstrued as a political view in a discussion that, on the face of it, appeared simply to be about everyday childhood experiences, is very telling. It illustrates the difficulties faced by easterners who wish to express a link to their past. As a result of the negative and often politicised connotations of *Ostalgie*, the participants continuously clarified and justified their sentiments in an attempt to prevent them from being misunderstood.

It is important to note, however, that although the participants emphasised their depoliticised attachment to the GDR in discussions about *Ostalgie*, they did express politicised identification elsewhere in the interviews. The participants identified a number of the sociopolitical structures from the GDR as being better than those in unified Germany. Although they were highly critical of the influential role that the SED played in individuals' everyday lives, they claimed that the GDR offered a higher standard of state provision and that there was more social equality under socialism. The following extract, also taken from Stefan's interview, is typical of the participants' narratives about the benefits of the social system in the GDR:

> I mean, I think that there were positive things in the GDR, but I don't support a kind of glorification or anything like that. [...] What was positive for me personally was, it was... a relatively, I mean, educational opportunities were fairer than they are now. I mean, this split, this division that now separates people from one another, I'd like to claim that didn't exist there.

There are clear tensions between this finding and the narratives analysed hitherto, where the participants went to great lengths to distance themselves from the political meanings of *Ostalgie* and made no reference to the sociopolitical aspects of the GDR in this context. In fact, at times they went as far as explicitly stating that their sentiments were not political, even when they were discussing themes that held no politicised connotations whatsoever. The point here is that participants did, indeed, express politicised forms of attachment to the GDR, albeit tentatively, when they were not discussing *Ostalgie*. That these did not come to light in the context of *Ostalgie* suggests that the participants feared that their politicised attachment would be misconstrued as being stuck in the past or showing an overall preference for socialism. It seems that they anticipated that the nuances of their politicised identifications would be overridden by the problematic connotations of *Ostalgie*, which pigeonhole easterners as backward-looking and anti-western. This finding, then, provides insight into the role of *Ostalgie* in perceptions of east Germanness. When talking about themselves, participants were able to negotiate dominant discourse and express their depoliticised attachment to the GDR. However, they appeared to be unable to negotiate the problematic political connotations of the term in order to ensure that their own politicised views come through. They therefore did not attempt to express politicised attachment to the GDR in the context of *Ostalgie*.

During the interviews, several participants addressed this issue more explicitly, explaining *Ostalgie* to be an unclear term which potentially distorted their understandings. For example, Marie claimed:

> In that way it's not a good term because it doesn't differentiate between people who want the Wall back and people who, like I just said, want to remember their childhood and things in a normal way, in a positive way, yeah. The term leaves everything open, so after the term you always need to explain, to say afterwards, actually I don't want the Wall back, or the GDR either. Otherwise it's a bit of a malleable, unconcrete term.

Marie's explanation of *Ostalgie* suggests that the term is extremely broad, and that this lack of definition presents a problem in itself. Without clarifying the term to avoid misunderstanding, it cannot act as an unproblematic expression of positive attachment to the GDR past, but is overridden by dominant memory which disparages the socialist past.

Other participants who problematised *Ostalgie* were more precise in their criticism. In the following extract, Elisabeth focuses on her own politicised attachment, and explains how this can be misconstrued:

> I think something that is often misinterpreted is when people say that things that were better, I mean, people can objectively say, that was better. And now, as soon you say, wow, yeah, childcare was really great...I mean, we've experienced two systems.

Elisabeth explicitly explains that she struggles to express her opinion that some of the sociopolitical features of the GDR were better in the face of perceptions that any politicised attachment is akin to an uncritical identification with socialism as a whole. The pause in her narrative is very telling – she makes it clear that politicised conceptions are often met with scepticism, but hesitates to explain explicitly the way that they are misconstrued. Given Elisabeth's exasperated tone in this account, this seems to indicate how disillusioned she feels about the difficulties she faces when attempting to communicate a more nuanced politicised attachment to the GDR. Her attachment to the past and mention of her dual experiences fit more closely with the claims made by postcolonial scholars such as Cooke that *Ostalgie* constitutes a critical appraisal of both the GDR and of the western system. Elisabeth cannot, however, confidently make this appraisal because, once again, she appears to be restricted by dominant perceptions.

Conclusion

The interviews analysed above have revealed that, in line with claims made by some postcolonial scholars, the hegemonic discourse which disparages the east tends to prevent *Ostalgie* from being used to assert positive perceptions of the east. Instead, this popular memory is appropriated by the dominant memory discourse and interpreted as a problematic form of glorification. In addition, however, the findings have provided greater insight into how easterners interact with *Ostalgie* in their identity construction, showing that the influence of dominant memory shifts in different types of social perception. When presenting their perceptions of other easterners, participants largely echoed mainstream stereotypes, using the label *Ostalgie* to refer mainly to a group of older east Germans living outside Berlin, whom they perceived as having difficulties in adjusting to unified Germany and from whom they explicitly distanced themselves. The lack of understanding that they showed towards the group, together with their frustration and consistent use of the third person, made it clear that they firmly distanced themselves from these easterners and, importantly, from *Ostalgie*. When discussing themselves, participants ensured that their own attachment to the past was not misconstrued as *Ostalgie* by explicitly distinguishing between their own perceptions and the term, and by emphasising the importance of depoliticised memories relating to childhood. Significantly, however, participants did not communicate forms of politicised attachment to the past when discussing *Ostalgie* – these emerged in other parts of the interview. It seems, therefore, that while participants managed, to some degree, to negotiate the negative connotations of *Ostalgie* and express depoliticised attachment to the past, mainstream stereotypes did appear to overshadow politicised perceptions.

In conclusion it is useful to return to the quotation entitling this chapter, which was taken from one of the interviews. In his claim '*Ostalgie* doesn't fit', the participant was referring to his own memories. However, this claim can be taken a step further, for *Ostalgie* also appears unsuitable for more general processes of remembering the GDR, and thus for understanding eastern identities. This form of popular memory does have the potential to be an outlet for positive attachment to the GDR, and even for a critical appraisal of both east and west, as scholars such as Cooke suggest. This potential is not fulfilled, however, because the dominant memory which portrays the east in a negative light ultimately turns *Ostalgie* into an undesirable and problematic expression of attachment to the past. The comparison of participants' own memories with their perceptions of others suggests that the influence of hegemonic discourse has made *Ostalgie* an inappropriate and potentially damaging label when it comes to easterners' identity construction. Participants rely on the negative connotations of *Ostalgie* to make sense of other easterners even though it does not correspond to their own perceptions or to those of people whom they have met. This suggests that the negative connotations of *Ostalgie* effectively override personal experiences, and by drawing on it to make sense of others, participants are perpetuating precisely those meanings of which they are so critical.

Notes

1. *Ein Kessel DDR* is a reference to the prime-time GDR television variety show *Ein Kessel Buntes* (*A Pot of Colour*), which was broadcast from 1972 to 1992.
2. The PDS merged with WASG in 2007, becoming *Die Linke*, as it is known today.
3. *Knusperflocken* were a confectionary product which existed in the GDR, and have since become a staple item in *Ostalgie* shops and hampers. The *Ampelmann* was the pedestrian crossing figure in the GDR, and became something of a cult figure of the east after unification. It now exists as a brand in its own right which is strongly associated with *Ostalgie*, and *Ampelmann* sweets are just one of many products sold within the brand.
4. It should be noted that, during the interviews, the participants frequently labelled apparently 'ostalgic' easterners as *Ossis*. They made a clear distinction between an *Ossi* and an *Ostdeutscher*, presenting *Ossis* as stereotypically 'ostalgic' and *Ostdeutsche* simply as people born in the east. Much of the section

on perceptions of others, therefore, deals with the participants' perceptions of *Ossis*, as well as how their understandings correspond to *Ostalgie*.

References

Ahbe, T. (1999) 'Ostalgie als Laienpraxis. Einordnung, Bedingungen, Funktion', *Berliner Debatte INITIAL*, 10 (3), 87–97.

Ahbe, T. and R. Gries (2009) 'Einleitung', in T. Ahbe, R. Gries and W. Schmale (eds) *Die Ostdeutschen in den Medien: Das Bild von den Anderen nach 1990* (Bonn: Bundeszentrale für politische Bildung), 11–15.

Bach, J. (2002) ' "The Taste Remains": Consumption, (N)ostalgia, and the Production of East Germany', *Public Culture*, 14 (3), 545–56.

Belke, J. (2009) 'Das Bild der Ostdeutschen im öffentliche-rechtlichen Fernsehen. Eine Diskursanalyse des ARD-Politmagazins KONTRASTE in der Zeit von 1987 bis 2005' in T. Ahbe, R. Gries and W. Schmale (eds) *Die Ostdeutschen in den Medien: Das Bild von den Anderen nach 1990* (Bonn: Bundeszentrale für politische Bildung), 135–79.

Berdahl, D. (1999) '(N)Ostalgie for the present: Memory, longing, and East German things', *Ethnos*, 64 (2), 192–211.

Brabazon, T. (2005) *From Revolution to Revelation: Generation X, Popular Memory and Cultural Studies* (Aldershot: Ashgate).

Buchstein, H. (1995) 'Shadows of the Wall – the Postcommunist PDS and Perspectives of the Democratic Left In Germany', *Constellations*, 2 (1), 31–50.

Cooke, P. (2003a) 'Performing 'Ostalgie': Leander Haussmann's Sonnenallee', *German Life and Letters*, 56 (2), 157–67.

Cooke, P. (2003b) '*Ostalgie*'s not what it used to be', *German Politics and Society*, 22 (4), 134–50.

Cooke, P. (2005) *Representing East Germany since Unification* (Oxford: Berg).

Knischewski, G. and U. Spittler (2006) 'Remembering The Berlin Wall: The Wall Memorial Ensemble Bernauer Strasse', *German Life and Letters*, 59 (2), 280–93.

Popular Memory Group (1998) 'Popular memory: theory, politics, method' in R. Perks and A. Thomson (eds) *The Oral History Reader* (London: Routledge), 75–86.

Schroeder, K. (2008) 'Ostalgie und Glorifizierung – Unkenntnis der Nachgebornen' in Konrad Adenauer Stiftung (ed.) *Wie schmeckte die DDR? – Wege zu einer Kultur des Erinnerns*, Dresden, 18 September, http://www.ferien-im-gebirge.de/CDU-Pockau/pdf/kas_ostalgie%20und%20glorifizierung.pdf [accessed 19 January 2012].

Theobald, J. (2000) 'Disgraceland GDR: locating the admirable amongst the abject' in P. Stevenson and J. Theobald (eds) *Relocating Germanness. Discursive Disunity in Unified Germany* (London: Macmillan), 131–49.

7
Reflective Nostalgia and Diasporic Memory: Composing East Germany after 1989

Elaine Kelly

The redrawing of borders in post-communist Europe led to a significant transformation of the continent's diasporic landscape. The migration that followed the collapse of the Iron Curtain resulted in the reintegration of certain long-established diasporas into their ethnocultural homelands. 25 per cent of Bulgarian Turks, for example, were repatriated to Turkey in 1989 (Stewart, 2003: 30), while the following decade saw an influx of 1,630,000 Russian Germans to Germany (Pohl, 2009: 280). At the same time, entirely new diasporas were created, not by the movement of people across borders, as has traditionally been the case, but by the movement of borders across people. With the fragmentation of Yugoslavia and the Soviet Union into smaller nationalising states, various ethnic communities were separated from their national homelands and subjected to processes of othering. Rogers Brubaker (2000: 2) describes this type of diasporic formation as 'accidental'. 'Accidental diasporas', he observes, 'crystallize suddenly following a dramatic – and often traumatic – reconfiguration of political space'.

The fate of East Germans following the fall of the Berlin Wall was initially cast as one of reintegration. German unification was framed as the bringing together of a single ethnocultural community, and the reclassification of East Germans as citizens of the Federal Republic as the closing of a historic rift. Characteristic was the significance placed on Willy Brandt's alleged declaration on 10 November 1989 to a demonstration in West Berlin: 'Now that which belongs together can grow together.'[1] As the sociocultural differences between eastern and western

Germany became apparent, however, this narrative of reunification lost some of its resonance. With unemployment rife and perceptions of otherness in the new federal states increasingly acute, a consciousness emerged among east Germans that was distinctly diasporic in nature. East Germany, it must be said, does not fall neatly into Brubacker's concept of an accidental diaspora. East Germans are neither an ethnocultural minority in the Federal Republic nor stranded far from an ethnic homeland. Moreover, given the steady flow of emigration to the West prior to 1989 and the fact that East Germans themselves actively participated in their state's downfall, the GDR represents a nebulous concept of *Heimat* at best. Yet, in the wake of its sudden demise, its citizens encountered circumstances that were replicated across Europe's newly created minority groups. In particular, the removal of agency that accompanied the rapid absorption of the GDR into the Federal Republic has echoes of the impotence that Brubaker (2000: 2) ascribes to other accidental diasporas. The rhetoric of colonisation that emerged from certain east German quarters in the 1990s might well be considered in this light.

Paradigms of diaspora and exile resonated strongly with east Germany's compositional elite in the 1990s. Georg Katzer notably remarked in 1992 that many of them felt like 'emigrants in their own country' (cit. in Nauck, 1993: 37). Born either before or during the Second World War, this generation of composers, which includes Reiner Bredemeyer (1929–95), Paul-Heinz Dittrich (b. 1930), Friedrich Goldmann (1941–2009), Katzer (b. 1935), Günter Kochan (1930–2009), Siegfried Matthus (b. 1934) and Friedrich Schenker (b. 1942), had begun their careers in the GDR and were beginning by the late 1980s to assume the mantle of senior statesmen. In the wake of unification their status changed considerably. From a position at the centre of a small musical scene, they found themselves demoted to the peripheries of a much larger one. Music was spared the acrimonious debates that played out in other spheres of German culture in the 1990s; unlike visual artists and writers, composers were not subject to public accusations of complicity with the totalitarian regime by their west German counterparts. Instead their reception in western Germany was one of silence. With the exception of the seminal *Musik in Deutschland 1950–1990* compact-disc series, which presents composers from East and West side by side,[2] few attempts were made to incorporate GDR artists into narratives of contemporary German music. Faced with this silence, many east German composers assumed an exilic identity, loosely assembling as a group united by experiences of exclusion and a shared past.

Composing from the sidelines

The experience of exile is rarely negative in all respects. Hamid Naficy (1993: 6) counters monolithic interpretations of it as a 'dystopic and dysphoric experience stemming from deprivation', and ventures that 'exile must also be defined by its utopian and euphoric possibilities'. In a 1990 interview, the musicologist Frank Schneider notably described the pervading atmosphere among East German composers as one of 'great hope as well as great fear' (cit. in Oehlschlägel, 1990: 35). In terms of creative stimulus, the opening of the German border brought with it promises of increased freedom and the opportunity to regenerate the insular and often stagnant compositional scene of the GDR. Schneider recalled the envy with which East Germans had viewed the vibrant new-music scene of the Federal Republic (ibid.: 39), and heralded the possibility that a freer exchange between East and West might result in a 'synthesis' or 'third way' for German composition as a whole (ibid.: 43). This optimism was tempered, however, by no small degree of trepidation. The compositional world of the GDR in the 1970s and 1980s had been a comfortable one, all things considered. Following the relaxation of cultural policy by the Honecker regime in the early 1970s, composers had enjoyed a relatively free aesthetic reign, avoiding, for the most part, the attention of the censor.[3] Moreover, the well-subsidised cultural system had provided ample opportunities for performances and commissions. While East German composition was by no means synonymous with the GDR state, it did exist predominantly within the realms of the state's cultural infrastructure. As such, the question of whether it could survive in the state's absence was a very real one.

As the practicalities of unification unfolded, Schneider's fears found a more concrete realisation than his hopes. Certain composers flourished in the freer climate. Friedrich Goldmann, for example, who was appointed professor of the Hochschule der Künste (now Universität der Künste) in what was formerly West Berlin in 1991, embraced the wealth of opportunities available. In an interview in 1995 he observed 'There are certain GDR-specific obstacles that I don't encounter in the west. And I find it wonderful that these are not there' (cit. in Danneberg, 1995a: 108). Goldmann, however, was in the minority among east Germany's compositional elite. For many of his compatriots unification brought with it both a loss of status and economic hardship. The rapid privatisation of the east German economy had significant implications for the dissemination of new music. The transformation in 1990 of the state-owned record company VEB Deutsche Schallplatten into the short-lived Deutsche Schallplatten GmbH Berlin resulted in the discontinuation of the GDR's contemporary music label, Nova. Similarly, composers found themselves without publishers as state-run publishing houses were closed, sold, or, in the case of historic companies, restored to their pre-war status and reunited with their western counterparts.[4] The fate of C.F. Peters Musikverlag is typical in this regard; the absorption of the Leipzig house into the Frankfurt office entailed a curtailing of the eastern end of the business and a subsequent orientation away from the company's support for east German music (Links, 2009: 226–31). Bredemeyer provided a bitter summation of the situation in 1994, remarking that 'the publishing houses have shaken us off as dogs shake off fleas' (cit. in Danneberg, 1995d: 42).

The difficulties engendered by the depressed economy were compounded as east Germany's leading musical institutions adopted an increasingly western profile. The Semperoper in Dresden and the Berlin Staatsoper both appointed west German directors at the start of the 1990s,[5] while a host of international conductors were drafted in to lead east Germany's orchestras: the Danish conductor Michel Schønwandt was appointed to the Berlin Sinfonieorchester, the Italian Giuseppe Sinopli to the Dresden Staatskappelle and Daniel Barenboim to the Staatsoper all in 1992, while the Spanish conductor, Rafael Frühbeck de Burgos, who had trained in Munich, took over the Rundfunk Sinfonie two years later. This shift of personnel, which was endemic across the upper echelons of east German society, led among other things to the dissolution of the professional and personal networks upon which artists depend for performances and commissions. In the absence of patrons or advocates, composers were confronted with the prospect of reinventing themselves for the west German contemporary arts scene. This was an issue even for those who had enjoyed some prominence in the Federal Republic prior to 1989. No longer deemed 'exotic' (Amzoll and Katzer, 2002: 648–9), they were compelled to explore new performance avenues as invitations from traditional routes dried up. The process of starting anew was one on which few of the GDR's senior figures embarked with enthusiasm. As Katzer explained in 1994:

> The situation is such that with the switch of the artistic elite in the new federal states, opportunities for performances have become more remote. To put it precisely: many of the directorships have changed. The new directors have naturally brought their own clientele with

> them. And I cannot be bothered to hawk my pieces around and advertise myself (it would also certainly have little point).
>
> (cit. in Danneberg, 1995b: 285)

The practical experience of exclusion prompted a series of common internal tensions that emerge prominently in interviews conducted with east German composers in the 1990s. As is frequently the case with diasporas, the question of what it meant to be east German appears to have assumed greater significance in the 1990s than it had ever done prior to the *Wende*. For those who had remained in the GDR until the end, the past unleashed conflicting and often irreconcilable emotions. Composers reminisce about an environment that was supportive and culturally stimulating but simultaneously corrupt and invalid. There is guilt and resentment towards the GDR – Katzer (1999: 454) speaks of the 'stigma of complicity' that east Germans must bear – but also a desire to retain ownership of this past. Kochan, for example, railed bitterly against an identity being imposed on east Germans by the west: 'You are supposed to have the decency to be ashamed that you were a citizen of the GDR und must now finally be proud and happy to be allowed to live as a free, authentic German in a free, authentic, great German state' (cit. in Nauck, 1993: 41).

Underpinning concerns of national identity were those of aesthetic identity. In his study of German exiles in Los Angeles during the Second World War, Ehrhard Bahr (2007: 20) discusses the crisis of continuity experienced by figures such as Brecht and Schoenberg as they struggled to reconcile an aesthetic in which they had believed with the failure of the society that had spawned it. A similar crisis of identity can be observed in the case of east German composers; in particular, the impact of the *Wende* on the continuity of compositional aesthetics was a fraught topic. While certain individuals, notably Matthus and Dittrich, argue that 1989 should not be considered to be a creative landmark (Danneberg,1995c: 337, 1995e: 169), a claim that in Dittrich's case can be read as a declaration of aesthetic independence from the GDR, others allude to the sense of loss prompted by the demise of the state. Frequent references are made, in particular, to an aesthetic of resistance that was rendered defunct after 1989 (Nauck, 1993: 39–40; Ullmann, 1999: 497). Katzer describes how the defiant conclusions that had once characterised his compositions became obsolete after the *Wende* (Amzoll and Katzer, 2002: 659). Bredemeyer goes a step further and associates the collapse of the GDR with the failure of an entire genre of political art: 'If music is an instrument of intervention, in the sense of Eisler

[...] then I have to say, very well then. Eisler lost, I too, it doesn't work any more' (cit. in Nauck, 1993: 38). From Bredemeyer's perspective, the *Wende* had removed not only his oppositional force but also his audience: 'The listeners don't need it any more, this type of comfort. They have completely new concerns too' (ibid.: 39).

Diasporic memory and memories of East Germany

James Clifford (1994: 307) distinguishes diasporic from immigrant communities by their relationship with the past. Immigrant communities, he argues, 'may experience loss and nostalgia, but only en route to a whole new home in a new place'. For diasporas, however, the past casts a far lengthier shadow. The collective history of displacement and accompanying nostalgia that defines such communities significantly delays assimilation into the new nation state. The centrality of nostalgia to diasporic identity has rendered it problematic for scholars in the field of memory studies. Andreas Huyssen (2003: 312) suggests that 'diasporic memory remains seriously understudied, perhaps because it often falls prey to nostalgia, and nostalgia by and large remains a negative category, something to be shunned'. Once a medical term for the physical symptoms of homesickness, nostalgia has come to be perceived as a 'social disease' (Stewart, 1993: 23). It is dismissed by its critics as an escapist and uncritical engagement with the past. Michael Kammen (1993: 688) describes nostalgia as 'essentially history without guilt', while David Lowenthal (1985: 6) classes it as populist and indiscriminate. 'The remembrance of times past', he observes, 'is a burgeoning business in almost every country, and any epoch will do.' Nostalgia is frequently portrayed as the antithesis to rational modernity; it obstructs the narrative of progress, is unironic and sentimental. Charles Maier relates it to memory, 'as kitsch is to art' (cit. in Boym, 2001: xiv). Nadine Attewell (2004: 23) elaborates: 'Like kitsch [...] nostalgia is problematic because it is perceived both as insufficiently mediated (that is nostalgia doesn't know enough to be ironic about itself) and altogether too mediated (it's false, a lie, a forgery of desire).'

Such readings of nostalgia, which assume a fixed idealisation of the past, are not particularly helpful in the context of diasporic memory. The diasporic existence is a double-sited one, shaped not only by a shared affinity with the lost homeland but also by a continuously evolving relationship with the new home. This suspension between two conflicting temporal and cultural spaces results in a fractured and ambiguous diasporic consciousness, a consciousness that reflects the tensions arising not only from the continuous juxtaposition of old and new, but also from the social and emotional ruptures, both positive and negative, that characterise the exilic condition. As Clifford (1994: 312) observes, 'diasporic consciousness lives loss and hope as a defining tension'. In contrast to traditional readings of nostalgia, which tend to focus on the phenomenon of *nostos* or returning home, diasporic memory is arguably more concerned with *algia* or longing. Pertinent here is Svetlana Boym's separation of nostalgic tendencies into two categories, restorative and reflective. Restorative nostalgia, she argues, 'evokes national past' (2001: 49). It 'stresses *nostos* and attempts a transhistorical reconstruction of the lost home.' Reflective nostalgia, in contrast, is an inherently individual process. It 'thrives in *algia*, the longing itself, and delays the homecoming – wistfully, ironically, desperately' (ibid.: xviii). Restorative nostalgia, like national memory, is concerned with reconstruction, authenticity and tradition. Reflective nostalgia, in contrast, 'does not pretend to rebuild the mythical place called home'. Instead it 'dwells on the ambivalences of human longing and belonging and does not shy away from the contradictions of modernity.' It is 'ironic, inconclusive and fragmentary' (ibid.: 49).

Boym's distinctions are particularly useful for interpreting the status of the GDR in the post-*Wende* music of east German composers. Nostalgia looms large in this body of work. Bredemeyer and Katzer, in particular, deal repeatedly with themes of loss and longing. Their preoccupation with the past is, however, far removed from the reconstructive conceptions of *Ostalgie*. Allusions to the GDR are neither escapist nor sentimental. Extra-musical metaphors are laden with irony, and while the styles and genres that had characterised East German composition before 1989 continue to dominate, they now betray a cynicism and absence of closure. Ultimately, this is a reflective nostalgia that centres on dislocation rather than any desire to return to a past age. It is a nostalgia that seeks to critique rather than transcend the present.

An early example of this phenomenon can be observed in Katzer's electroacoustic tribute to the end of the GDR, *Mein 1989* (*My 1989*, 1990a). One of a number of works commissioned by the Bourges International Festival of Experimental Music in 1990 to commemorate the various revolutions of 1989, *Mein 1989* does not position the fall of the Wall as a unique and radical event. Instead, Katzer's use of the past to contextualise it renders it as simply another stage in a cyclical historical process. The work builds on two of Katzer's earlier compositions, *Mon 1789* (*My 1789*, 1989), ostensibly a commemoration of the French Revolution but also a sharp critique of the revolutionary principles that underpinned the GDR, and *Aide mémoire* of 1983, which charts the course of the Third Reich through a series of sonic nightmares. Drawing on source sounds from the former and a sizeable excerpt from the latter, *Mein 1989* offers a similarly unheroic narrative of German history. Katzer mourns not for the passing of the GDR, but for the accompanying loss of idealism.

The piece starts, like *Mon 1789*, with a recording of Katzer reading Anaximander's fatalistic comment on the ephemeral order of things: 'The things that are perish into the things from which they come to be, according to necessity, for they pay penalty and retribution to each other for their injustice in accordance with the ordering of time.'[6] This text serves as a précis of the compositional events, which reduce Germany's recent past to a series of interrelated beginnings and ends. Katzer alludes first to the Third Reich, quoting the section from *Aide mémoire* that deals with the final years of the Second World War. Depicted first is the exhilaration of war; rousing speeches by Goebbels and the strains of Liszt's *Les préludes*, which served as the theme to the daily wartime radio bulletin, the *Wehrmachtbericht*, are accompanied by the cheering of crowds. This gives way to sonic portrayals of destruction, loss and ultimately silence, a *tabula rasa* characterised by sounds of fire crackling, the wind whistling, and a lone, ominous raven. Katzer's imagining of the GDR, which emerges from this abyss, follows a similar trajectory of ascent and decline. Its birth is heralded by a dawn call of blackbirds and Katzer reciting 'all men are equal' from the Declaration of Human Rights. The state's innocence is undermined almost immediately, however, by a recording of Katzer singing a frail, unaccompanied rendition of the popular nineteenth-century paean to freedom, 'Freiheit, die ich meine' ('The freedom I mean'). His voice is interrupted repeatedly by construction noises – an allusion perhaps to the erection of the Wall – and becomes increasingly strangulated as the song progresses. It is finally cut short by sounds of confinement and oppression, manifest here through the sonic events of keys jangling and a door slamming shut. The return of the raven and the whistling wind marks the end of the hopes that were invested in the GDR.

Katzer's depiction of the demise of the GDR itself is comical rather than momentous. The juxtaposition of unsynchronised carnival bands in the spirit of Charles Ives captures the undirectional nature of the dissent that characterised 1989. The delusion of the GDR's leaders, meanwhile, is evoked through the inclusion of the recordings of Honecker's ill-fated prophecy that the Wall would still be standing in 50 or even 100 years, and Mielke's plaintive claim to the East German public in

November 1989 that 'I love, I love all [people].' Katzer loops and distorts both statements, reducing their owners to cartoon-like figures of ridicule. The actual fall of the Wall is presented in a similarly unceremonious fashion. The euphoria that accompanied the build-up to the event is palpable in the sounds of jubilant crowds, which are combined with the ominous fate motif from Beethoven's Fifth Symphony. This cuts sharply, however, to a far more subdued recording of Katzer whistling the chorus of the spiritual 'Joshua Fought the Battle of Jericho'. Notably, the song's revolutionary significance – both in the context of nineteenth-century slavery and the civil rights movement – is undermined by Katzer's low-key performance. He switches from whistling to song for the final line – 'and the walls came tumbling down' – and for the last word of the phrase, substitutes his voice with the unclimactic sounds of bricks falling. The GDR is laid to rest by a chorus of hammering 'Wall peckers' ('Mauerspechte') and, subsequently, a return of the windswept *tabula rasa* soundscape. A solitary blackbird tentatively signifies the start of a new era, the uncertainty of which is underlined in Katzer's final gesture, a play on the word 'liberté'. He stutters over the word as if encountering it for the first time, constructing it gradually from its phonetic components like a child learning to read. His final questioning statement of it suggests a degree of hope but no great confidence in what the future might hold.

Blooming landscapes

The expectations, however mild, that conclude *Mein 1989* dissipated in the years following unification. A diasporic aesthetic is increasingly pronounced in the early 1990s, colouring not only compositions that deal explicitly with the German situation such as Bredemeyer's *Wendepunkt* (*Turning Point*, 1992), but also more oblique explorations of exile. Friedrich Schenker, for example, remarked of his 1992 orchestral piece *...ins Endlose...* (*...to infinity...*), which was inspired by Kafka's emigration novel *America*: 'images of abrupt change, new beginnings and unrest [...] of people as masses and/or individuals accompanied me and motivated me in my compositional work' (cit. in Mayer, 2010). Perhaps the strongest expressions of a diasporic consciousness can be found in a group of works that use as a reference point Helmut Kohl's notorious proclamation on the occasion of the currency union on 1 June 1990 that 'through our joint efforts, we will soon succeed in restoring Mecklenburg-Vorpommern and Saxony-Anhalt, Brandenburg, Saxony, and Thuringia into blooming landscapes where it is worthwhile to live and work' (Kohl, 1990). As this prophecy failed to materialise, the notion of 'blooming landscapes' was seized upon as a metaphor of loss, symbolising not only the defunct GDR, but also, and perhaps more importantly, the promised utopias that had failed to materialise both before and after the *Wende*.

These disjunctions are paramount in Reiner Bredemeyer's *Aufschwung OST* (*Soaring East*, 1993), a four-movement work for piano and a trio of oboe, percussion and tuba that was premiered at the Musik-Biennale Berlin in 1993. The work's title functions on two levels. In its literal sense it alludes to Kohl's vision, translating as a soaring or upswing of the east, a sentiment that is countered by Bredemeyer's opening performance direction, 'Leider nicht...' ('Unfortunately not...'). From a musical perspective, it describes the two starkly contrasting sound worlds that are juxtaposed throughout: 'Aufschwung' refers to Robert Schumann's piano piece of the same name from the *Fantasiestücke* op. 12, composed in 1837, which Bredemeyer subjects to 'faithful misuse' to serve as the piano part for the composition; 'OST' is an acronym of the trio of instruments – percussion translating as *Schlagzeug* –, which provide an atonal and often jarring counterpart to Schumann's romanticism. The conflicts implicit in the title are augmented in the cryptic preface to the score. Highlighting Schumann's move from East to West and subsequent madness, Bredemeyer underpins his contemporary relevance in the score with wordplays on Endenich, where Schumann was incarcerated at the end of his life, and on the Federal Republic's claims to sole representation of Germany during the Cold War ('Alleinvertretungsanspruch'):

> The Zwickauer who went to the West, went, as is well known, insane there (that the proximity of Bonn may have played a role in this is surely speculation). The final, eighth work from his op. 12 is called 'End of the Song' and it should be played 'with good humour'. This presupposes the minor but rare capability for self irony and great artistry; the pianist in the '4 Quartet Pieces' shall also have this requirement. He starts self-governing [*souverän*] but 'Endenich' [ends] claiming sole representation [*alleinvertretungsansprüchig*].

In the score itself, the polarisation of *souverän* and *alleinvertretungsansprüchig* translates into modes of conflict and indifference. Bredemeyer overrides the sonata rondo form of Schumann's original, dividing 'Aufschwung' instead into a repeated binary format that contrasts the stormy rondo theme (A) and the lyrical first episode (B), as

Schumann, 'Aufschwung', *Fantasiestücke* op. 12, no. 2

Exposition			Development	Recapitulation		
A	B	A	C	A	B	A
b./1–16	b./17–40	b./41–52	b.53–114	b./115–22	b./123–46	b. /147–54
Mov. 1	Mov. 2	Mov. 3			Mov. 4	

Reiner Bredemeyer, *Aufschwung OST* – piano part

Figure 7.1 Bredemeyer's transformation of Schumann's formal structure in *Aufschwung OST*

illustrated in Figure 7.1. This division of thematic material results in two distinct levels of engagement between the piano and the trio. In the first and third movements, in which the irascible rondo theme sets the tone, there is constant tension between the two sound worlds. The OST trio contradicts, parodies, and makes various unsuccessful attempts to synchronise with Schumann's piano part. In the third movement in particular, the oboe and tuba frequently imitate the piano's gestures and contours. The resulting effect, however, is one of caricature rather than reconciliation, highlighting the chasm between the musical languages of past and present. In the second and fourth movements, this chasm is heightened through a portrayal of indifference. Both movements open with a pensive oboe passage, punctuated by percussion and tuba. Against this, the piano enters unobtrusively with Schumann's introspective B episode. Its interaction with the trio is minimal; each sphere appears all but oblivious to the other's existence.

Like Katzer's *Mein 1989*, *Aufschwung OST* belongs to a critical aesthetic that long predates the *Wende*. Bredemeyer similarly drew on the Germanic musical canon as a vehicle for registering discontent in works such as *Bagatellen für B.* (*Bagatelles for B.*, 1970) and *Einmischung in unserer Angelegenheit* (*Meddling in our Affairs*, 1985), which quote excerpts by Beethoven and Schubert respectively. *Einmischung*, for example, involves a perestroika speech by Gorbachev, which is framed by excerpts from 'Muth!' from Schubert's *Die Winterreise*, triumphantly orchestrated to reflect the 'moments of the "Marseillaise"' that Bredemeyer (Bredemeyer and Wollny, 1983: 488) claimed to have discovered in Schubert's piano accompaniment. Any such revolutionary impetus is strikingly absent from *Aufschwung OST*. Following the final statement of Schumann's rondo theme at the end of the fourth movement and the failure of any synthesis to emerge between the piano and the trio, the pervading atmosphere is one of despondence. Günter Olias (1995: 85) notably describes the final series of questioning sustained notes and lengthy intermittent pauses, in which the trio ultimately subsumes the piano, as an expression of 'defiant pained resignation'.

The changing dimensions of Kohl's 'blooming landscapes' emerge particularly clearly in three compositions by Katzer: *Offene Landschaft mit obligatem Ton e* (*Open Landscape with an Obligato Pitch e*, 1990b) for chamber orchestra; *Landschaft mit steigender Flut* (*Landscape with Rising Tide*, 1992) for orchestra and tape; and *Les paysages fleurissants* (*Blooming Landscapes*, 2001) for four-channel tape. The first of these, like *Mein 1989*, captures the equivocal emotions that dominated in the immediate aftermath of the *Wende*. Katzer explained that the pervasive E pitch, which acts as a leitmotif throughout the piece, could be interpreted variously 'as expectation [Erwartung], as unity [Einheit], as termination (of the GDR) [Ende (der DDR)]' (Fuhrmann, 2005). The second piece is equally ambiguous but deals with nostalgia and disappointment rather than hope. It opens with natural water sounds, which evoke the sinking of the Atlantis of the Baltic Sea, Vineta, the demise of which, according to legend, was brought about by the depravity of its citizens. The water references do not allude only to the failures of the past. Katzer (Amzoll and Katzer, 2002: 659–60) asserts a second impetus for the piece in the wave or 'flood' of right-wing radicalism that overwhelmed east Germany in 1992.

The most provocative of Katzer's works in this vein is *Les paysages fleurissants*, which is dedicated to 'all shareholders'. A sardonic response to Kohl's economic predictions for the east, the programme note delineates the trajectory of the piece as follows:

> The labours of the beginning, the continual frustrations, the relapse to beautiful melancholy, resignation, silence –. But then the redeeming bell, a rise in the stock exchange, progress is booming, greedily devouring itself, accompanied by a triumphant, resounding, 16-foot Laudate! Laudate!
>
> (Katzer, 2001)

The composition is constructed from two source sounds: a recording of an ageing truck engine, which Katzer wryly describes in the programme note as a 'modern symbol of trade and prosperity'; and a synthetic 16-foot organ pipe, which sounds a three-note phrase emulating the contours of the word 'Laudate'. The work opens to the strains of the truck engine trying and repeatedly failing to start. For the first four minutes, as this source is subjected to various transformations, the soundscape is one of tension, rupture, and ultimately lackadaisical surrender as the choking gestures become increasingly intermittent. The second section of the piece opens similarly. This time, however, the engine stutters into action, its laborious success accompanied by repeated statements of 'Laudate'. Notably, the low resonant pitch of the latter produces an effect that is far from triumphant; the chugging and disjointed sounds arising from the engine do not warrant any such elation. In the final moments of the piece the engine cuts out entirely, giving way to a silence that is broken only by two final 'Laudate' statements. Distorted and descending in pitch, these speak of ironic failure.

Boym has observed that 'at its best, reflective nostalgia can present an ethical and creative challenge' (2001: xviii). Certainly, the shadow cast by the GDR in post-*Wende* compositions makes for uncomfortable listening. The defunct state exists not in the evocative and universalising symbols that have come to be associated with the variants of the past narrated by *Ostalgie* and totalitarianism, but in modes of loss and irony. The works share not the unifying tendencies of collective memory but the more fractured tropes of individual remembering that are born of the diasporic experience. For disenfranchised and alienated East German composers, reflective nostalgia represents a means of engaging critically with their political environment; compositional memories of the GDR mediate the often stark chasm that exists between individual experience and the undifferentiated nationalising narratives of past and present that have dominated in post-unification Germany. Ultimately, the irreconcilability of these spheres has resulted in an aesthetic that is characterised by displacement and disillusion. As Katzer recently observed, even 'if there naturally can be no return – the hopes that I, as an artist and composer, placed in the *Wende* have been disappointed' (Königsdorf, 2009).

Notes

1. Brandt never actually made this statement during his historic speech, but rather later that day. See Emmerich (2009) and Rother (2000).
2. Issued by Deutsche Musikrat in conjunction with Red Seal SONY/BMG Music Entertainment.
3. Katzer (Amzoll and Katzer, 2002: 655) recalls that except in cases where controversial texts were used, 'composing in the GDR was never really dangerous'.
4. In contrast to East German writers, few composers had established links with West German publishing houses prior to 1989.

5. Christoph Albrecht was appointed to the Semperoper in 1991 and Georg Quander to the Berliner Staatsoper in 1992. The Leipzig Oper was unique in its decision to appoint the east German composer Udo Zimmermann as artistic director in 1991. The musical director, appointed in 1990, however, was the west German Lothar Zagrosek.
6. Translated in Cohen, Curd and Reeve (2011: 13). Katzer reads from Nietzsche's German translation.

References

Amzoll, S. and G. Katzer (2002) '"Man muß die Ränder wachsen lassen": Im Gespräch mit Stefan Amzoll', *Utopie kreativ*, CXLI-II, 647–65.

Attewell, N. (2004) '"Bouncy Little Tunes": Nostalgia, Sentimentality, and Narrative in Gravity's Rainbow', *Contemporary Literature*, XLV, 22–48.

Bahr, E. (2007) *Weimar on the Pacific: German Exile Culture in Los Angeles and the Crisis of Modernism* (Berkeley, CA: University of California Press).

Boym, S. (2001) *The Future of Nostalgia* (New York: Basic).

Bredemeyer, R. (1992) *Wendepunkt*, for male-voice choir, 3 clarinets, tuba and percussion (unpublished).

Bredemeyer, R. (1993) *Aufschwung OST* für Klavier, Oboe, Schlagzeug und Tuba (Quartettstücke 4) unter treuhändlerischen Missbrauch der Nr. 2 aus den Phantasiestücken op. 12 von Robert Schumann (Berlin: Neue Musik, 2004).

Bredemeyer, R. and U. Wollny (1983) '"Ihr lacht wohl über den Träumer, der Blumen im Winter sah?" Wilhelm Müllers "Winterreise" und ihre Wiedervertonung durch Reiner Bredemeyer', *Musik und Gesellschaft*, XXXV, 486–90.

Brubaker, R. (2000) 'Accidental Diasporas and External Homelands in Central and Eastern Europe: Past and Present', *Institute for Advanced Studies, Vienna, Political Science Series*, 71, 1–19.

Clifford, J. (1994) 'Diasporas', *Cultural Anthropology*, IX, 302–38.

Cohen, S. M., P. Curd, and C. D. C. Reeve (2011) *Readings in Ancient Greek Philosophy: From Thales to Aristotle* (Indianapolis, IN: Hackett).

Danneberg, W. (1995a) 'Damit hat sich jeder herumzuschlagen: Gespräch mit Friedrich Goldmann', *Musik in der Schule*, XLVI, 108–10.

Danneberg, W. (1995b) 'Ein leicht herablassender Ton: Gespräch mit Georg Katzer', *Musik in der Schule*, XLVI, 283–5.

Danneberg, W. (1995c) 'Ich habe die Absicht, eine Kinderoper zu schreiben: Gespräch mit Siegfried Matthus', *Musik in der Schule*, XLVI, 169–71.

Danneberg, W. (1995d) 'In den Hintergrund gedrängt: Gespräch mit Reiner Bredemeyer', *Musik in der Schule*, XLVI, 41–3.

Danneberg, W. (1995e) 'Nicht für'n Appel und'n Ei! Gespräch mit Paul-Heinz Dittrich', *Musik in der Schule*, XLVI, 335–8.

Emmerich, W. (2009) 'Cultural Memory East v. West: Is What Belongs Together Really Growing Together?' in K. Leeder (ed.) 'From Stasiland to Ostalgie: The GDR Twenty Years After', *Oxford German Studies*, 39 (3), 278–87.

Fuhrmann, W. (2005) 'In jeder Musik steckt eine Haltung: Zum 70. Geburtstag des Komponisten Georg Katzer', *Berliner Zeitung*, 10 January 2005, http://www.berliner-zeitung.de/archiv/zum-70–geburtstag-des-komponisten-georg-katzer-in-jeder-musik-steckt-eine-haltung,10810590,10247562.html [accessed 1 January 2012].

Huyssen, A. (2003) 'Diaspora and Nation: Migration into Other Pasts', *New German Critique*, LXXXVIII, 147–64.

Kammen, M. (1993) *The Mystic Chords of Memory: The Transformation of Tradition in American Culture* (New York: Vintage).

Katzer, G. (1983) *Aide mémoire*, for tape; available on *Angewandte Musik [b] Musik für Radio: 1950–2000* (RCA Red Seal, 2001).

Katzer, G. (1989) *Mon 1989*, for tape; available on *Elektroakustische Musik – Komponierte Zeitgeschichte* (RCA Red Seal, 2008).

Katzer, G. (1990a) *Mein 1989*, for tape; available on *Elektroakustische Musik – Komponierte Zeitgeschichte* (RCA Red Seal, 2008).

Katzer, G. (1990b) *Offene Landschaft mit obligatem Ton e*, for chamber orchestra (Edition Peters).

Katzer, G. (1992) *Landschaft mit steigender Flut*, for orchestra and tape (Wergo: WER 62742).

Katzer, G. (1999) 'Das Vergangene trotz Zukunft weiter bewältigen. Referat zur Generalversammlung des deutschen Musikrates in Bonn' in U. Dibelius and F. Schneider (eds) *Neue Musik im geteilten Deutschland. Dokumente aus den achtziger Jahren* (Berlin: Berliner Festspiele), 454–6.

Katzer, G. (2001) *Les paysages fleurissants*, for tape (unpublished).

Kohl, H. (1990) 'Fernsehansprache des Bundeskanzler Kohl anlässlich des Inkrafttretens der Währungs-, Wirtschafts- und Sozialunion, 1 Juli. 1990,' *Bulletin des Presse- und Informationsamt der Bundesregierung*, LXXXVI, 741–2.

Königsdorf, J. (2009) 'Ultraschall Festival 2009 in Berlin', *tip Berlin*, 30 January 2009, http://www.tip-berlin.de/kultur-und-freizeit-theater-und-buehne/ultraschall-festival-2009-berlin [accessed 1 January 2012].

Links, C. (2009) *Das Schicksal der DDR-Verlage: Die Privatisierung und ihre Konsequenzen* (Berlin: Links).

Lowenthal, D. (1985) *The Past is a Foreign Country* (Cambridge: Cambridge University Press).

Mayer, G. (2010) 'Advanced Composition and Critical (Political) Ambition', http://guentermayer.wordpress.com/category/musikgeschichte [accessed 22 August 2011].

Naficy, H. (1993) *The Making of Exile Cultures: Iranian Television in Los Angeles* (Minneapolis, MN: University of Minnesota Press).

Nauck, G. (1993) 'Anpassen, Widersetzen, Aufgeben. Komponieren nach einem politischen Umbruch. Zur Situation der DDR-Komponisten im wiedervereinigten Deutschland', *Positionen: Beiträge zur neuen Musik*, XVII, 37–41.

Oehlschlägel, R. (1990) 'Große Hoffnung, große Furcht: Gespräch zwischen Komponisten und Musikologen aus der DDR und der BRD', *MusikTexte*, XXXIII–IV, 35–43.

Olias, G. (1995) 'Dokumentarisches und Gleichnishaftes in neueren Werken: Anregungen zur musikdidaktischen Interpretation', *Musik in der Schule*, XLVI, 84–98.

Pohl, J. O. (2009) 'Volk auf dem Weg: Transnational Migration of the Russian-Germans from 1763 to the Present Day', *Studies in Ethnicity and Nationalism*, IX, 267–86.

Rother, B. (2000) 'Gilt das gesprochene Wort? – Wann und wo sagte Willy Brandt "Jetzt wächst zusammen, was zusammengehört"?', *Deutschland Archiv*, 33, 90–93.

Schenker, F. (1992) ...*Ins Endlose*... (Wergo: WER 62982).

Stewart, M. (2003) 'The Hungarian Status Law: A New European Form of Transnational Politics?', *Diaspora: A Journal of Translation Studies*, XII, 67–101.

Stewart, S. (1993) *On Longing: Narratives of the Miniature, the Gigantic, the Souvenir, the Collection* (Durham, NC: Duke University Press).

Ullmann, J. (1999) 'von wende zu wende – verspätete nachrichten aus einem fernen land' in U. Dibelius and F. Schneider (eds) *Neue Musik im geteilten Deutschland. Dokumente aus den achtziger Jahren* (Berlin: Berliner Festspiele), 497–500.

8

Colour and Time in Museums of East German Everyday Life

Chloe Paver

A feature of post-GDR cultural memory is the clear division between museums documenting the inhumanity and criminality of the East German state and museums documenting so-called 'everyday life'. This term ('DDR-Alltag') is widely used for those areas of East German life which, while subject to varying degrees of political and ideological pressure, were, for most people, free of state violence: the home, the workplace and leisure time. Even if Federal institutions such as the Zeitgeschichtliches Forum Leipzig (Leipzig Forum for Contemporary History) attempt to encompass both the state and the everyday, and even if museums of the everyday are beginning to address dictatorial terror, the two types of museum are likely to remain a feature of the German culture industry.

Given that this chapter focuses on museums of everyday life, one might question its inclusion in the section 'Beyond Nostalgia'. With their vibrant displays of manufactured objects, museums of everyday life in the GDR are a ready target for accusations of *Ostalgie*. If this chapter nevertheless positions itself 'beyond nostalgia' it is partly because scholarship has come to understand *Ostalgie* in more complex terms, no longer just as a 'dangerous form of selective amnesia', but as a 'multi-layered phenomenon' which implicates both easterners and westerners and is known to Germans partly through caricature (Cooke, 2005: 104–5; Berdahl, 2008: 363). Anselma Gallinat argues later in this volume (Chapter 9: 150) that, in field interviews with easterners, 'memories are not easily categorisable into "critical" and "nostalgic"', while in her chapter Patricia Hogwood (Chapter 2: 44) views *Ostalgie* as a position that resourceful easterners have actively adopted to help 'manage the cognitive dissonances of transition from socialism to capitalism'.

Rather than pronouncing museums 'guilty' or 'not guilty' of peddling *Ostalgie*, this chapter takes for granted that *Ostalgie* is a social position well known to museum curators and their visitors. Some curators may wish to distance themselves from *Ostalgie*;[1] others are ready to exploit its commercial advantages to support their museums. It is also possible to pursue both these strategies at once; but in 2012 almost everyone views *Ostalgie* from a distance. Thus, a museum which issues a promotional DVD titled *'Es war nicht alles schlecht!': Lebensart DDR 1949–1989* (*'It wasn't all bad!': Life in the GDR 1949–1989*, no date, after 2008) positions itself in the *Ostalgie* debates and invites visitors to take this attitude or leave it. While this tactic is unlikely to win friends at Germany's state-run museums, the private DDR-Museum 'Zeitreise' in Dresden-Radebeul, which sells the DVD, is currently working with the BStU (Office of the Federal Commissioner for the Stasi Files) to introduce a narrative strand on the role of the Stasi in GDR society; in the meantime it is showing a BStU poster exhibition about the Berlin Wall.

Proceeding from this initial insight that museums may occupy more than one position simultaneously, this chapter examines the contrasting metaphors of colour and drabness which are used – sometimes at the same time – to envision the GDR in museums of everyday life. My analysis of a second source of complexity – the difficulty of calibrating the relative 'pastness' of GDR objects – draws on a growing body of scholarship on GDR material culture and its afterlife. The chapter attempts to draw out complexities in what can easily be dismissed as straightforward or populist museum displays.

The chapter draws examples from two types of museum. The DDR-Museum in Berlin and the Dokumentationszentrum Alltagskultur der DDR in Eisenhüttenstadt show a carefully ordered selection of their collections supplemented by professionally researched historical data. The DDR-Museum Malchow and the DDR-Museum 'Zeitreise' in Dresden-Radebeul – two of four similar museums visited by the author – are privately run and display a significant proportion of their holdings, including repeats of the same object. Thus, the Radebeul museum displays not just one GDR fire extinguisher, but nine, and not just one typewriter, top-loading washing machine, toaster, voltmeter, accordion or set of skis, but several, and in some cases dozens, of each (see Figure 8.1). This second type of museum supplies information about individual exhibits and themes without offering a systematic framework

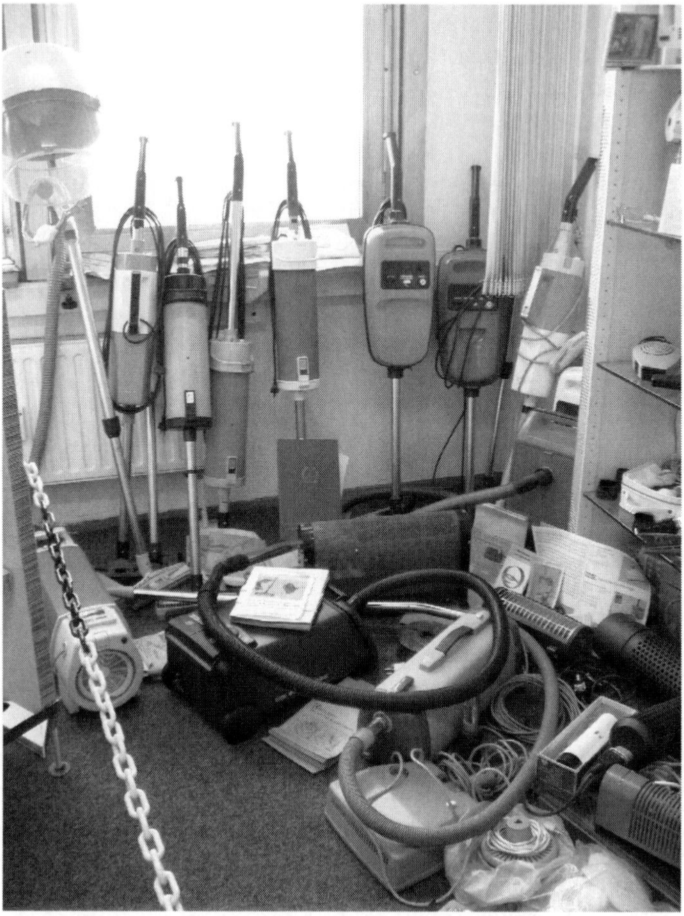

Figure 8.1 Display of objects at the DDR-Museum 'Zeitreise' in Dresden-Radebeul (Chloe Paver; image reproduced with the permission of Hans-Joachim Stephan).

of interpretation. For ease of reference I refer to each museum by its geographical location.

The *grau–bunt* spectrum

An admittedly unscientific survey of usage of the phrase 'der graue Alltag' (the greyness or drabness of everyday life) indicates that it collocates strongly with 'DDR' and that the phrase 'der graue DDR-Alltag' is used not only by westerners (for whom it may confirm prejudices about the former East) but also, both with and without irony, by former citizens of the GDR. The metaphor can readily be literalised in the realm of objects. In an interview to mark the twentieth anniversary of the *Wende*, journalist Annette Ramelsberger (2009) explained her motives for preserving Günter Schabowski's telephone, found in his abandoned office:

> It's typical. When you think about it, it's an iconic symbol of everything that typified the GDR: it's made of plastic and it's grey. And yet its form reminds me more of the 1960s than the 1980s and 1990s. And that's also typical of the GDR: rather stuck in the grey of the 1960s.

The association between drabness and everyday life in the GDR is evidently so automatised that Ramelsberger does not connect Schabowski's telephone, as one might anticipate, with the GDR elite and its exercise of power. Instead, she draws an associative bridge from the object's colour to life in the GDR as a whole, which she sees as having been characterised by synthetic materials and by a 'greyness' that persisted long after it was appropriate.

Given that Ramelsberger herself calls the grey telephone an icon, it may seem superfluous to stress the mythicising tendency of her comments. Nevertheless, a visit to any museum of everyday life in the GDR would show that Schabowski might just as well have owned a brightly coloured plastic East German telephone: the brand of telephone used for the hotline to the Kremlin came in a rather jaunty lime green, for instance (DDR-Museum; see also Bertsch and Hedler, 1990: 102). Far from being 'grau', museums of the everyday culture of East Germany are 'bunt' – in both its senses, of 'colourful' and 'varied'.

To point this out is not to propose a literal-minded approach which seeks to establish how colourful the GDR was in physical reality. We can take for granted both that the East was subject to the universal laws of physics and that former East Germans can invoke the psychological 'greyness' of the GDR without being in denial of its varied manufacturing design palette. In analysing statements about the GDR past I follow Gallinat (Chapter 9), who argues that such statements should not be judged as correct or incorrect, but understood as rhetorical gambits in ongoing social conversations. What interests me from a rhetorical point of view is that, in memory discourses about the GDR, speakers tend to invoke one pole of the *grau–bunt* spectrum to suit the context, sometimes oddly conflating literal and metaphorical meanings and sometimes creating odd dissonances between the literal and the metaphorical.

On its home page, a tour company lists attractions in Berlin: 'Nearby is the DDR-Museum where one can experience at first hand what the grey everyday life of socialism looked like' (Humboldt Tours Berlin, 2011). Here it is assumed that 'greyness', despite its conventional lack of marketing appeal, will sell, since it promises the reliable fulfilment of the tourist's expectations about communism. Indeed, such is its confidence in this selling point that the tour company neglects to tell the customer that the museum is, in fact, remarkably 'bunt'. Following criticism that it presented the former GDR in terms that were too attractive and depoliticised, the Berlin museum extended its display in 2010 to present more clearly the workings of the dictatorship. To demonstrate its move to a more 'realistic' political reading of the GDR, the curators chose the colour grey – in the form of a semi-circular bank of black and white photographic enlargements – though this quickly dissolves into colour if one opens the display cases or walks around to their reverse side.

This metaphorical association of the state with greyness is interesting because it is a retrospective reading at odds with the regime's historical self-presentation through colour, most obviously in banners and commemorative items, and in youth and sport uniforms, all of which are amply represented in museums. Two other categories of colourful objects much in evidence at museums – children's toys and plastics – can also be said to have been produced partly in the service of the regime. A small but significant minority of toys had a propaganda message. The Malchow museum displays an 'Electric Quiz' board game whose questions include 'What is the name of the largest Pioneers' House in the GDR and when was it handed over to our government by our Soviet friends?' As the Eisenhüttenstadt museum explains particularly well, plastics, for which vibrant colour or *Farbenfreude* was a key selling point, were a product of the chemistry programmes of the 1960s that attempted to supply East Germans with cheap and appealing household goods to rival the West (Rubin, 2003). One might therefore speak of 'verordnete Farbe' (colour by command). Since this element of command doubtless contributed to the psychological greyness of the era, the conflation of these opposites in memory is understandable.

Objects in museums about the Stasi tend, by contrast, to be muted in tone: a succession of office equipment, stationery and photographs. Since this drabness can usefully stand for the moral murk of state oppression, museums tend not to liven it up. The Museum in der 'Runden Ecke' (Museum at the 'Round Corner') in Leipzig inserts a critical frame around any colourful state self-representations that it feels obliged to show. A red fabric banner woven with the SED's emblem and the slogan 'United we are everything' is juxtaposed with a statement in the museum's distinctive 'handwriting' of black marker pen applied to corrugated cardboard (in imitation of protest placards): 'The Ministry for State Security was an instrument of terror in the hands of the SED and was to a large degree a criminal organisation.' Elsewhere, in a room devoted to sport in the GDR, the visitor is greeted by lurid flags and tassels which afford relief from the surrounding gloom and might seem to celebrate the sporting spectacles documented on photographs around them. However, information boards explain that spectators in Leipzig's athletics stadium were drilled to raise and lower the flags in choreographed displays that spelled out propaganda slogans for the cameras. Other information in the room explains the various ways in which sport was subject to Stasi and state interference.

At its permanent exhibition in Berlin, the BStU banishes all the SED's own colours. The background is grey, with enlarged black and white photographs covering much of one wall. In sharp contrast, vibrant lime green is used as an accent colour to pick out the representative biographies of six Stasi victims. This has the effect of stressing their value in the present over the 'grey' system that oppressed them, and arguably of evoking their agency within their victim role.

Colour is also commonly invoked in memory discourses about the *Wende*. At the modest Malchow museum, a sheet of typed A4 paper offers a 'Leitgedanke' or interpretative framework for the displays. It explains the purging of East German households after the *Wende*: 'People escaped from the grey monotony of "real existing socialism" by plunging into the torrent of capitalist colour'. Here, the opposition grey = East, colourful = West (which is invoked in almost identical terms by the Dresden museum; see DDR-Museum 'Zeitreise', 2011) is used to explain the rejection of the eastern products since donated to the museum. Yet these same objects suggest that in reality – as opposed to metaphor – eastern consumers are just as likely to have been fleeing in the opposite direction: away from the gaudy patterns of the 1970s with which consumers remained lumbered even in 1989 towards a more restrained western design palette. Certainly, in their displays Malchow's curators seem at pains to offer a 'bunt' version of the GDR, not only in material terms but also in terms of a complex social structure and domestic culture.

An essay by Wendy Westphal on Florian Henckel von Donnersmarck's 2006 film *Das Leben der Anderen* (The Lives of Others) touches on the question of colour and memory. In interview, Donnersmarck recalls studying the colour palette of GDR television. Having noted a lack of strong reds and blues, he endeavoured to exaggerate this muted palette in his *mise-en-scène*, on the grounds that memory exaggerates visual effects, and was surprised to find audiences telling him that this was exactly what the GDR (rather than GDR television or a stylised memory of GDR television) was like:

> Everywhere people said 'That's exactly what it was like, it looked exactly like that.' But in reality that's what it looks like *in memory*, when you try to imitate memory, the inner truth of the GDR as it were. And yet there were blue objects in the GDR, of course there were. But in the inner truth of the GDR there weren't any.
>
> (cit. in Westphal, 2010: 10)

Though Westphal does not comment further on this phenomenon (and it would need more than Donnersmarck's observation to prove its existence) it adds weight to the idea that real colours and their figurative attributes become confused in memory.[2]

Anachronism

These comments suggest that colour has a temporal dimension, to which I now turn. 'The museum object', writes Gottfried Korff (2007: 141), 'belongs to another time, but places itself face to face with the present-day spectator.' While anachronistic effects are thus fundamental to all museums, in the case of the GDR the familiar effect is complicated. Beyond the primary anachronism noted by Korff (the 'pastness' of all museum objects) lies one alluded to by Ramelsberger in her comment on Schabowski's telephone: despite some success in the 1960s, East German industrial design subsequently fell behind that of the West, causing many objects to appear 'stuck' in an earlier decade. Ina Merkel (2006: 254) adduces this as one reason why objects quickly moved through the rubbish phase to the museum phase: because equivalent designs in the West were already 'museum pieces'. This secondary anachronism requires the museum visitor to employ a kind of double vision to see the 'double life' that some objects led in the GDR: one and the same product may have enjoyed a first life phase in the 1960s or 1970s when it appeared modern to consumers and therefore, as Eli Rubin (2003: 112) argues, helped to stabilise the regime, and a second life phase, in the 1970s and 1980s, when it was proof of the GDR's inability to keep up with the West and caused increasing disillusion. Even with captioning, which is not always on offer, it can be hard for visitors without first-hand knowledge of the GDR to keep those object life phases and likely emotional responses to them in view, and there is a danger that GDR wares are viewed in one simplified time dimension, as 'old stuff'. Elsewhere in this volume, Gabriele Mueller (Chapter 12: 209) sees a similar, though more deliberate, flattening out of time differences in television dramas about the late phase of the GDR, and expresses concern that this offers an attractive simplification for younger viewers who can simply write the GDR off as 'past': 'The films condense all the visual elements which have become markers of GDR life in complex post-*Wende* discourse into one "representative" tableau, which contains several layers of time and which is clearly identifiable as the past.' The Eisenhüttenstadt museum is the most careful to avoid this temporal flattening, giving a clear chronological account of developments in East German manufacturing and design, including contemporary consumer views, though even this museum does not seem to address head-on the 'ageing' of objects during the last decade of the GDR, nor to help the visitor distinguish between objects which were perceived as new in their day and objects that were already outdated when produced.

Another force may conspire to muddy the chronological waters in museums of the GDR. Writing of a visit to the Eisenhüttenstadt museum in the late 1990s, Charity Scribner (2003: 640) argues that objects made from poor-quality materials may look older than they are: 'The lightest collectibles – books, food wrappers, and the like – are of materials so fragile, so acidic, that they appear much older than their true fifteen or twenty years.' While such items form only a small proportion of those on view in museums and while indestructibility is a more typical characteristic of GDR objects, Scribner's essay also draws a fruitful comparison between three exhibitions which she sees as embodying different stances towards the GDR: Josef Beuys' *Wirtschaftswerte* (*Economic Values*) of 1980, which presented autographed GDR consumer goods as artistic 'ready-mades'; the West German exhibition *SED. Schönes Einheits Design* (*SED: Stunning Eastern Design*) of 1989; and the exhibition at the Eisenhüttenstadt museum, then called the 'Open Depot'. Though *Schönes Einheits Design*, a mean-spirited Western exhibition mounted just months before the *Wende* at the Habernoll Gallery in Dreieich-Götzenhain, might with some justification be seen as a diversion from the concerns of today's museums of the GDR, it has had an interesting afterlife and can be used to bring into focus some of the practical curatorial challenges faced in museums today.

The fall of communism intervened unexpectedly between the opening of *Schönes Einheits Design* in August 1989 and the publication of a retrospective catalogue the following winter.[3] The catalogue (Bertsch and Hedler, 1990) made no bones about the exhibition's contempt for the backwardness of East German design and has been roundly criticised in the scholarly literature. Scribner (2003: 642) notes that 'the selection of GDR products depicted [...] appears aimed to confirm the superior tastes of sophisticated Westerners'. Paul Betts (2000: 739–40) calls it 'a rather smug West German assessment', arguing that it was part of a wider 'ideological sleight of hand' that cast East Germany as the enemy of modernity and therefore as ripe for rejection by its people. For Merkel (2006: 259) the catalogue is 'a mockingly sarcastic book' in which 'the product culture of the GDR is devalued as cheap, old-fashioned and profane'. To this general censure one might add that the sneering introduction, written by designer Georg Bertsch, speaks with a *wir*, or 'we', that excludes East Germans,[4] despite the fact that they were by this time (early 1990) at liberty to buy the catalogue from the same shops as their soon-to-be compatriots.

While there is thus ready agreement about the catalogue's *Besserwesserei*,[5] more could be said about the oddly anachronistic effects that it documents and helps create. To underline her point about its anti-Eastern bias, Scribner (2003: 642) notes that the packaging depicted in the catalogue is 'faded' and cites the publisher's own cover text, which speaks of the 'pallid world of uniform consumer goods'. Yet despite the catalogue's standard invocations of a 'grauer DDR-Alltag',[6] the photographed objects are neither uniformly drab nor photographed with anything like the derision expressed in Bertsch's introduction. The photographic aesthetic is in fact close to the marketing aesthetic used today by professional museums of the GDR. The objects, many of them brightly coloured, are carefully lit against monochrome backgrounds to draw out the characteristics of their materials and forms. Where objects are photographed alone, as many are, the images have the quality of reverent portraits. The photograph of a well-designed set of bathroom scales with a shocking-pink plastic casing might be said to represent the high point of this aesthetic (Bertsch and Hedler, 1990: 84).

Thus, while *Schönes Einheits Design* was certainly a cruel exhibition at the time it was mounted, the catalogue, as an artefact that persists over time, has entered into a temporal limbo. Some objects, such as the cockerel-shaped egg cups now widely on sale in museum shops, have been singled out as design classics and thereby withdrawn from the ageing process. At the same time, readers will, over the intervening years, have gradually lost the ability to calibrate the crudity and outdatedness of products at the time of their manufacture (and original exhibition display). If I make a conscious effort to remember, I can say with confidence that in 1989 tampons in the West were notably more sophisticated than their Eastern counterparts shown in the catalogue; but I am much less sure that the audio-visual equipment documented in its pages would have looked behind the times from the day it went on sale. As if to confirm this loosening of our temporal moorings, Taschen re-issued the *Schönes Einheits Design* catalogue in 2004 – now in a pocket format and with a more neutral title and introduction – in its 'Icons' series (Ulrich and Hedler, 2004); this version is currently on sale in the Berlin museum's shop. The fact that Taschen was able to re-use the same photographs means that the photographer's aesthetic functions equally well as sarcastic mockery and as realism aimed at a sympathetic viewer.

At first sight, the new 'Icons' edition of the catalogue is easily assimilable to the category of 'retro'. Elizabeth Guffey notes that technological obsolescence creates many objects in this category, arguing that the utopian ideals of an earlier modernist era are part of retro's appeal. She invokes Raphael Samuel's notion of 'retrochic' as 'a sensibility that sidestepped established historical accounts and questions of chronology and context' and she proposes to analyse retro 'as a non-historical way of knowing the past' (Guffey, 2006: 17). While Guffey is writing about lifestyle and collecting choices, one might reasonably assume that many visitors will come to a museum with a more diffuse retro 'sensibility' which leads them to apprehend objects without a clear sense of 'chronology and context' and in a 'non-historical way'.

Once more, however, the GDR context seems to complicate matters. First, Beuys' exhibition of 1980 suggests that GDR objects had already been through a retro phase (albeit in fine art rather than popular culture) even before the GDR's demise. Beuys had individually autographed paper grocery bags to create saleable 'multiples', in a provocatively engineered collision between lack of consumer value and art-market value (Staeck and Steidl, 1990: 75). By 1989, two pages of the catalogue for *Schönes Einheits Design* were devoted to mocking such paper bags (Bertsch and Hedler, 1990: 148–9). Yet they now serve as one of a select group of icons chosen for the website of the Berlin museum's shop (DDR-Museum Berlin, 2011). A further complication is that the 'Icons' version of the *Schönes Einheits Design* catalogue has not, as one might expect of a retro product, selected a limited number of design classics. The full series of photographs is reproduced and many of the objects remain irredeemably mediocre. It may be, then, that – as with the tour company selling the 'greyness' of the GDR – Taschen can sell its book on 'iconic' GDR design safe in the knowledge that readers are happy to embrace within their conception of the GDR the poor design quality of many of its wares. This duality is corroborated by museum shops in which selected GDR products (both original and reproduction) are sold alongside postcards with motifs that make fun of the *Mangelwirtschaft* (economy based on a lack of supply), including a popular series by Thomas Hoepker. A shop sign photographed by Hoepker in 1974 reads 'Opening Times: Every last Wednesday of the month from 3–5 p.m.'. In museums of everyday life the GDR is thus simultaneously mocked for 'failing to deliver the goods' (Berdahl, 2008: 360) and welcomed as a source of consumer products that promise distinction.[7]

This discussion of two catalogues documenting a long-forgotten exhibition has taken us some way from the concerns of today's museum curators, and it is important to stress that the 'iconic' treatment of objects, which singles them out visually for praise or mockery, is largely a feature of the museum periphery (advertising, postcards and other souvenirs). Museum displays place objects in visible relation to many others. At its crudest, this may take the form of a taxonomical exercise in placing like with like. Room reconstructions are also common, and in the best displays selected objects are placed within a personal, social and/or political framework. If Ramelsberger cared to look for telephones in museums of the GDR, for instance, she would find most of them in reconstructed offices, accompanied by commentary on GDR bureaucratic structures. In that setting it would be much less easy to use a telephone to represent the state of a whole nation.

Nevertheless, it remains the case that the complex 'pastness' of the GDR object is both difficult to contextualise in museum displays and, as Mueller suggests in her analysis of television dramas (see Chapter 12), easy to simplify for political purposes. The clearest way to illustrate successive life phases of GDR objects would be to have two rows of objects, one Eastern, one Western: in the 1950s and 1960s objects would look similar in design, but through the 1970s and 1980s it would become apparent that Western design is speeding ahead. Yet the Haus der Geschichte in Bonn has been criticised for such parallelism. For Betts (2000: 740) its exhibition is typical of cultural phenomena of the 1990s that 'cast East German culture as fundamentally pre- or anti-modern' and therefore as rightly discarded.

The temporary exhibition *Normiert, Möbliert, Variiert. Eine Ost-West-Berliner Wohnstudie um die 70er* (*Standardised, Furnished, Customised: A Study of the East and West Berlin Home in the 1970s*) at the Mitte

Museum in Berlin deployed a parallel display while resisting anti-Eastern readings. In a deliberately stylised 'face-off' between East and West, an Eastern *Wandschrank* (modular shelving system) faced a Western one across a divided coffee table; even the curtains, one in an eastern fabric and one in a western one, were drawn into the game. By choosing the 1970s the museum was able to level the playing field: although the eastern catalogue for *Wandschränke* was of inferior design and print quality to the western one, the displays showed much more commonality than difference, especially in matters of taste, including the schmaltzy background music, which alternated between eastern and western popular songs. Thus, if the objects looked dowdy to the contemporary visitor, they at least looked *equally* dowdy. The Mitte Museum's emphasis on East–West commonalities (echoed in its permanent display) reflects the fact that it was formed from the merger of three museums, Mitte and Wedding in the East and Tiergarten in the West.

The Radebeul museum hints at a different alternative to the confident leaps and bounds of western design progress. While the museum offers no overarching interpretation, it provides highly detailed information on individual objects, such as:

> Technically, the RS 2510 corresponds more or less to the RS 2500, except that in addition it has a memory for 16 channels. There are three push buttons to allow the user to choose a channel or to switch to manual, and the information is displayed using a 2-digit, 7-segment LED display.

Like all texts in the museum, this has been researched and authored by the director, Hans-Joachim Stephan. The distinction he makes between closely related but discrete object types addresses itself particularly to collectors, since acts of taxonomy constitute the field of collectible objects. If the average museum visitor finds the sudden excess of detail odd, this may be because the unit of time has been set unusually small. Even in an industrial design museum the narrative would move forward in larger leaps (conceivably from the RS 2500 to the RS 5000, but certainly not from the RS 2500 to its variant, the RS 2510). However, this sudden deceleration of design time brings us closer to life-time, to time as it is experienced both in forward movement and in retrospective appraisal by individuals. Gallinat (see Chapter 9) argues for the social value of taking east Germans' sense of their own life achievements seriously rather than dismissing their personal milestones or *Errungenschaften* as now irrelevant by-products of a corrupt state, and

Irene Lazda (2010: 215–16) argues that 'in the lives of [GDR] individuals objects marked milestones of success or disappointment'. The addition of the 16-channel memory represents a life achievement to an engineer, at the very least, and perhaps also to the workers on the assembly line. The testimony of eyewitnesses ('Zeitzeugen'), which is largely absent from permanent displays in museums of everyday life, though sometimes offered in the form of guided tours, might be used to draw this out. While museum professionals would probably look down their noses at the narrative techniques of the DDR-Museum 'Zeitreise', its acknowledgement of small steps in design progress – even in the technologically less advanced GDR – has the potential to foreground positive personal endeavours of GDR citizens.

In its analysis of metaphor and rhetoric, this chapter adds 'colour', so to speak, to Katrin Kohl's survey of typical metaphors used in memory discourses about the GDR (Kohl, 2009). In its analysis of time it proposes that the material residue of East German production may become steadily less able to evoke the chronological stages in the GDR's 40-year span as the *Wende* recedes, especially given the complication of the East's gradual industrial stagnation. The final example from the Radebeul museum raises a key question: how should this stagnation feature in museum narratives? Should it be used to tell a political story of failure or personal stories of achievements in politically difficult times? In her comparative analysis of the state-run Zeitgeschichtliches Forum Leipzig and an amateur museum of the everyday, Daphne Berdahl clearly favours the latter. While the Leipzig museum is symptomatic of the 'devaluation of East German histories since reunification', excluding all life narratives other than resistance (Berdahl, 2008: 354), the amateur museum Zeitzeugen *Ostalgie*, in an unnamed town, 'connects personal biographies to collective memory' and is itself an achievement in the biographies of unemployed former easterners (ibid.: 356). Berdahl sees such museums as less subversive than their detractors fear, given that they focus on manufactured products and therefore on consumer choice as 'a fundamental right' (ibid.: 362). But she sees a value in their giving expression to 'a highly complicated relationship between personal histories, disadvantage, dispossession, the betrayal of promises, and the social worlds of production and consumption' (ibid.: 359). The context of this remark suggests that the 'betrayal of promises' is an experience in the new Germany, despite the obvious material 'disadvantage' of the East. It remains to be seen whether the state-run Sammlung Industrielle Gestaltung (Collection of Industrial Design), which is set to have a permanent display space in Berlin and will focus more clearly on the 'everyday' than the Zeitgeschichtliches Forum, will make up for the perceived deficiencies of the Forum and allow space for the expression of a diversity of pre- and post-*Wende* experiences of material culture.

Notes

1. In conversation with the author (April 2011), Andreas Ludwig, Director of the Dokumentationszentrum Alltagskultur der DDR, noted that distancing the museum from *Ostalgie* was important to securing continued funding. I am grateful to Herr Ludwig for information on this and other matters.
2. In Chapter 12 (209), Gabriele Mueller notes the use of a clichéd *mise-en-scène* in television dramas about the GDR. They show 'cramped apartments carefully composed in brown, grey, and yellow hues'.
3. The 'catalogue' includes new objects acquired since the exhibition; no indication is given as to which these are. Possibly, Merkel (1998: 283) confuses the exhibition and its catalogue when she writes that the exhibition was mounted *after* the *Wende*, a confusion compounded by Betts (2000: 739), who states that the exhibition opened in December 1989. The catalogue dates the opening to 29th August 1989 (Bertsch and Hedler, 1990: 176, note 53).
4. For instance: 'These things seem alien to us; we aren't quite sure how to handle them; at first sight we find them shabby' (Bertsch and Hedler, 1990: 9).
5. A punning coinage from the 1990s, combining the word for 'being a know-all' and the word for 'Westerner'.
6. On the inside cover we read: 'The objects depicted here are "real existing" goods from the grey everyday life of the GDR'. See also Bertsch's Introduction (Bertsch and Hedler, 1990: 7).
7. Museum shops are still relatively under-studied, but for a good model in a related field, see Dittrich (2010).

References

Berdahl, D. (2008) 'Re-Presenting the Socialist Modern: Museums and Memory in the Former GDR' in K. Pence and P. Betts (eds) *Socialist Modern: East Germany Everyday Culture and Politics* (Ann Arbor: University of Michigan Press), pp. 345–66.

Bertsch, G. C. and E. Hedler (eds) (1990) *SED. Schönes Einheits Design. Stunning Eastern Design. Savoir Eviter le Design* (Cologne: Taschen).

Betts, P. (2000) 'The Twilight of the Idols: East German Memory and Material Culture', *Journal of Modern History*, 72, 731–65.

Cooke, P. (2005) *Representing East Germany Since Unification* (Oxford: Berg).

DDR-Museum Berlin (2011) http://www.shop.ddr-museum.de/index.php [date accessed 1 September 2011].

DDR-Museum 'Zeitreise' (2011) http://www.ddr-museum-dresden.de/cod/php/ddr-museum.php?lang=deu&thm=home&thmsub=gedankeninhalte&id=1&sid=3&pdf=1&dr=1&thmid=99 [date accessed 1 September 2011].

Dittrich, U. (2010) 'Pieces of the Past: Souvenirs from Nazi Sites – The Example of Peenmünde' in B. Niven and C. Paver (eds) *Memorialization in Germany Since 1945* (Basingstoke: Palgrave Macmillan), pp. 114–23.

Guffey, E. E. (2006) *Retro: The Culture of Revival* (London: Reaktion).

Humboldt Tours Berlin (2011) http://www.humboldttoursberlin.com/touren-berlin-sehenswuerdigkeiten-berlin-stadtrundgang-stadtfuehrung-de.phtml [date accessed 1 September 2011].

Kohl, K. (2009) 'Conceptualizing the GDR: 20 Years After', *Oxford German Studies*, 38, 265–77.

Korff, G. (2007) 'Zur Eigenart der Museumsdinge' in M. Eberspächer, G. M. König and B. Tschofen (eds) *Museumsdinge. Deponieren, Exponieren*, 2nd rev. edn (Cologne: Böhlau), pp. 140–45.

Lazda, I. (2010) 'The *Alltag* Becomes *Alltagsgeschichte:* The Haus der Geschichte in Lutherstadt Wittenberg and the DDR-Museum Berlin' in S. G. Figge and J. K. Ward (eds) *Reworking the German Past: Adaptations in Film, the Arts, and Popular Culture* (Rochester: Camden House), pp. 203–22.

Merkel, I. (1998) 'Consumer Culture in the GDR, or How the Struggle for Antimodernity was Lost on the Battleground of Consumer Culture' in S. Strasser, C. McGovern and M. Judt (eds) *Getting and Spending: European and American Consumer Societies in the Twentieth Century* (Cambridge: Cambridge University Press), pp. 281–99.

Merkel, I. (2006) 'From Stigma to Cult: Changing Meanings in East German Consumer Culture' in F. Trentmann (ed.) *The Making of the Consumer: Knowledge, Power and Identity in the Modern World* (Oxford: Berg), pp. 249–70.

Ramelsberger, A. (2009) Interview with D. Stawski, ' "Ikone für alles, was die DDR ausgemacht hat" ', *Süddeutsche Zeitung*, 9 November.

Rubin, E. (2003) 'The Order of Substitutes: Plastic Consumer Goods in the *Volkswirtschaft* and Everyday Domestic Life in the GDR' in D. F. Crew (ed.) *Consuming Germany in the Cold War* (Oxford: Berg), pp. 87–119.

Scribner, C. (2003) 'Object, Relic, Fetish, Thing: Joseph Beuys and the Museum', *Critical Inquiry*, 29 (4), 634–49.

Staeck, K. and G. Steidl (eds) (1990) *Joseph Beuys. Das Wirtschaftswertprinzip* (Heidelberg: Edition Staeck).

Ulrich, R. and E. Hedler (eds) (2004) *DDR Design. East German Design. Design de la RDA. 1949–1989* (Cologne: Taschen).

Westphal, W. (2010) ' "Truer than the Real Thing": "Real" and "Hyperreal" Representations of the Past in *Das Leben der Anderen*', unpublished conference paper delivered at the GSA conference, Oakland, California, September.

Part IV

Past Memories for Present Concerns

9
Memory Matters and Contexts: Remembering for Past, Present and Future

Anselma Gallinat

The East German past has been the focus of much debate and scholarly work in Germany since reunification in 1990. The official and government-sponsored discourse on this past is known as *Aufarbeitung*, the 'reworking' of the past, which regards the era of socialism as one part of the nation's *doppelte Vergangenheit*, the 'double burden in history'. *Aufarbeitung* comes with a very clear view of what the GDR was, the 'SED-dictatorship', and of what the present is, the free and democratic republic, a dichotomic mirror image of the 'unjust' and totalitarian socialist regime.[1] While the term SED-dictatorship, which is central to this discourse, seems to limit dictatorial rule to the ruling socialist party, it is fundamentally underpinned by an understanding that this aspect of the GDR shaped everything else: from the outcomes of elections to individual professional choices, cheap foodstuffs and low rents. More often than not it is thus used to mean the 'GDR-as-dictatorship' (see Beattie, 2008). Faced with a population that does not always seem to agree with these basic premises, *Aufarbeitung* has become a technique of governance that tries to form collective memory through commemoration, musealisation, education and research. The discourse is fashioned largely by concerns in the present, about citizens' disengagement with politics and nostalgic sentiments about socialism, the loathed *Ostalgie*, which 'whitewash' the former regime. Indeed, in this realm nostalgia is perceived as the 'Other' to 'correct remembering', and that 'Other' needs to be countered. While here memory matters to legitimise government in the present and safeguard the nation's future in freedom, for individual and social memory the cards are differently stacked. In this regard the relationship between past, present and future is less unidirectional and memories are not easily categorisable into 'critical' and 'nostalgic', just as lives in the GDR cannot easily be ordered into 'perpetrators' and 'victims'.

Considering first the context of *Aufarbeitung* and then that of a local newspaper editorial office, this chapter explores which contexts give rise to which kind of remembering and why the past matters to individuals in those moments. The chapter thus seeks to engage with Silke Arnold-de Simine and Susannah Radstone's question of 'why some aspects of the past are constantly revisited' (Chapter 1: 19). It is based on data collected during ethnographic research which sought to explore the construction of narratives about the East German past in two settings in the eastern German state of Mittelland and its capital, Tillberg.[2] Over a period of 14 months two researchers (the author and Dr Sabine Kittel) conducted participant observation in relevant institutions and life-story interviews with employees.

Opinions on the question of the degree to which memory is shaped by present concerns or determined by the past events it recalls differ in the literature, and it is highly likely that these balances shift between different discourses. For *Aufarbeitung*, Friedman's statement (1992: 207) that 'The past is, thus, constructed according to the conditions and desires of those who produce historical texts in the present' appears to hold true. For individual and socially shared memories, however, past and present appear to interact in more complex ways. As Arnold-de Simine and Radstone posit, 'memory is understood to emerge through the mutual interactions of the past on the present *and* the present on the past' (Chapter 1: 20). In this vein, Birth (2006: 181) argues that we should concern ourselves more with the phenomenological presence of the past in the present, which he terms the 'immanent past', rather than its objectification. He puts it thus:

> Although the phenomenological existence of the past is in the present, [...] the present does not determine the immanent past. In some cases, the conspicuous nature of vestiges from the past demand attention; in other cases, such vestiges haunt and subtly structure intersubjective relations; and in still other cases, present experience evokes unwanted, anxiety-provoking flashbacks. In significant ways the past in the present structures the reproduction of knowledge and subjectivity, as much as present concerns can shape the past.
>
> (Birth, 2006: 186)

The first part of this chapter will therefore consider how the realm of government is writing the East German past through a preoccupation with the democratic present and future of the nation. This discourse makes this memory more linear and orderly than it appears in individual experiences, which the second part of the chapter considers. In the realm of social interaction and individual belonging, memory creates, as Birth (2006) states, new views, knowledge and experiences which in turn point to different conceptions of present and future.

Memory matters, for democracy

The Working Group *Aufarbeitung* in Tillberg, where the first phase of fieldwork took place, was founded in 1996 as a formalisation of already existing collaborations between institutions involved in similar 'memory work'. It coordinates activities, organises teacher training courses and other projects, and informs policymaking. Its remit concerns both German dictatorships, although during fieldwork its focus was clearly on the East German past. At the core of the group are the Office for Political Education (Landeszentrale für politische Bildung; LpB), Mittelland's Stasi Commissioner (Stasi-Beauftragter; LStU), the local Office of the Federal Commissioner for Stasi Files (Bundesbeauftragter für Stasi-Unterlagen; BStU), and memorials/museums such as the Stasi Prison Memorial. The LpB, which chaired the group, is a part of Mittelland's State Chancellery (at the time of fieldwork led by the conservative Christian Unity Party) and links the Working Group closely to the state government and its politics. To allow for efficient decision-making all institutions are usually represented by their directors, who in the main were men and western German. This fact, however, was rarely acknowledged openly as the group seemed united by their shared moral endeavour of safeguarding the memory of the dictatorship. Underpinning the group's concern with how the GDR is remembered today is a sense that the character of this memory influences how individuals position themselves in the current state (see Chapter 1).

This underlying logic was voiced very explicitly by the State Chancellery in response to findings of a survey on the 'political attitudes [of the population] between past and present', published in the summer of 2007. The survey had been commissioned by the government after a number of incidents that appeared to point to problems with democracy in the population (such as a very low turnout at local elections) and after long-standing concerns in the Working Group about popular nostalgia for socialism. The survey sought to explore questions on democracy, anti-Semitism and xenophobia, and the socialist past, as well as data on work and social backgrounds. The survey report provided a complex picture of the relationships between past and present, and of individuals' relationship to politics. However, both the State Chancellery, which needed to make a political response, and the Working Group *Aufarbeitung* focused on a few select responses. Much attention was paid to the fact that a majority had agreed with the statement that 'not everything was bad in the GDR' (however, a slightly smaller majority also agreed that the GDR had been a dictatorship, and furthermore most expressed support for democracy as the better order). Moreover, many respondents had evaluated the GDR's health care and education systems as better than today's. These responses were understood as showing nostalgic tendencies among a majority of the population, and related to another response which apparently revealed 'incorrect' understandings of parliamentary democracy. The Working Group *Aufarbeitung*, and staff at the LpB in particular, thus concluded that sentimental attachment to the socialist past prevented many of Mittelland's citizens from fully embracing the new democratic order.

This meant in turn that *Aufarbeitung* could and should be used to further a positive relationship to the political system. As the State Chancellery's press release stated, 'a selective remembering of the GDR past and a partly incomplete understanding of democracy are interconnected and interdependent in various ways'.[3] In response, the anniversaries of 2009 and 2010 would be used to 'reflect experiences with the building of democracy'. Events and texts (such as a governmental position paper published later that year) would tell a narrative of East German history that re-emphasised moments of civil action (endeavours for a multiparty system in 1945, demonstrations for regime change, escapes to West Germany, lack of popular support for SED rule, etc.), which would provide a view of democracy as the only possible regime that secured the civil rights people had been longing for during 40 years of totalitarian rule.

The LpB was identified as heading this task for the state government. Both GDR and Third Reich history, previously central aspects of the LpB's work in their own right, now became instruments in this all-commanding drive for 'democracy education'. While the term 'democracy' was never clearly defined, some of the debates reveal the underlying assumptions. In the survey question on parliamentary democracy that had raised eyebrows, for example, a majority of respondents had agreed with the statement that it was 'the task of the political opposition to support the government in its work and its decisions'. This jarred with schoolbook views which posit that opposition parties are integral to the plurality of political opinion in democracy through their criticism and literal 'opposition'. After years of observing protracted and seemingly unhelpful debates the population of Mittelland had, however, found that political parties should work together to achieve the best outcome. This in turn may have been understood in the political realm, and by the many western German actors in *Aufarbeitung*, as an expression of attitudes fostered in the socialist era when all parties belonged to the 'national front', a mass organisation overseen by the ruling SED. In either case, it is clear that the term 'democracy' is used here to refer to political practices that go back to the foundations of parliamentary democracy in the West German Republic. In this vein, the Federal Office for Political Education (BpB) made the sixtieth anniversary of the *Grundgesetz* (federal constitution) which symbolises the foundation of West Germany in 1949, one of the historical milestones to be remembered alongside the autumn of 1989 in the anniversary year of 2009. This determined view of 'democracy' as the West German political system means that other views came to be castigated as 'failures to understand' and 'failures to engage' in general. From a viewpoint of democracy as critical engagement with plurality and as participation, however, this is a rather un-democratic position.[4]

It appears that in the political field of *Aufarbeitung*, memory is very well organised (see Gallinat, forthcoming).[5] It comes in clear categories: nostalgic or critical, whereby 'critical' means recognition of the truth of the dictatorship. It has a clear purpose in the present, in that it fosters attachment to democracy, or rather to the political realities practised in West Germany for the past 60 years, and for the future of the nation in that it safeguards these political views, which are the basis of civil rights and freedom in the long term. Not only that, but signing up to this view of the SED-dictatorship and, if eastern German, reconsidering one's own life in that regard, has become a precondition of citizenship in the present. As the title of the survey suggests, refusing this view means remaining caught '*between* past and present' (emphasis added).

Remembering matters, for belonging

The findings of the survey reveal more than the government's narrow reading gives away. What these political actors chose to overlook was that a majority of respondents had also agreed that the GDR had been a dictatorship and expressed support for democracy as the better order.

A majority rejected a return to socialism, and more than half of the respondents stated that the benefits of unification outweighed its drawbacks. It thus seems that neither nostalgia nor democracy are as easily definable and categorisable as political *Aufarbeitung* suggests.

Ochs and Capps (2001: 56) argue that while many narrative exchanges seek to 'imbue an experience with a linear causal and temporal structure and conventional moral stance [...] these narrative formats may not resonate with actions, conditions and mindsets of the tellers or, more important, those participating in a set of life events'. This argument seems particularly apt in the East German context given the deep ambiguities inherent to life under socialism. As Havel (cit. in Skultans, 2001: 334) explains, it is very difficult, if not impossible, to categorise the population into victims and perpetrators 'for everyone in his or her own way is both a victim and a supporter of the system'. This is because 'society is not sharply polarised on the level of actual political power, but [...] the fundamental lines of conflict run right through each person' (ibid.: 334). In turn, memories will often reflect the tensions that individuals experienced during the socialist past as well as since (see Gallinat and Kittel, 2009). The remainder of this chapter will explore these complexities through material gathered during participant observation at the second site of fieldwork, the *Daily Paper*. While news reporting necessarily has a different relationship to the past than politics, the focus here is rather on how memories are invoked by individuals. Three particular areas will be considered: the question of judging the past, the past as resource in the present and belonging through memory.

The past in the present

The *Daily Paper* is the main daily in the northern part of Mittelland. Its headquarters in Tillberg feature an open plan office combining six desks, which hosted approximately 20 members of staff, most eastern German, of a range of ages. One of our interviewees, Thorsten Seifert, was in his late thirties and thus belonged to the younger cohort.

Thorsten had, like the vast majority of his peers, followed the socialist life course by joining the GDR's children's and youth organisations, but he had always struggled with authoritarian structures. He wore his hair long, went to his final exams wearing batik jeans despite a ban on jeans and, most notably, refused to sing a propaganda song in his music exam because it had previously been rejected in class discussions as being untrue. Thorsten had hoped to join a relative's private photography business but his apprenticeship saw him faced with an insufferable employer. When drafted for army service he therefore volunteered for the longer service period of three years but had not appreciated that he would be sent to the border troops and stationed at the Berlin Wall. This was an immensely difficult time for him and he soon requested to be moved elsewhere. His time with the army ended with the first free elections in the spring of 1990, and he soon applied to the *Daily Paper*, where he found that journalism suited him because 'I was somewhere where it was important to cause objection. To not just toe the line but, in contrast, explore the subtext behind a certain statement.'

Thorsten's story highlights how lived lives defy the easy categorisation of opponent versus supporter and good versus bad citizen that political *Aufarbeitung* inevitably supports. While he rejected arbitrary authoritarianism he fulfilled all the obligations of GDR citizenship; in fact he volunteered for additional army service. Thinking of this life in terms of resistance or complicity, and of Thorsten's memory as either sympathetic to the dictatorship or nostalgic, thus seems nonsensical. In the same way that his life was multifaceted, Thorsten's response to our interview questions on how the socialist past is managed today was complex: 'I don't like it when people talk about "the" GDR. Everything gets overshadowed by the Stasi and the SED. You get tiny pieces that can never give you the whole picture.' For Thorsten, current representations of the past lack depth and this is not only a failure of *Aufarbeitung*: 'On the one hand there is this reduction to Stasi, and on the other a weird cult around particular GDR symbols'.

The problem that Thorsten's response highlights concerns mechanisms of alienation that are inherent in the reproduction of the past for present-day purposes. Thorsten struggles with the 'distanciation' (Skultans, 2001; Gallinat, 2011) that representations of the past seem to require of him. He observes how in their reproduction symbols have been removed from the context that gave them their meaning, opening them to new readings (Thompson, 1984: 180) and usages. Light-hearted adaptations of the blue shirt of the socialist youth organisation (FDJ) by young people today can only suggest fashion to anyone who did not grow up in socialism. To those who recognise these uniforms as part of their daily life (or those of others), the new usage suggests a similarly light-hearted approach to memory which happily mixes the political with both the everyday and state control and thus does not do justice to the deep emotional rifts experienced by those who lived through these times. The continued focus on the Stasi, on the other hand, may cause those who did not experience such difficulties to feel alienated, as it suggests only perpetrators and victims inhabited the past society.

Like many of our informants, Thorsten does not contest the truth of the totalitarian aspects of socialist rule, neither does he engage in nostalgia. In contrast, he takes issue with both, if they claim exclusive status. Engaging with the presence of the past in the present, he is taken back to his own experiences under the socialist regime and argues that life in the GDR needs to be seen as multifaceted. 'There was never a "the" GDR', he asserts in the interview.

Suspending past and present

When it appears in conversations as casual off-the-cuff remarks and comparisons, the past takes on a rather different form. Such throw-away comments ('it wasn't all bad in the GDR') are often understood as expressions of nostalgia for socialism. Seeing them in their rhetorical context, however, reveals that they have much more elaborate functions as metaphors in the present. Metaphors, argues Burke (1973: 262), are 'for socializing losses, for warding off evil eye, for purification, propitiation, and desanctification, consolation and vengeance, admonition and exhortation, implicit commands or instructions of one sort or another'. They are part of 'linguistic politics' (Crocker, 1977: 42), which very much concerns the present and may thus leave remembering behind.

At the *Daily Paper* a source of such comments, remarks and jokes was Markus Winkler, a journalist in his fifties who had worked at the paper since the 1970s and was now head of the politics desk. My fieldnotes record how, one morning in December chatting with colleagues, Markus 'recalls how he spoke to his neighbour yesterday when they were "collectively" clearing the snow off the pavement in front of their houses'. In another instance we were in the canteen for lunch, having just settled at our table. Another colleague came belatedly looking for a spare seat: 'Markus points to a free chair and says: "We need to keep that one free. The general secretary is joining us". "Oh", says the colleague, "comrade Stalin coming too?" "Yes", agrees Markus, "for observational purposes", he grins'. In a third example, we were again at lunch talking about politics. Markus explained that he would love to write an opinion piece on the recent strikes among delivery service workers for the minimum wage, highlighting the fact that the people distributing this very paper are also paid below minimal wage. A colleague cautioned him, "This is dangerous, think of your career". 'Markus: "Well, then today is not much better than back then, then you were also only allowed to write politically correct stuff. And today, you have also got *the scissors in your mind*. And you are not allowed to write things just the same." '

In these three examples Markus draws on the past rhetorically to describe moments in the present. What he achieves in the first two is first of all ambiguity. Discussing the creation of ambiguity in *tāupōu* dance performances in Samoa, Mageo (2008: 72) observes:

> Psychologists tell us that people, beset by the need to take a course of action or a position, are apt to resolve ambiguity by a reductive judgement that distorts a situation's true complexity [...]. But colonial contradictions and ambivalence fuel zones of ambiguity, such that their authors seek to keep all manner of heterogeneity in play.

Similarly here, Markus uses metaphors that invoke the past, without quite being the same as the past, in order to create an almost uneasy sense of ambiguity that leaves both past and present suspended in the moment.

His first comment refers to the well-known East German collective activities, where groups of people (often school children) would come together to tidy neighbourhoods, plant trees, maintain parks. Yet he talks about a situation in which two neighbours – hardly a 'collective' – clear snow off pavements for which they are individually responsible. This happenstance of working simultaneously – not together – is rhetorically moved into the realm of state-enforced togetherness, which in turn ridicules both the clearing of snow in the present and state collectivity of the past. It is unclear whether Markus is trying to achieve anything beyond comic appeal with this comment, as the comment itself is directionless. One thing it does, however, is both assume and evoke a community of memory, an *Erinnerungsgemeinschaft* (Nünning and Erll, 2006).

Something similar happens in the second instance: Markus indicated that the 'general secretary' may come for lunch and keeps a chair free for this ghostly character. A conversational partner joins the joke driving the sense of ambiguity further by adding the name Stalin: the infamous leader of the Soviet Union had little to do with either the 'general secretary' of the SED committee or with Stasi surveillance. The person thus referred to remains anonymous; no one takes their place. Was Markus playing games with the past, or was he actually referring to someone in the present? Maybe it was the editor-in-chief, who occasionally joins his staff for lunch, or some other colleague who may be interested in overhearing lunchtime conversations. Again, Markus brings aspects of the GDR, some of them contradictory, not quite connected, into the present. He constructs a figure from the past 'that both reproduce[s] and belie[s] the original' (Mageo, 2008: 72). The mimesis thus created causes ambiguity, suspending both periods in obscurity. Despite all this, as the brief exchange with the colleague shows, his arbitrary comments can only ever engage individuals with the same experiential knowledge of life and work in socialist East Germany GDR and its metaphorical reappearance in the present. Despite all mimetic contradictions, Markus creates *Erinnerungsgemeinschaften.*

The final example is the clearest of the three. Markus draws on a metaphor from the GDR, 'the scissors in your mind', which stands for strict party control and journalists' struggle with party preferences of ideology over reality in news reporting, to comment on a situation in the present. This comparison moves today's democratic state rhetorically into the domain of repressive state systems. There is little ambiguity here. The past is brought forward to embrace the present, leaving its imprint. This stark critique, however, has to be seen in the context in which it does its politics. As Markus makes clear in his interview, he is aware that, despite being channelled by the interests of publishing houses, journalism today is still much freer than it ever was in the socialist era. Yet in that moment at lunch he had a point to make and did so by drawing on the past for metaphorical 'firepower'.

These three instances of the past being invoked in the present for 'linguistic politics' highlight two points. First, in everyday talk the relationship between past and present is not unidirectional. Rather, it moves back and forth and on occasion leaves both spheres existing simultaneously, which impacts on how they can be perceived, creating new knowledges and relationships. Second, however, this means that some invocations of memory are metaphoric references which are highly context-dependent; they may not relate to the past as remembered and they contrast starkly with the complexities apparent in biographical remembering.

And belonging

Creating community, whether through shared memory or culture, is a crucial part of belonging. In Anthropology, 'home' has been described as a cognitive space: ' "home" [. . .] "is where one best knows oneself" – where "best" means "most" if not always 'happiest" ' (Rapport and Dawson, 1998: 9). Kondo (1996: 97) contends that home is a safe place where 'one does not need to explain oneself to outsiders'. This sense of familiarity is also part of the German term *Heimat,* or homeland (Applegate, 1990; Bausinger, 1990: 33), which also has strong nationalist connotations. Many people use it interchangeably with the phrase of being or feeling 'at home' (Gallinat, 2008) which is based on a familiarity that is created through time and continued 'dwelling' (Ingold, 2000): 'home is the place "you know the history of", "where you have seen developments" and "changes for the better and the worse" ' (Gallinat, 2008: 676). In this view, personal history and the history of place intertwine in the unfolding of time. Such a sense of home *through* time also requires an immanent past that matches remembering; that is, it requires more public, shared visions of the GDR that can accommodate the various and ambiguous experiences that many eastern Germans had.

Another of our informants at the *Daily Paper* expressed the importance of remembering for belonging in his interview. Karl Schäfer was a senior editor at the paper. He had worked as a foreign correspondent in the Middle East for some years during GDR times but now held a managerial role. In our interview Schäfer discussed some turmoil that had developed around the administrative committee of the newly founded Memorial Foundation of Mittelland, appointed by the state parliament and made up of representatives of the main parties. One of the party representatives had been a Stasi informant and, furthermore, a solicitor who had dealt with political convictions. As soon as this transpired, the Association of Victims of Stalinism made their committee membership in the Foundation dormant. At the time of the interview the parliament was working on a political solution to this conundrum to save the future of the Foundation. Schäfer did not understand how it could have come to this. His view was that, first of all, the representative in question should have refrained from volunteering for this sensitive post. If he wanted to help *Aufarbeitung*, this could be done in other ways. Even worse was the fact that the state parliament had voted the former solicitor into post, overlooking his controversial biography. In this discussion Schäfer shows empathy for the victims' association and a general support for *Aufarbeitung*. In contrast, however, his initial response to the question of how he thought the GDR past was dealt with today sounded defensive of East German, if not 'nostalgic', identity: 'in principle, the GDR past is being ignored today'. Schäfer explicated:

> Well, there are certain aspects that keep being emphasised, like dealing with the State Security Police. But the life achievements of individuals in the GDR, or also, this feeling of being at home [*Heimatgefühl*], which existed in the GDR, that's the kind of thing that is pushed away today. I mean, I am not a fan of nostalgia, lots of things were not good back then, if not to say, crap. But, we lived in the GDR, we were happy, and of course we didn't have the material

> wealth of our brothers and sisters in the West. But we didn't walk around all day with our head down either. And we also enjoyed our work. Not studying, but the youth camps, when we got out at the weekend for a couple of days and did a work initiative [*Aufbaueinsatz*] and partied and so on. As I said, the approach to the history of the GDR is very selective. That's how I see it.

Schäfer states the inevitable: 'we lived', 'we were happy' in the GDR. With regard to trauma narratives, Antze and Lambek (1996: xviii) warn that the creation of 'an excessively determined story in which there is an over-identification with a particular character' bears dangers for the self. For Schäfer and for Thorsten the complexity of experiences in the GDR finds itself at odds with the over-determined narratives of both *Aufarbeitung* and *Ostalgie*. These dissonances create difficulties for individual belonging in the present.[6]

For eastern Germans the state and country of origin have transformed radically. Memory has remained, but remembering selves find their recollections do not quite fit the official discourse with its distinct binaries (see Chapter 1: 28). Due to the emotional power of its messages about suffering this discourse has, however, become part of the narrative framework and for individuals to be recognised as morally acceptable beings they have to acknowledge the 'dictatorship' when talking about the GDR. However, the 'truth' of this notion cannot become all-determining because for individuals to feel 'coherent' (Linde, 1993), maintain a sense of self-worth and feel at home – for better or worse – in the new nation they also need to be able to recount life achievements (*Errungenschaften*). This term, common in corner-shop conversations, is usually called upon when East German culture is to be defended, when a sense of being colonised by a hegemonic West Germany (Cooke, 2005) is countered. It means 'achievements' but strongly implies struggle and difficulties that had to be overcome. In its broad sense the term is often used to refer to East German institutions, from the *Ampelmann* to free childcare.[7] But it can also be applied to biographies, where it signposts milestones like marriage, family, career, and so on. This seems to be what Schäfer suggests. For many working in *Aufarbeitung*, however, the term is the harbinger of nostalgic tendencies, as it entails the reappraisal of aspects of the past that were dependent upon mismanagement, repression of civic liberties and indoctrination in the totalitarian regime. Certainly in Schäfer's usage it has connotations of reminiscing, which are furthered by the example of youth camps. However, he himself also rejects uncritical glorifications of the GDR.

It appears that nostalgia is not necessarily a unidirectional return to the past in defiance of the present. Schäfer's reminiscing here seems similar to what Boym (2001) calls 'reflective nostalgia', which she distinguishes from 'restorative nostalgia'. Reflective nostalgia 'thrives in *algia*, the longing itself and delays the homecoming.' It 'dwells on the ambivalences of human longing and belonging and does not shy away from the contradictions of modernity' (Boym, 2001: xviii). Nostalgia in this view is much more than a reproduction of the past in the present, which loses sight of that present. Rather, it is a remembering that layers the remembered past over the present, without the forced ambiguity that metaphorical uses of the past can create. This layering can then give rise to new realisations and further critiques of the present (see Cashman, 2006). A degree of such reminiscing is inevitable in the remembering of lived lives which also – and quite simply – concerns childhood, youthful mischief and family, in contexts fundamentally different from today's. Schäfer's comments seem to suggest that some liberty to reminisce might be what is required to make the new nation a home for the future for those who can and want to remember the past in all its ambivalences.

Conclusion

The question raised by Arnold-de Simine and Radstone (Chapter 1) of who validates memory discourses remains a pertinent one in eastern Germany but it is through contestations around this question that individual remembering and invocations of the past in social contexts take place. As this chapter shows, in the social matrix of everyday life where memory is fashioned, there is little need to fear the development of divergent *Erinnerungsgemeinschaften*, as individuals move in and out of different discourses and different usages of the past, often keeping several in play simultaneously.

Against the backdrop of the 'collective instruction' (Sontag, 2003: 76) that *Aufarbeitung* appears to constitute, individuals remember the socialist past and draw on it as a resource, conscious of the underlying politics but nevertheless on their own terms. While the very orderly, categorised discourse of *Aufarbeitung* assumes direct correlations between memories of socialism and political attitudes in the present, individuals' usage of the past reveals much more fluid and ambivalent relationships between past, present and future. Just as these usages show that the experienced past is too complex to fit the simplistic binaries that the vision of the 'GDR-as-dictatorship' inevitably creates, they show that attitudes to the present cannot easily be categorised either. The layering of past and present through nostalgia, or their ironic suspension through linguistic politics, point to a future that is either more open, or has more potential and is less determined than the future of 'parliamentary democracy' which is assumed by the work of political *Aufarbeitung*. This layering of periods in memory allows, exactly, the creation of new possibilities and unknown paths (Birth, 2006: 186) born out of the experience of fundamental regime change.

Notes

1. The SED was the ruling party, the Socialist Unity Party.
2. The project was kindly sponsored by the ESRC (Economic and Social Research Council, UK; RES0061-23-0035). To protect informants' anonymity, all names appearing here are pseudonyms, including that of the *Bundesland*, its capital and the newspaper; the names of government institutions are generic.
3. To protect informants' anonymity, details of references to texts and articles published by the institutions involved in the project are also excluded here. These may be obtained by contacting the author.
4. As Hogwood (Chapter 2) suggests, eastern Germans may have different relationships to such western German concepts.
5. Arnold-de Simine and Radstone comment on the problematics of the many binaries this creates (Chapter 1).
6. Similar problems are evident in other post-socialist contexts (cf. Wanner, 1998; Richardson, 2004).
7. The *Ampelmann* is the figure of a green and red man on pedestrian traffic lights in the GDR.

References

Antze, P. and M. Lambek (1996) *Tense past: Cultural Essays in Trauma and Memory* (London: Routledge).

Applegate, C. (1990) *A Nation of Provincials: The German Idea of Heimat* (Berkeley, CA: University of California Press).

Bausinger, H. (1990) 'Heimat: Über eine vieldeutige Beziehung', *Narodna Umjetnost*, 27, 33–58.

Beattie, A. (2008) *Playing Politics with History: The Bundestag Inquiries into East Germany* (New York: Berghahn).

Birth, K. (2006) 'The immanent past: Culture and psyche at the juncture of memory and history', *Ethos*, 34 (2), 169–91.

Boym, S. (2001) *The Future of Nostalgia* (New York: Basic).

Burke, K. (1973[1957]) *The Philosophy of Literary Form*, 3rd edition (Berkeley, CA: University of California Press).

Cashman, R. (2006) 'Critical nostalgia and material culture in northern Ireland', *Journal of American Folklore*, 119 (472), 137–60.

Cooke, P. (2005) *Representing East Germany since Unification* (Oxford: Berg).

Crocker, J. C. (1977) 'The social functions of rhetorical forms' in J. C. Crocker and J. D. Sapir (eds) *The Social Use of Metaphor: Essays on the Anthropology of Rhetoric* (Philadelphia, PA: University of Pennsylvania Press).

Friedman, J. (1992) 'Myth, history and political identity', *Cultural Anthropology*, 7 (2), 194–210.

Gallinat, A. (2008) 'Being "East German" or being "at home in eastern Germany"? Identity as experience and as rhetoric', *Identities: Global Studies in Culture and Power*, 15 (6), 665–86.

Gallinat, A. (2011) ' "The rush to (East) German history": Recognising memory and belonging' in J. McLaughlin, D. Richardson, and P. Phillimore (eds) *Contesting Recognition: Contemporary Cultural and Institutional Disputes* (Basingstoke: Palgrave Macmillan).

Gallinat, A. (forthcoming) 'Inside discourse: Governing the memory of the East German past', (under review).

Gallinat, A. and S. Kittel (2009) 'Zum Umgang mit der DDR-Vergangenheit heute: Ostdeutsche Erfahrungen, Erinnerungen und Identität' in T. Großbölting (ed.) *Friedensstaat, Leseland, Sportnation? DDR-Legenden auf dem Prüfstand* (Berlin: Links).

Ingold, T. (2000) *The Perception of the Environment: Essays on Livelihood, Dwelling and Skill* (London: Routledge).

Kondo, D. (1996) 'The narrative production of "home", community, and political identity in Asian American Theatre' in S. Lavie and T. Swedenburg (eds) *Displacement, Diaspora and Geographies of Identity* (Durham: Duke University Press).

Linde, C. (1993) *Life-Stories: The Creation of Coherence* (Oxford: Oxford University Press).

Mageo, J. (2008) 'Zones of ambiguity and identity politics in Samoa', *Journal of the Royal Anthropological Institute*, 14, 61–78.

Nünning, A. and A. Erll (2006) 'Concepts and methods for the study of literature and/as cultural memory' in A. Nünning, M. Gymnich, and R. Sommer (eds) *Literature and Memory: Theoretical Paradigms, Genres, Functions* (Tübingen: Francke).

Ochs, E. and L. Capps (2001) *Living Narrative: Creating Lives in Everyday Storytelling* (Cambridge: Harvard University Press).

Rapport, N. and A. Dawson (1998) 'The Topic and the Book' in N. Rapport and A. Dawson (eds) *Migrants of Identity* (Oxford: Berg).

Richardson, T. (2004) 'Disciplining the past in post-Soviet Ukraine: memory and history in schools and families' in F. Pine, D. Kaneff and I. Haukaness (eds) *Memory, Politics and Religion* (Münster: Lit).

Skultans, V. (2001) 'Arguing with the KGB archives: Archival and narrative memory in post-Soviet Latvia', *Ethnos*, 66 (3), 320–43.

Sontag, S. (2003) *Regarding the Pain of Others* (New York: Picador/Farrar, Straus and Giroux).

Thompson, J. B. (1984) *Studies in the Theory of Ideology* (Berkeley, CA: University of California Press).

Wanner, C. (1998) *Burden of Dreams* (University Park, PA: Pennsylvania State University Press).

10
The Politics of Memory in Berlin's *Freiheits- und Einheitsdenkmal*

Anna Saunders

Since the mid-1990s, Berlin has often been diagnosed as suffering from an acute case of 'monumentitis', an affliction which relates to both the number of monuments being constructed, and the protracted and controversial debates which accompany their construction and reception. On the one hand, this trend can be witnessed internationally as part of the contemporary 'memory boom'; on the other, Berlin proves to be an extreme example, as demonstrated by a plethora of recent publications about the role of memory in this city (e.g. Ladd, 1997; Till, 2005; Jordan, 2006; Verheyen, 2008; Webber, 2008). Indeed, as the capital of a new, united Germany, Berlin has become a national 'theatre of memory' (Samuel, 1994) in which new cultural and political symbolism is being staged, and where the reconfiguration of a 'normalised' identity has – in the wake of two dictatorships and a divided Germany – challenged politicians and artists alike. Although the role of monuments has changed considerably during the twentieth century, from overt expressions of power to more ambiguous or subversive forms (Mittig, 1987), they continue to act as 'symbols and repositories of memories' (Ladd, 1997: 4), and play an important role in the construction – or rejection – of collective identities.

Perhaps inevitably, a large number of contemporary monuments in Berlin are concerned with the process of 'reworking' Germany's more difficult past. It is, for instance, hard to keep track of the numerous memorials, monuments and installations in remembrance of Holocaust victims, not to speak of the volumes which have been written about them (e.g. Jeismann, 1999; Stavginski, 2002; Young, 2002; Leggewie and Meyer, 2005; Klabach, 2009; Thünemann, 2009). While monuments relating to the GDR past may not yet have attracted so much scholarly attention, they have equally dominated the German media in recent years. The early 1990s, for example, witnessed impassioned debates over the proposed demolition of socialist realist monuments, whereas 10 to 15 years on, questions of how best to remember the Berlin Wall and its victims became paramount. By 2009, however, a rather different monument debate – one which proposed celebrating pride in the past – was making headlines: that of the proposed *Freiheits- und Einheitsdenkmal* (Monument to Freedom and Unity), a Bundestag-backed project to remember the demonstrations of 1989 and German unity in 1990. Although several other eastern towns had already erected monuments to these events,[1] the proposed monument in Berlin proved highly contentious, and despite initial plans for its completion by the twentieth anniversary of the fall of the Berlin Wall in 2009, the project experienced a series of setbacks, with a final winner being announced only in April 2011.

An examination of the motivations behind this project offers significant insight into the functioning of political memory, as well as, more specifically, the role of GDR memory in contemporary German politics. Political memory is understood here in Aleida Assmann's terms (2006: 36–58), as a form of 'top-down' memory which is staged by state institutions, and adopts a functional and ritual purpose in the creation of collective identities. In this way, the Berlin project indicates the desire to promote a more defined, symbolic representation of the events of 1989 than previously, perhaps because we are now looking back to the GDR from a greater distance. Yet as this chapter will show, the existence of social – or 'bottom-up', lived – memories of this period provides a counterbalance, and demonstrates that such categories of memory are porous, and regularly change constellation. Most importantly, previous cultures of remembrance in Germany have also become bound up with the quest for a *Freiheits- und Einheitsdenkmal*, meaning that the project has often been shaped by factors far removed from the historical events of 1989 themselves. Indeed, as this example demonstrates, memory of the GDR does not exist in a vacuum, and should always be understood within a broader context; as Aleida Assmann (2006: 17) states, 'Memories do not exist as self-contained systems, but rather in social reality they always touch, strengthen, cross over with, modify and became polarised with other memories and impulses of forgetting'.[2] It is precisely this interaction between different memories and remembrance traditions which is at the heart of Berlin's *Freiheits- und Einheitsdenkmal*.

Chronology and milestones

As with many national monuments, the history of this project is long and complex. It dates back to May 1998, when the newly formed Initiative Denkmal Deutsche Einheit (Initiative for a Monument to German Unity) published an open letter calling for an international design competition for a monument to the demonstrations of 1989 and German unity. The main impetus was the forthcoming tenth anniversary of the fall of the Berlin Wall in 1999. While the letter was supported by a number of politicians, intellectuals and public figures, the initiative was driven by four individuals: Florian Mausbach (then President of the Federal Office for Building and Regional Planning), Lothar de Maizière (first and only democratically elected Prime Minister of the GDR), Günter Nooke (co-founder of *Demokratischer Aufbruch* [Democratic Awakening], later Christian Democratic Union [CDU] politician) and Jürgen Engert (journalist). Although they viewed their project as a 'citizens' initiative' (Mausbach, 2008: 3), it clearly came from a group of leading figures, the first three of whom were members of the CDU. Despite this political allegiance, they succeeded in proposing a motion to the Bundestag in April 2000 which was signed by 177 members from four different parties (CDU/Christian Social Union [CSU], Social Democratic Party [SPD], Free Democratic Party [FDP] and Green Party). On 9 November 2001, however, after lengthy debating in subcommittees and in the Bundestag, the proposal for a monument failed to gain a majority, largely due to opposition votes in the SPD and the Party of Democratic Socialism (PDS). It was not until six years later, under Angela Merkel's chancellorship, that the motion was accepted by the Bundestag on 9 November 2007. A public design competition was finally launched in December 2008, with a view to announcing the winner on 9 November 2009. However, the competition was halted in April 2009, when the jury failed to select any of the 533 entries for a second round. A revised, two-stage competition was subsequently launched, in which 33 designs were invited to compete from a larger pool of applicants in March 2010; on 3 October 2010, three first prize winners were announced, and after minor modifications, the design by 'Milla und Partner' was announced as the winner in April 2011. This design proposes a huge shallow bowl-like construction, which tilts like a see-saw under the amassed weight of pedestrians, and on which the slogans 'Wir sind das Volk. Wir sind ein Volk' ('We are the people. We are one people') can be read in large lettering; on the golden undersurface of the bowl, visitors will see images from 1989/90. While it is projected that the design will be built for the twenty-fifth anniversary of 1989, it remains to be seen – at the time of writing in 2012 – whether this will be the case.

This chronology reveals two interesting points relating to the timings of decisions. First, the project has been driven by anniversaries of the peaceful revolution and in particular the fall of the Berlin Wall. Initially, for example, the project was to be completed by the twentieth anniversary on 9 November 2009, but as the process stumbled, this date was then to mark the laying of the founding stone, and then the announcement of the winner. The Bundestag decisions were also symbolically made on 9 November, and although the competition failed to meet any of the 9 November targets, the winners were finally announced on 3 October 2010, yet another significant milestone: the twentieth anniversary of unification. The continual efforts on the part of politicians and competition organisers to appropriate specific dates and round anniversaries for the monument indicate their desire to embed this past into the active cultural fabric of the contemporary community. By linking concrete memorial form to nationally celebrated anniversaries, the hope is to create a specific and renewable tradition of remembrance even before the monument is built, thus ensuring a secure and lasting memory culture which will extend beyond the memories of those who experienced 1989 first hand.

Second, the time-span of decisions made in the Bundestag reveals an interesting pattern, for the discussions in 2000 and 2001 saw objections on the part of SPD and PDS members that the time was too soon for a monument and that the proposal required more reflection. Some stated that unification was not yet complete, thus calling into question the suitability of the monument for the present day, while others questioned the motives of the monuments' advocates – many of whom had been active in the demonstrations of 1989 – as little more than an act of self-celebration (Deutscher Bundestag, 2000b: 9328). Social memory of this period thus provided arguments both for and against the creation of a monument, demonstrating that it was not simply first-hand experience of the demonstrations that influenced opinions, but rather the nature and extent of individuals' participation. By 2007, however, objections had become less vociferous, and although criticism of the tight time-frame around 2009 persisted, it was not only a different political configuration in the Bundestag that secured success the second time round, but also the passing of time. The mediation of the past into a more deliberate, fixed form of political memory clearly demands time; in this case, however, far less than the passing of a generation or the 80-year period suggested by Jan Assmann's model (1999).

On first impressions, this project thus appears to be rooted in the apparently straightforward desire to remember the increasingly distant demonstrations of 1989 and the subsequent event of German unity while living memory still exists. The decision to call it the *Freiheits- und Einheitsdenkmal* (rather than the other way round) was to be a clear indication that 'freedom' came before 'unity', and that the former was the precondition for the latter (Deutscher Bundestag, 2000b: 9331). It was also intended to be a monument about the future aspirations of Germany as a nation, and one which would highlight the historical importance of the 'peaceful revolution' to Germany's young generation. As the following section demonstrates, however, a more detailed examination of the competition outline and the hopes of the initiators show that this monument has become inextricably linked to Germany's past cultures of remembrance and to periods of history much older than the GDR itself, thus demonstrating the strong influence of past memory traditions.

Establishing breaks and continuities with past traditions of remembrance

All monuments must be viewed in relation to the memorial landscape which existed prior to their creation, for they are likely either to provide continuity with, or seek to break away from past traditions of form. In the case of the *Freiheits- und Einheitsdenkmal*, the desire for a monument which displays three key elements – democratic credentials, national symbolism and positive historical connotations – responds directly to the post-unification memorial landscape, and proposes a new direction from old traditions. The first of these, the desire for a monument that celebrates democracy in both content and form, thus not only reflects the political order of Germany today, but also aims to provide distance from the remembrance cultures of previous regimes, in which party colours dictated the shape of the memorial landscape. The most recent example of this was, of course, in the GDR, where monumental socialist realist structures were erected in memory of historical figures such as Lenin, Marx and Ernst Thälmann, in order to demonstrate through symbolic means the primacy of the socialist ideology. Other heroic structures, however, remain from earlier times, with numerous Prussian equestrian statues, whose origins were often also far from democratic, still in evidence across Germany. In response to such structures, it is little surprise that abstract and unheroic monumental forms were anticipated by advocates of the *Freiheits- und Einheitsdenkmal*. As Markus Meckel (SPD) claimed, 'It should not be a heroic monument'

(Deutscher Bundestag, 2000b: 9328), and Nooke even called for it to become a 'Mecca for democrats' (Deutscher Bundestag, 2000b: 9327). Regarding process rather than form, Mausbach (2008: 3, 6) has also been at pains to emphasise that their project has come 'from the midst of society', and should not be seen as 'a representative state monument [...], but rather a citizens' memorial'. The monument as a symbolic vehicle for the democratic transmission of memories thus became an integral part of the project from its inception, and paved the way for an open, public competition. Although the competition process proved problematic, it is notable that all entries to both competitions were publicly exhibited in Berlin, followed by an eight-month open-air exhibition in 2011 (see Figure 10.1); together with the numerous associated public discussions, websites and documentations, these exhibitions testify to the desire for a democratic project, themselves becoming an important part of the process.[3] Many politicians have, indeed, voiced the opinion that while the failed competition of 2009 was regrettable, the fact that time was taken and opinions were sought only underlines the concern to uphold as democratic a competition as possible.

As well as displaying democratic credentials, the monument is also intended to be a 'national symbol in the centre of the German capital' (*Gestaltungswettbewerb*, 2008: 4). As such, it is to mark another break

Figure 10.1 2011 open air exhibition on the designated site for Berlin's *Freiheits- und Einheitsdenkmal* (Anna Saunders).

with the past: that of a nation which has struggled for years with the concept of 'negative nationalism'. Although the GDR erected unequivocally heroic antifascist national monuments, the tradition in the FRG, which has largely provided continuity with unified Germany, rested rather on the cautionary notion of the *Mahnmal*: a memorial to be understood as a warning to future generations. This tradition culminated in the 'Memorial to the Murdered Jews of Europe' – more commonly termed the 'Holocaust Memorial' – which was completed in 2005 in central Berlin. In accordance with the notion of 'negative nationalism', the prime location of this monument implies that the German nation should incorporate shame into its national memorial landscape, rather than constructing a national identity based on positive historical continuities, such as the French tradition of *liberté, égalité, fraternité*. This is a perception which is further heightened by the growth of monuments and exhibitions featuring repression and victimhood in the GDR. The proposed *Freiheits- und Einheitsdenkmal* thus attempts to break with this tradition by enabling the celebration of a national tradition of freedom and unity, much in the same way that other European nations have done for years; to quote Wolfgang Thierse (SPD): 'Let us finally be a normal, an average, an ordinary European people' (Deutscher Bundestag, 2007b: 12965). As a 'national' project, this monument also aims to create a focal point for both eastern and western Germans, and by focusing on an element of eastern heritage, it responds to other recent memory debates in which western narratives have frequently dominated (as seen in the destruction of the Palast der Republik, the dismantling of socialist realist monuments or the renaming of streets). Nooke thus viewed the monument as a significant contribution to the ongoing unification project:

> I even believe that such a monument would rather speed up the process of so-called inner unity. This is especially important from the viewpoint of eastern Germans, because in past years they have sometimes had the feeling that their own primary contribution towards German unity, namely the peaceful revolution, has taken somewhat of a back seat in terms of public interest.
>
> (Deutscher Bundestag, 2001: 19507)

Preliminary debates have, indeed, invested great faith in the potential symbolic power of a new monument for the nation, and the willingness of the German state to invest €10 million in the project at a time of economic downturn suggests its political importance.

The desire for a 'positive' monument, or a 'Freudenmal' (Deutscher Bundestag, 2007b: 5), is also inextricably linked to the notion of 'negative nationalism'. Ever conscious of this tradition, advocates have consistently tried to turn the tide; Thierse, for example, has attempted to link the cautionary tradition with a celebratory one: 'We should erect a *Mahnmal* to our historical happiness, so that we do not forget how precious and vulnerable freedom and unity are, nor the values to which our national fortune commits us.' (Deutscher Bundestag, 2007b: 12965) Similarly, yet in a more direct tone, Nooke (2006: 122) claimed: 'Let us intone a new key for our national memory, in the major not in the minor.' In light of such comments, it is difficult to disentangle the proposed *Freiheits- und Einheitsdenkmal* from the Holocaust Memorial, for a new, positive monument is inevitably viewed as an 'anti-monument' to the Holocaust Memorial. Although Nooke explicitly denied this intention, he also claimed: 'But we will not let ourselves be defined as a nation by twelve terrible years of Nazi dictatorship' (Deutscher Bundestag, 2000b: 9327–8). It is thus little surprise that many cynics view this monument as an antidote to the Holocaust Memorial, with some even suggesting that the initial plan to include an information centre was intended as a direct parallel to that of the Holocaust Memorial (Janzing, 2000; Schönfeld, 2009: 165). Furthermore, the tone of the parliamentary debates indicated that monuments to the victims of the Holocaust were deemed a prerequisite for a 'Freudenmal', and it is significant that the *Freiheits- und Einheitsdenkmal* was not approved before the Holocaust Memorial was completed. Once again, this case study clearly shows that the monument as a form of political memory is highly dependent on the physical landscape in which it is placed, and whether seen as competing or complementary, other memory debates form a constituent part of a monument's evolution.

The hopes and desires placed in this project represent something of a dichotomy. On the one hand, the construction is to represent a new start: a break with numerous traditions of remembrance and the end of the so-called 'short twentieth century', a period marked by two world wars, two dictatorships, a divided Germany and the Cold War. On the other hand, however, the choice of location and the associated political rhetoric indicate a desire to demonstrate continuity with two longer-standing German traditions: freedom and unity. The first of these concerns one of the central values for which demonstrators campaigned in 1989, yet significantly the attempt to draw on a broader tradition of freedom has steered the debate away from the GDR. Advocates of the monument, for example, have looked back to the nineteenth century, and proposed that the monument should demonstrate the 'overcoming of a martial nationalism and the completion of the democratic revolution of 1848' (Deutscher Bundestag, 2000a: 4), as well as highlight the importance of other movements for freedom in previous centuries (Deutscher Bundestag, 2007a: 4). Others have been keen for the monument to represent Germany's debt to neighbouring eastern European countries, whose reform movements proved significant in giving courage to GDR citizens (Deutscher Bundestag, 2007b: 12950). In the aftermath of September 2001, Cornelia Pieper (FDP) even promoted the proposed monument as a '*Mahnmal* against war and terrorism', thus linking it to much broader global trends (Deutscher Bundestag, 2001: 19507). The battle for freedom from different regimes and at various historical junctures was thus to be incorporated in equal measure with the East German demonstrators' fight for freedom from SED control. The timing of the monument was also critical in this respect, for 2009 marked not only 20 years since the fall of the Wall, but also 160 years of the Paulskirche in Frankfurt, 90 years of the Weimar constitution and 60 years of the Federal Republic. This was clearly to be about a longer tradition of freedom, rather than uniquely that of GDR demonstrators, thus revealing the attempt to organise political memory in a systematic way, with the aim of creating a stable tradition in the present which would retain the emotional pull of past traditions.

Alongside freedom, unity was also intended to draw on a longer tradition, largely through the proposed location (as seen in Figure 10.1): a platform which was built to support a colossal monument to Kaiser Wilhelm I, completed in 1897 for the hundredth anniversary of his birth. Although the monument itself was dismantled by the GDR regime in 1949–50, the platform remains today and provides a sizable area of derelict land in the heart of Berlin, next to the site on which the Berlin Palace once stood, and is due to be rebuilt. The fact that this platform does not mark the location of the 1989 demonstrations is problematic for those who value a sense of authenticity, and indeed many advocate Leipzig as a preferable location, for it was here that the demonstrations began. Historically, however, this choice of location highlights continuity with the past, for the Imperial monument was also designed as a national monument for the German people, in celebration of the unification of Germany in 1871. Thus by drawing a line between 1871 and 1989–90, the project attempts to highlight a longer historical tradition, once again demonstrating a concern with constructing a stable national identity, rather than with the historical complexities of 1989.

This is particularly problematic for those on the left, who fear that it highlights 'a national-conservative continuity which has nothing to do with the freedom movement in the GDR' (Luc Jochimsen [PDS], cit. in 'Einheitsdenkmal...', 2008). There is little doubt that the choice of location says more about the needs of present-day political identities than a direct concern with the past it intends to celebrate, and as this example shows, the geographical fixity of monuments often provokes a confrontation with other political memories that different representative forms are less likely to encounter; in short, there can never be a clean slate on which to build a monument.

Competition process: changing the goalposts

In light of the numerous hopes and desires that were invested in this project, it is little surprise that the first competition ran aground. The desire to embed the 'peaceful revolution' firmly in the cultural memory of the Berlin Republic proved too ambitious, in terms of both procedure and expectations of form. The attempt to promote a genuinely democratic competition demonstrates some of the problems. Most notably, the open competition attracted so many entries that jury members had at most one minute to pass judgement on each design – clearly not enough time to draw any well-considered conclusions. Furthermore, the broad spectrum of entrants provided for a wide range of quality, and while there were clearly a number of original and thought-provoking designs, a large number were more questionable. Critics, for example, commented on the 'deficient inspiration' of artists (Mania, 2009), as well as the 'symbolic harmlessness' and 'irrelevance' of many designs, some of which have been described as 'naïve' and 'embarrassing' (sfk, 2009). The media inevitably highlighted the more absurd entries, such as those including a large yellow banana, a 25-metre high giraffe, and a group of demonstrating smurfs (Kilb, 2009). As one of the jury members, writer Thomas Brussig (2009), summarised: 'The lesson learned from the whole exercise: an open competition, in which the weight of artistic merit holds sway – through fully democratic means – is an illusion. Word has got out that democracy favours mediocrity.' As this process indicates, a true 'citizens' monument' is, perhaps, an unattainable quest. The problem of quality, however, also resulted from the complex demands placed on entrants, for not only did the competition outline call for designs to incorporate German and European traditions of freedom and unity from 1848 onwards, but three further requirements were included.

First, designs were to refer to other towns and cities, especially Leipzig, where demonstrations had taken place; second, they were to point the public towards associated nearby sites of memory, and third, they were to include plans for an information centre (*Gestaltungswettbewerb*, 2008: 33). In overloading the symbolic meaning of the monument, it seems that organisers were in danger of promoting amnesia rather than remembrance of 1989. Additionally, the looming date of 9 November 2009 pushed the competition out of its comfort zone, for not only had it become highly complex, but there also appeared to be little time to allow for reflection.

These facts were all recognised by the Federal Committee for Culture and Media, which discussed the future of the project in July 2009 and set recommendations for a revised competition which was launched early in 2010. A number of changes were made: the requirement to link Berlin to other locations of protest was removed (as Leipzig is now to receive its own monument), the inclusion of an information centre was withdrawn (as the German Historical Museum can house such information) and the requirement to link the monument to other relevant sites of memory was dropped. Most significantly, however, the call to draw on historical continuities was also removed, and as the committee stressed: 'the memory of the peaceful revolution in the autumn of 1989 and the act of regaining German unity should be the artistic focus of the *Freiheits- und Einheitsdenkmal*' (Presse- und Informationsamt, 2009a). Finally, the new competition was to invite competitors from a pool of applications, thus ensuring a much smaller number of professional entries. The decision to back down on a significant number of the initial requirements demonstrates an important element of political memory: namely that – in being imposed 'from above', rather than growing organically 'from below' – it is always likely to be subject to simplification, particularly when dealing with symbolic forms such as monuments. As a journalist from *Die Zeit* polemically suggested: 'Perhaps a national monument can only function under the conditions of propaganda' (Finger, 2009). Evidently, one single monument can never satisfy the needs of a whole nation, and as such, this representative form cannot be fully 'democratic' either in process or form. Even the winning design by 'Milla und Partner', which highlights the weight of democracy in a highly visual way, has been controversial, and accused of being both monumental in proportion and too closely associated with the political elite. Instead, this project is perhaps most successful in highlighting the nature of the national community both as 'imagined', and as one in which myth-building is intrinsic.

Memory, form, and the GDR legacy

The majority of discussions during the first phase of the *Freiheits- und Einheitsdenkmal* took place with a view to taking stock of the GDR during the twentieth anniversary year of its demise. On 9 November 2009, the day on which the monument was initially to be completed, the Minister for Culture, Bernd Neumann, claimed that the 'reworking of the SED-dictatorship remains a central duty of society' (Presse- und Informationsamt, 2009b). As discussions surrounding this project have demonstrated, however, the GDR has not always remained its central focus; the monument has often come to stand for a much wider panoply of meanings, thus suggesting a certain instrumentalisation of GDR history for the purposes of contemporary politics. While the second competition – stripped bare of the demands to include longer historical traditions – demonstrated the intention to interact more fully with the events of this year, the duo of freedom and unity still poses a problem for some critics. *Die Linke* (the Left party, formerly the PDS), for instance, has consistently argued against remembering the demonstrations of 1989 together with the event of unity, for a unified Germany was not on the agenda for demonstrators in October and early November 1989 (e.g. Deutscher Bundestag, 2007b: 12963). By bringing these events together, such a monument would suggest to future generations that the desire for unity was one of the principal aims of the demonstrators in 1989, thus rewriting history. A further criticism on the part of left-wing critics has been that the peace groups of the early 1980s, as well as the 'swords into ploughshares' movement and the critical role of the churches, would be downplayed – if not forgotten – in such a monolithic reading of history (e.g. Deutscher Bundestag, 2001: 19509). It seems, indeed, that historical detail may be in danger of being brushed aside in the interests of future aspirations, and in light of persisting differences between east and west, one could claim that the proposal still fails to correspond to present-day realities. As one critic insisted in 2009, 'Germany needs the unity of the country not on a pedestal, but rather in everyday life' (Hübner, 2009), and jury member Matthias Flügge (2011) disagreed with the choice of the winning design, claiming that it 'polishes away all critical and contrary elements [...] under gold leaf'. It must be remembered, however, that – as a form of state-sponsored political memory, in which symbolic, ritualised forms are deliberately sought – this proposed monument cannot seek to represent the demise of the GDR in all its complexity. As Jennifer Jordan (2005: 61) states, 'any landscape of memory also exists with a shadow landscape of forgetting', and it is the timing of this debate which particularly highlights such a shadow landscape. The attempt to commemorate an event in a national memorial only 20 years after its passing is, indeed, ambitious, and with social memory of this period still prevalent, conflicting opinions and motives are inevitable. Above all, this debate reminds us that attempts to instil commemorative symbolism at the heart of a nation tell us more about the present and future aspirations of that nation, rather than the past it seeks to represent.

Memory of the GDR is clearly entrenched in contemporary politics and the building of future identities, yet this chapter also shows that its physical representation in memorial form has as much to do with past traditions. In calling for a democratic, national and positive monument, this project seeks to demonstrate a break with past cultures of remembrance; the desire to counter authoritarian GDR traditions of remembrance, as well as more self-reflexive western forms, proves as important as the historical events of 1989 themselves. While this monument may not represent the pillar of democracy that was initially hoped for, efforts to make the competition process transparent, as well as the willingness to recognise other sites of memory and afford more time for the project – rather than shoehorning it into a tight time-frame centred around 9 November 2009 – suggest that lessons have been learned from the past, and that this is more than simply an exercise in political propaganda. As the monument landscape of twentieth-century Germany demonstrates, however, its future – if erected – may not be guaranteed. In Andreas Huyssen's words (1995: 250), 'the permanence promised by a monument in stone is always built on quicksand', and forms of political memory may, ironically, be shorter-lived than social memory of the same event. It is for this reason that we must recognise the palimpsestic nature of political memory, which can only fully be understood if the process of its writing and rewriting is exposed. Memory of the GDR must thus be understood within the broader context of contemporary politics and past cultures of remembrance, for it is the pull of both past and future traditions which shape present-day preoccupations with memory and identity.

Notes

1. For example, the pillar erected on Nikolaiplatz in Leipzig (1999), the 'Friedensglocke' (bell of peace) in Dessau (2002), and the 'Bürgerdenkmal' (citizens' monument) in Magdeburg (2003).
2. All translations from German are my own.

3. Designs from the first competition were exhibited in the Kronprinzenpalais in May 2009, and from the second competition in the Martin-Gropius-Bau in October 2010. Published documentations include Apelt (2009) and *Gestaltungswettbewerb* (2009). The main website is managed by the *Deutsche Gesellschaft e.V.*: http://www.freiheits-und-einheitsdenkmal.de/.

References

Assmann, A. (2006) *Der lange Schatten der Vergangenheit. Erinnerungskultur und Geschichtspolitik* (Munich: Beck).

Assmann, J. (1999), *Das kulturelle Gedächtnis* (Munich: Beck).

Apelt, A. H. (ed.) (2009) *Der Weg zum Denkmal für Freiheit und Einheit* (Schwalbach/Ts: Wochenschau).

Brussig, T. (2009) 'Brussig: "Nicht die Künstler, wir haben versagt" ', *Tagesspiegel*, 8 May, http://www.tagesspiegel.de/kultur/Einheitsdenkmal-Thomas-Brussig-Mitte;art772,2792018 [date accessed 8 September 2009].

Deutscher Bundestag (2000a) 'Antrag', Drucksache 14/3126, 6 April.

Deutscher Bundestag (2000b) 'Plenarprotokoll, 14/99', 13 April.

Deutscher Bundestag (2001) 'Plenarprotokoll 14/199', 9 November.

Deutscher Bundestag (2007a) 'Beschlussempfehlung und Bericht', Drucksache 16/6974, 7 November.

Deutscher Bundestag (2007b) 'Plenarprotokoll 16/124', 9 November.

'Einheitsdenkmal soll auf den Berliner Schlossplatz' (2008) *Süddeutsche Zeitung*, 13 March.

Finger, E. (2009) 'Mehr Revolution wagen!', *Die Zeit*, 9 July, 48.

Flügge, M. (2011) Interview on *Deutschlandradio Kultur*, 14 April, http://www.dradio.de/dkultur/sendungen/thema/1435816/ [date accessed 8 September 2011].

Gestaltungswettbewerb für ein Freiheits- und Einheitsdenkmal Berlin (2008) *Auslobungstext – 1. Stufe* (Berlin: Bundesamt für Bauwesen und Raumordnung).

Gestaltungswettbewerb für ein Freiheits- und Einheitsdenkmal in Berlin (2009) *Dokumentation des offenen Wettbewerbs 2009* (Berlin: Bundesamt für Bauwesen und Raumordnung).

Hübner, W. (2009) 'Einheit ohne Sockel', *Neues Deutschland*, 7 July, 6.

Huyssen, A. (1995) *Twilight Memories: Marking Time in a Culture of Amnesia* (New York: Routledge).

Janzing, G. (2000) 'Ein neuer Boom der Memorialkultur', *die tageszeitung*, 8/9 April, 25.

Jeismann, M. (1999) *Mahnmal Mitte. Eine Kontroverse* (Cologne: DuMont).

Jordan, J. (2005) 'A Matter of Time: Examining Collective Memory in Historical Perspective in Postwar Berlin', *Journal of Historical Sociology*, 1, 37–71.

Jordan, J. (2006) *Structures of Memory: Understanding Urban Change in Berlin and Beyond* (Stanford, CA: Stanford University Press).

Kilb, A. (2009) 'Einheitsdenkmal: Freiheit für die Schlümpfe', FAZ.NET, 5 May, http://www.faz.net/s/RubCF3AEB154CE64960822FA5429A182360/Doc~ED2741788EED34C36BA131847A4F9D83D~ATpl~Ecommon~Scontent.html [date accessed 8 September 2009].

Klabach, K. (2009) *Das Holocaust-Denkmal Berlin: Ein Sühnemahnmal des Deutschen Volkes?* (Munich: Grin).

Ladd, B. (1997) *The Ghosts of Berlin* (Chicago: University of Chicago Press).
Leggewie, C. and E. Meyer (2005) *Ein Ort, an den man gerne geht* (Munich: Hanser).
Mania, A. (2009) 'Ausstellung zum Wettbewerb für ein Freiheits- und Einheitsdenkmal, Berlin', artnet, http://www.artnet.de/magazine/kommentar/mania/mania05-29-09.asp [date accessed 8 September 2009].
Mausbach, F. (2008) *Über Sinn und Ort eines nationalen Freiheits- und Einheitsdenkmals* (Berlin: Bundesamt für Bauwesen und Raumordnung).
Mittig, H.-E. (1987) 'Das Denkmal' in W. Busch and P. Schmoock (eds) *Kunst. Die Geschichte ihrer Funktionen* (Weinheim: Quadriga), pp. 457–89.
Nooke, G. (2006) 'Ein Denkmal für die Einheit in Freiheit? Formen der Auseinandersetzung mit der DDR' in P. März and H.-J. Veen (eds) *Woran erinnern? Der Kommunismus in der deutschen Erinnerungskultur* (Cologne: Böhlau), pp. 111–22.
Presse- und Informationsamt der Bundesregierung (2009a) 'Neues Wettbewerbsverfahren zu Berliner Freiheits- und Einheitsdenkmal beschlossen' (Pressemitteilung Nr.: 293), http://www.freiheits-und-einheitsdenkmal.de/edenkmal-exposee.php?id=46 [date accessed 7 September 2009].
Presse- und Informationsamt der Bundesregierung (2009b) 'Kulturstaatsminister Bernd Neumann: Aufarbeitung der SED-Diktatur bleibt zentrale gesellschaftliche Aufgabe' (Pressemitteilung Nr. 439), 9 November, http://www.bundesregierung.de/nn_1494/Content/DE/Pressemitteilungen/BPA/2009/11/2009-11-09-bkm-aufarbeitung-sed-diktatur.html [date accessed 4 February 2001].
Samuel, R. (1994) *Theatres of Memory* (London: Verso).
Schönfeld, M. (2009) 'Kritisches Denkzeichen und restauratives Denkmal' in T. Flierl and E. Müller (eds) *Vom kritischen Gebrauch der Erinnerung* (Berlin: Dietz), pp. 141–74.
sfk (2009) '"Kompletter Schrott" Wettbewerb für Einheitsdenkmal', *Welt Online*, 28 April, http://www.welt.de/kultur/article3641729/Wettbewerb-fuer-Einheitsdenkmal.html [date accessed 8 September 2009].
Stavginski, H.-G. (2002) *Das Holocaust-Denkmal* (Paderborn: Schöningh).
Thünemann, H. (2009) *Holocaust-Rezeption und Geschichtskultur* (Idstein: Schulz-Kirchner).
Till, K. (2005) *The New Berlin: Memory, Politics, Place* (Minneapolis, MN: University of Minnesota Press).
Verheyen, D. (2008) *United City, Divided Memories? Cold War Legacies in Contemporary Berlin* (Lanham: Lexington).
Webber, A. (2008) *Berlin in the Twentieth Century: A Cultural Topography* (Cambridge: Cambridge University Press).
Young, J. (2002) *At Memory's Edge: After-images of the Holocaust in Contemporary Art and Architecture* (Yale: Yale University Press).

11
'We were heroes.' Local Memories of Autumn 1989: Revising the Past

Alexandra Kaiser

The year 2009 in Germany was dominated by the remembrance of the twentieth anniversary of the autumn of 1989. A vast number of books and articles were published and various films and television documentaries were made. But memory activities were neither restricted to the media nor exclusively a top-down phenomenon. Autumn 2009 saw commemorative events taking place throughout the whole of eastern Germany; cities from Plauen to Rostock and from Erfurt to Görlitz recalled their demonstrations against the regime of the Socialist Unity Party of Germany (SED) of 20 years earlier. Various exhibitions, lectures and discussions were organised and numerous local days of remembrance were initiated to celebrate local contributions to the fall of the Berlin Wall and the dismantling of the GDR. Apart from the anniversary of the fall of the Wall on 9 November, an undoubted highlight of the commemorative efforts in autumn 2009 was the *Lichtfest* (festival of lights) in Leipzig on 9 October.

Based on detailed fieldwork, this chapter focuses on local memory culture and policy in Leipzig. Following an outline of the various commemorative activities in Leipzig, it will analyse the contexts and meanings of the significant boom in the remembrance of autumn 1989. By discussing the narrative of the *Friedliche Revolution* (peaceful revolution) and its function in current German memory culture, this study shows how attempts are being made to create a new, positive national tradition and even a national myth for the post-1990 FRG.

Leipzig 1989: The historical background

As the situation in the GDR with its ruined cities, disastrous environmental conditions and political and economic decline became ever more precarious in the 1980s, those who struggled to achieve reform within the GDR gained increasing strength (Neubert, 1997). While it was not possible to pronounce an opinion in public, the (Protestant) church offered a sanctuary-like space and a public forum, albeit small in size. Opposition groups had been forming under its aegis since the early 1980s. In Leipzig, the most important meeting place was the Nikolaikirche (St. Nicholas Church) where, beginning in 1982, *Friedensgebete* (peace prayers) were held every Monday. The prayers provided a forum to discuss and exchange ideas, yet in 1988 their character changed from more or less intimate circles into mass events, as people wishing to leave the country increasingly used the Nikolaikirche as a space to meet and demand their rights. The process of creating a critical and public culture of resistance accelerated in 1989. After the *Friedensgebet* on 4 September, approximately 1500 people gathered for a demonstration in the churchyard of the Nikolaikirche, and the number of participants increased steadily over the following weeks. On 7 October, during the festivities for the fortieth anniversary of the GDR, public protests and demonstrations took place in different places all over the GDR. As a result people became aware of the significance of the following Monday, 9 October, and with the massacre in Beijing on 4 June in mind, many people feared that the SED would react in the same way. Indeed, the GDR government prepared for a violent 'solution': 3000 members of the armed forces were placed on alert. However, in spite of the threat that the police might open fire, about 70,000 people gathered in the city centre and some carried candles. Faced with such large numbers the state retreated and the demonstration proceeded peacefully, with people moving in a huge protest march from Augustusplatz along the city ring road to the Runde Ecke, the headquarters of the district administration of the Stasi, where the demonstration began disbanding (Mundus, 2009).

The course of events on 9 October was perceived as a signal that the state would not react violently to future protests, and Leipzig was declared a 'city of heroes' ('Heldenstadt') by the writer Christoph Hein. The number of people who joined the demonstrations in Leipzig and elsewhere continued to increase in the following weeks. Only a month later, the Wall came down.

Leipzig 2009: Revival of the past

The protest on 9 October 1989 has been an important date for local memory culture ever since (Jessen, 2009: 472–77). On the occasion of the twentieth anniversary of the protest, the date was introduced as a local public holiday (Stadt Leipzig, 2011c: 38) and the commemorative efforts reached a new high point with the celebration of the *Lichtfest*. Organised by the city of Leipzig, the Leipzig Tourismus und Marketing GmbH, and the Initiative 'Tag der Friedlichen Revolution – Leipzig 9. Oktober 1989' (abbr. Initiative 9. Oktober), it surpassed all expectations with 100,000 people in attendance.

The anniversary's official programme started with the dedication of a *Freiheitsglocke* (freedom bell). The dedication of the bell was followed by a state ceremony at Leipzig's Gewandhaus concert hall in the presence of both Chancellor Angela Merkel and Federal President Horst Köhler. In accordance with the historical events 'peace prayers' began at the Nikolaikirche at 5 pm. Afterwards, the great *Lichtfest* was opened on Augustusplatz. It was carefully designed to echo symbolic traditions.

As early as 2007 and 2008, a *Nacht der Kerzen* (night of candles) had been organised outside the Nikolaikirche. In 2009 the *Lichtfest* began with a 'candlelight display' on Augustusplatz: people created the words 'Leipzig 89' by placing thousands of candles in front of the opera house (see Figure 11.1). To simplify inclusion of this emotional moment in

Figure 11.1 Candle display on Augustusplatz, Leipzig, at the 2009 'Festival of Lights' (Alexander Schmidt/PUNCTUM).

news broadcasts, the beginning of the candlelight display was scheduled for 6 pm (Krutsch, 2009b). It was clear that the *Lichtfest* performance was intended to create new images for collective visual memory, challenging the highly emotional images of 9 November that had gone around the world.

After the candlelight display on the evening of 9 October 2009, the crowd moved from Augustusplatz to follow the historical route along the city ring road where lighting and multimedia installations by more than 20 artists were presented (Stadt Leipzig, 2009). Proceeding past the artworks, the crowd continued to the Runde Ecke, where its official route ended. The event had thus in essence been created as a performative happening and symbolic re-enactment, with the participants – citizens of Leipzig and visitors from elsewhere – as main actors walking in the footsteps of the demonstrators of 1989. The mayor of Leipzig, Burkhard Jung, expressed the aim of the *Lichtfest* as the creation of 'an emotional experience that will, above all, appeal to young people', and institutionalise 'a fitting commemoration which will attract attention both at home and abroad' (Stadt Leipzig, 2009: 4). The local authorities were therefore highly conscious of the new format they were about to establish.

Memory and the process of remembering the past is always influenced by the specifics of different media (see Erll and Nünning, 2004 and Chapter 1 this volume). While the importance of media characteristics has often been noticed in general, detailed studies, in particular of the specifics and the impetus of performative forms of remembering, are quite rare.[1] Performative media are not 'dogmatic' in transmitting a certain message, but open to different interpretations. At the same time, such forms as rites or ceremonies are highly effective strategies for passing on and creating traditions, values and perspectives, because significance is not merely represented passively but instead practised, created and executed with the body. The same is true for a re-enactive event such as the *Lichtfest*. Moreover, re-enactive commemorations represent a new quality among memorial signs: the differentiation between first- and second-hand experiences or between the mediation and bodily experience is being blurred. Even people who did not take part in the original protests of 1989 can now, 20 years later, achieve bodily involvement in an 'authentic' event modelled on the historic example, implying a very strong sense of emotional inclusion. We can assume that the commemorative potential of 9 October 1989 is decisively heightened by the affective quality of the *Lichtfest*.[2]

At the same time, due to its performative character, the *Lichtfest* allows for conceptual openness and various ways of understanding its message. The *Lichtfest* performance created a space which could accommodate the interests of many different parties and memory groups. By attracting tourists, it became a financial success for the city of Leipzig and fulfilled its role as a modern image campaign. It helped to confirm local identity but was also a means of promoting 9 October as an important national or even international date. Moreover, the event offered the possibility of identification with the past both for citizens of Leipzig who were active during the protests in 1989, and for younger people and those lacking any personal connection to autumn 1989. With regard to different understandings of the *Lichtfest,* I will distinguish between 'subversive' and 'national' readings.

Subversive readings

Among the complex narratives and conflicting memories of autumn 1989, one can differentiate not only between official narratives, personal memories, and eastern and western German memory communities, but also between differing views within the cohort of former members of the opposition. While some of the civil rights campaigners identify with today's political system and have gone on to political careers, a great number from the opposition retrospectively judge the protests of autumn 1989 as a revolution that was lost and betrayed. Their aim was not to end the GDR but to reform its model of socialism; thus 9 November was seen not as a breakthrough or critical step along the way to a long-awaited German unification, but rather as the abrupt end of a process of democratisation and reform within the GDR.

Voices that tried to link the commemorations with alternative, critical narratives of the 1989 protests were audible in 2009. Christian Führer, for example, former pastor of the Nikolaikirche and one of the best-known exponents of the autumn 1989 protests, proclaimed the start of a 'second part of the revolution' in order to continue the discussions of 1989 and challenge the FRG's current economic system (Führer, 2009). Like Friedrich Schorlemmer, another well-known protagonist of the GDR opposition, Führer is active within the Stiftung Friedliche Revolution (Peaceful Revolution Foundation), which was founded in 2009 and presents itself as a defender of the central principles of autumn 1989. Its home page points to civil disobedience, active citizenship and a critique of capitalism (Stiftung Friedliche Revolution, 2011).

In a more general sense, the celebration of 9 October and the numerous other local commemorations of autumn 1989 laid a new emphasis on events that took place in the GDR *before* the fall of the Wall, thereby refocusing on an east German perspective. By stressing the revolutionary movement itself, the events question the dominance of the west German narrative. The extensive commemorations could therefore be interpreted as a reaction to the disillusionment and dashed hopes resulting from German unification, as well as a critique of an earlier (self-)expression that saw the FRG as 'the promised land'. Confronted with the persisting social and economic imbalance between eastern and western Germany, many former East Germans retrospectively see the uprising itself as the only event they can celebrate. I would suggest that the potential for a 'subversive' reading of the commemorative events in 2009 was one of the most important reasons for the overwhelming support and participation of many thousands of people in the eastern part of Germany.

A subversive, anti-national tendency is also reflected in the symbolic language. With regard to the main political symbols that were used during the transformation of 1989–90, the cultural anthropologist Gottfried Korff has differentiated four categories: anti-socialist symbols, national and economic symbols (in favour of the FRG's free market system) and 'archaic' symbols (Korff, 1990: 136). Among the symbolic language of the commemorations in Leipzig in 2009 it is striking that only the last category was taken up, most impressively represented by candles. The candle was probably the most popular symbol used in 1989, and is not only reminiscent of the church roots of the Monday demonstrations, but also functions as a symbol of peace and freedom, and thus for autumn 1989 in a broader sense. Its connotations of bringing light into darkness, warmth, and spreading the revolutionary impetus (Korff, 1990: 151; Seidel, 1996: 137–40) highlight the positive image of the protests particularly well.

Apart from the candle, other symbols of the GDR opposition and of autumn 1989 were also re-used during the anniversary event in Leipzig. An advertising column installed on Augustusplatz was reminiscent of a similar pillar that had been put up in the same location 20 years earlier by Kurt Masur, ex-director of the Leipzig Gewandhaus, to provide a forum for people to express their opinions. In reference to the most popular symbol of the GDR peace movement, 'swords into ploughshares' ('Schwerter zu Pflugscharen'), and in imitation of an action performed at the Wittenberg church congress of 1983, a sword was forged into a sickle (Raulien, 2009). In view of the 'archaic' symbols used in 1989 – the use of the expression 'hero' is another example – Korff has pointed to the orientation they provide in a precarious and unknown situation. The re-use of the symbols in 2009 likewise satisfies that need for orientation; the same could be said of the performance of the *Lichtfest* in its entirety. Simultaneously, this memory practice could be understood in terms of resistance to an unduly western interpretation of the protests.

National readings

The day after the *Lichtfest*, various left-wing groups organised a demonstration in Leipzig, campaigning under the slogan 'Still not lovin' Germany' (Still not lovin' Germany, 2009). The demonstration's motto criticised the utilisation of commemorative activities as state propaganda in a fundamental way. Other critical objections to the nationalisation of autumn 1989 were made (see Schreier, 2009; Lila Offensive, 2010). Drawing on west German collective memory and disregarding the subversive reading, a national reading has always dominated in mass media and official politics and history. By neglecting the openness of the discussions and simplifying the historical facts, this reading declares 3 October 1990 to have been the final cause and end point of the protests by GDR citizens in 1989. However, the more recent vehement insistence on taking the protests of autumn 1989 as the basis for an all-German, positive national 'identity pool' (see Nooke, 2008) significantly shifts the emphasis. As early as 2007, a document titled '40 + 20 = 60 Jahre Bundesrepublik. Ruf aus Leipzig' ('40 + 20 = 60 Years Federal Republic. Call from Leipzig') was published. By including 9 October 1989 – an event that took place in the GDR – as an essential part of the democratic tradition of the FRG, it stated that Leipzig had made national history. Among the signatories of the appeal were the mayor of Leipzig, Kurt Masur and Christian Führer (Ruf aus Leipzig, 2007).

Another paper titled 'Leipziger Thesen' ('Leipzig Theses'), which was authored by the Initiative 9. Oktober and widely published in 2009, expresses the intentions of the new memory policy even more explicitly. Pointing to the democratic character of the 1989 protests, it glamorises the *Friedliche Revolution* as the first and only successful and nonviolent revolution in German history. However, according to the 'Leipziger Thesen', the people's pride in their achievements and their defeat of the SED dictatorship is now 'buried' ('verschüttet'). The quest to revive that pride and self-esteem is indicated as an important mission. Currently, the Initiative 9. Oktober, which incorporates various communal and public authorities, as well as research, educational and cultural institutions in Leipzig (see Autumn '89 Initiative, 2011), is one of the strongest forces in the public sphere demanding a reappraisal of autumn 1989 to upgrade its national relevance. In any case, the main architects of the nationalisation of autumn 1989 seem to be east German intellectuals with links to the opposition of 1989 – opposition members from the second tier, who 'long for attention today' (Geissler, 2011). The influence of certain individuals can hardly be overestimated, and one of the most important exponents pushing the debate is without doubt Rainer Eckert, director of the Zeitgeschichtliches Forum Leipzig and chief spokesperson of the Initiative 9. Oktober in 2008/09. He has published various articles and books on this subject and baulks at using the term *Wende* when talking about the autumn protests and the transformation processes of 1989–90.

From the '*Wende*' to the '*Friedliche Revolution*'

The debate about perspectives on 1989 and its reinterpretation is reflected on the linguistic level as well. In everyday German speech, the autumn of 1989 and the transformation processes leading to German unification are commonly referred to by the term *Wende* ('turn'). Despite its widespread use and its banality, the term is decried by some protagonists of the new direction in memories of 1989 and denounced in public declarations (see below). While earlier essays dealt with the question of whether the protests in 1989 merited identification as a 'revolution' at all (e.g. Kühnhardt, 1997), the current debate concerns – in crude terms – whether the designation *Friedliche Revolution* should be obligatory or not. A number of articles have addressed the matter (e.g. Eppelmann and Grünbaum, 2004; Eckert, 2007; Damm and Thompson, 2009; Jesse, 2011). In the meantime, even the German Federal government (Bundesregierung, 2009) has published a plea for the term's use on its home page.

Egon Krenz had spoken of a *Wende* in the politics of the SED when he succeeded Erich Honecker as Secretary-General in October 1989, and the term's 'abuse' by Krenz is presented as the main reason for the need to declare it as a taboo. After more than 20 years, this hardly seems to constitute a satisfactory argument. Moreover, the term *Wende* has a certain legitimacy simply because everyone – in eastern and in western Germany – uses it. A typical German sees no political implications and means to imply no belittlement of the GDR system, but uses the term as shorthand to refer to a distinct political, economic and social process and a distinct period of time (1989/90) (Richter, 2007; Beleites,

2011: 73–4). The heightened effort made to replace the term *Wende* with the expression *Friedliche Revolution* may therefore rather be explained by the political significance of the latter for the construction of a positive German national identity and mythology. While the term *Wende* does not necessarily imply an active role for the populace but covers different and quite complex changes, the expression *Friedliche Revolution* re-casts the 'East German' as a 'national revolutionary'. By transforming the events that led to German unification into a tale of effective heroism, it turns the protesters of 1989 into (active) heroes who caused the Wall to fall and therefore have a right to be proud of their achievement – and by implication proud of the post-unification FRG.

Lichtfest versus *Freiheitsdenkmal*

The attempt to control the usage of specific terms to refer to 1989–90 is an example of the conflict between official top-down and individual bottom-up memories. Another prominent example which the city of Leipzig has undertaken to highlight further the significance of 9 October is the project to erect a *Freiheits- und Einheitsdenkmal* (Monument to Freedom and Unity) as a complement to the one planned for Berlin (see Chapter 10). With its inauguration due to take place in 2014, the Federal government agreed to spend five million Euros on the monument. The government of the Free State of Saxony will pay another 1.5 million Euros.

In Leipzig there are already several monuments to remember 9 October. The first was built by artist Andreas Stötzner near the Nikolaikirche in 1999. Resembling a church pillar, it serves to remind viewers of the ecclesiastical roots of the 1989 protests. Later on, a bronze plaque designed by sculptor Markus Gläser, a fountain by David Chipperfield and the project 'public light_öffentliches licht' by Tilo Schulz completed the ensemble (Stadt Leipzig, 2011a). Proponents of the *Freiheits- und Einheitsdenkmal* cite the local character of these memorials to justify the building of an additional monument that will reference 9 October's national relevance. The Initiative 9. Oktober and the municipality are again the most dominant forces pushing forward the project. The mayor of Leipzig does not tire of emphasising the monument's importance for the city's image and identity. Stressing the argument that Leipzig should not reject the government grant, a large majority of the Leipzig city council supports its construction.

While the *Lichtfest* on 9 October, which has become an annual event and a local tradition, is widely accepted and appreciated by the people of Leipzig – in 2010 it attracted about 40,000 people, in 2011 more than 25,000– the plan for a national monument provoked harsh criticism, even though it refers to the same historic event. Since December 2008, when the plan for the monument was finally confirmed by the German Bundestag, the results of opinion surveys have suggested that a majority of citizens is unwilling to support the idea of a national memorial in Leipzig. A survey by the Institut für Marktforschung showed that the population was split roughly 50–50, with 48 per cent of the participants rejecting the monument and 47 per cent approving of it (Geissler, 2011). During a telephone VoteCall survey in January 2009, initiated by the local newspaper, 75 per cent of callers rejected the plans for the monument (Krutsch, 2009a), and in January 2011, 92 per cent of callers declared themselves against it (Orbeck, 2011). Letters to the editors of the local newspaper also show the same negative tendency.

In order to legitimise the project after the city council had refused to conduct a referendum, municipal authorities organised two workshops: one with selected 'experts' from Leipzig and elsewhere, and one with teenagers from Houston, Krakow, Hanover and Leipzig, who discussed the *Freiheits- und Einheitsdenkmal* and emphatically confirmed its importance. In February 2011, another opinion poll – this time at the behest of the city of Leipzig and based on a sample of 3,000 citizens – finally yielded 54 per cent assent (for more details see Stadt Leipzig, 2011b). The slightly more positive result may, however, rather be ascribed to the modified method of collecting data than to a shift in public opinion.

The monument's national significance – the main argument of its supporters – is at the same time a main argument of those who object to it. Others suggest spending the federal grant alternatively on social projects or point to the already existing memorials. Whereas the *Lichtfest* has the potential to integrate national and local intentions and to mobilise people for whom the memory of 1989 has nothing to do with a commitment to the post-1990 FRG, the monument rather detaches itself from local remembrance. This is evident in the choice of location, now fixed at the Wilhelm-Leuschner-Platz; while this location represents an ideal solution with regard to urban development, there is no direct link to the protests of 1989, as the protest march did not reach it.

The *Friedliche Revolution* as all-German national myth?

While the narrative of the *Friedliche Revolution* is based on its image as an essentially democratic movement from below, its construction occurs with pressure from above. Some would call the official strategy

Geschichtspolitik (politics of history). While the term *Geschichtspolitik* has typically been used in the sense of an – often critical – analytic tool for describing political procedures from the outside, it seems to have acquired another meaning in recent times. The casual openness with which policymakers and their supporters speak of deliberate mythmaking – of establishing the peaceful revolution as a 'master narrative' (Eckert, 2009b: 1069) and 'founding myth' of the new, larger FRG (Eckert, 2011) – is indeed astonishing. The activist perspective can possibly be seen as a consequence of the boom in memory studies; increasingly widespread awareness that memory – following Maurice Halbwachs and Aleida and Jan Assmann – is not merely neutral and 'given' but always constructed, may constitute sufficient grounds, for some, to take its construction into their own hands.

In his book *Die Deutschen und ihre Mythen* (The Germans and their myths), the political scientist Herfried Münkler discusses the mythological differences between the pre-1990 FRG and the GDR. While the GDR established its own system of political myths, concentrating on the heritage of the peasants' revolt, the Napoleonic wars and antifascism after 1945, the FRG drew its self-confidence primarily from its economic power and lacked a positive foundation myth. With regard to war crimes and the Nazi past, the FRG's national identity was marked by a negative 'signature' (Münkler, 2009: 9–10, 19–20, and 411–76). The unification of the two Germanys opened, however, a new chapter in German memory culture and the construction of national identity (Jeismann, 2001). After decades of focusing on the Holocaust and Nazism, a search for 'positive achievements' and 'happy moments' in German history began in the post-1990-FRG. The attempt to establish a narrative of the peaceful revolution is part of that new 'longing' for positive identification and even national pride. With regard to allegations that Germany's guilt and responsibility would be marginalised, a declaration titled 'Das Jahr 1989 zu feiern, heißt auch, sich an 1939 zu erinnern!' ('Celebrating 1989 also implies commemorating 1939!'), signed by public intellectuals, historians, and representatives of historical sites and political institutions was published in the newspaper *Die Zeit* and elsewhere (Das Jahr 1989 zu feiern, 2009).

Myths are legends that favour the creation of identity by confirming or contrasting with existing reality. Social groups, ethnicities, communities and nations refer to myths, and by reducing the complexity of history they lend significance to what cannot be altered or – alternatively – conjure up the vision of a better world. It is thus the function of myths that is important, rather than their 'falsehood' or 'truth'.[3] What, then, is the function of the narrative of the *Friedliche Revolution* in recent German culture and identity, and – most interestingly – does it function as a myth at all? Is it probable that 9 October, with its image as 'day of decision' (Eckert, 2009a; Kuhn, 1992), will turn into a nationwide commemorative day?

Following the 'Leipziger Thesen', the narrative of the *Friedliche Revolution* can be seen as an attempt to find an all-German tradition of remembrance that integrates people from both the east and the west. In equating the federal constitution (*Grundgesetz*) and its reference to human dignity with the demands of the protesters in autumn 1989, it serves to justify the political system of the FRG. By ignoring the specific circumstances of autumn 1989 – in particular, Mikhail Gorbachev's policies of glasnost and perestroika, the changes in eastern Europe and the ruinous state of the GDR's political and economic system – and the complexity of contemporary intentions, the narrative of the *Friedliche Revolution* turns the *Wende* into a heroic self-liberation by the East German people. Being portrayed as 'responsible citizens' ('mündige Bürger') and as a powerful force that caused the Wall to collapse, the East German people are described as the 'victors of history'. Against this background, the year 2009, incorporating the celebration of the sixtieth anniversary of the FRG and the twentieth anniversary of autumn 1989, was conceived as an important stage of 'crystallisation' in the self-assertion of a new Germany (Ruf aus Leipzig, 2007; Leipziger Thesen, 2009). In addition to its significance for German history, the European dimension of the *Friedliche Revolution* was also stressed in declarations that autumn 1989 neutralised the October Revolution of 1917 (Eckert, 2011: 332; Kielmannsegg, 2010: 5), following the argument that the 70,000 peaceful protesters in Leipzig brought not only the GDR, but communism and totalitarianism in Europe, to their final collapse.

Despite its positive image, there is little to suggest that the *Friedliche Revolution* will be accepted – and 'believed'[4] – as an all-German myth in the post-1990 FRG. As indicated above, many east Germans have been unwilling to interpret their protest against the SED government in a national sense, while in other parts of Germany a general lack of interest in the GDR's opposition movement and the *Friedliche Revolution* still prevails. While Ilko-Sascha Kowalczuk diagnosed 'Revolutionsneid' ('revolution envy') not least among the '68 generation in the west (Kowalczuk, 2009: 546–7), I would rather – following Münkler (2009: 479) – explain the typical attitude of west Germans as a result of their role as bystanders whose everyday lives and political opinions were not affected by the revolutionary events. Subsequently, the celebrations of autumn 1989 that took place in 2009 had no sustained effect on public perception in western Germany. Despite the elaborate performance of the *Lichtfest*, 9 October is neither popular nor well known in other parts of Germany, and the west German media are generally uninterested in reporting on such events. In view of the aspirations of its advocates to achieve nationwide significance, 9 October is thus somewhat reminiscent of 17 June. In memory of the uprising in the GDR against the SED government that took place in 1953, West Germany established the date as the 'Day of German Unity' and as a national holiday. However, 17 June never developed a real bonding force – most people in the FRG simply enjoyed the day off without worrying unduly about its political significance.

As the futile attempts to establish the *Friedliche Revolution* as a national myth show, a collective all-German memory culture has not yet been developed. Curiously enough, the disruption in current German memory culture is most prominently demonstrated by the doubling of the *Freiheits- und Einheitsdenkmal* with sites in Leipzig and in Berlin. Despite the location of the Berlin monument in a former GDR area, its symbolism is clearly connected with Berlin as federal capital of the FRG and with the federal government (see Chapter 10). While the Leipzig monument was supposed to emphasise the east German contribution to German unification, it resulted in the contrary, for instead of strengthening shared memories and values, it cut them off. Although the planned monuments in Berlin and in Leipzig are both dedicated to 'freedom and unity', the function has effectively been divided: while the Berlin monument corresponds to the paradigm of 'unity' and therefore to a west German perspective, the proposed monument in Leipzig rather connects with the conception of 'freedom' and thus with an east German perspective. The two monuments symbolise the contrary nature of 'unity'; they point to the existing and still seemingly insurmountable differences between east and west German memory culture.

Notes

1. An exception is Connerton (1989).
2. The celebration of the fall of the Wall in Berlin in 2009 was also realised as re-enactive event: the 'Wall' was rebuilt with oversized dominos, which were then toppled.
3. A great number of books have concentrated on the importance of myths for the construction of collective and national identity, see for example Flacke, 2001; Münkler, 2009: 9–30.

4. Herfried Münkler and Jens Hacke (2009: 29–30) assume that a myth's efficacy fails not only because of its content but because of its functionalism. In their view, myths must be 'believed' like religious dogma; they cannot simply be decreed with the aim of developing their legitimising character.

References

Autumn '89 Initiative (2011) Herbst '89 – Aufbruch zur Demokratie, http://www.herbst89.de/ [date accessed 10 July 2011].

Beleites, M. (2011) 'Die Zukunftsfragen nicht aus dem Blick verlieren. Gedanken nach zehn Jahren als Landesbeauftragter für die Stasi-Unterlagen', *Horch und Guck*, 20 (71), 70–5.

Bundesregierung (2009) ' "Wende"? "Friedliche Revolution"? "Mauerfall"?', http://www.bundesregierung.de/Content/DE/Artikel/20Jahre/2009-10-20-wende-oder-wie.html, [date accessed 7 August 2011].

Connerton, P. (1989) *How Societies Remember* (Cambridge: Cambridge University Press).

Damm, M. and M. Thompson (2009) 'Wende oder Friedliche Revolution? Ungleiche Deutungen einer historischen Zäsur', *Totalitarismus und Demokratie*, 6, 21–35.

'Das Jahr 1989 zu feiern, heißt auch, sich an 1939 zu erinnern!' (2009), *Die Zeit*, 20 August 2009, http://www.23august1939.de [date accessed 5 October 2011].

Eckert, R. (2007) 'Gegen die Wende-Demagogie – für den Revolutionsbegriff', *Deutschland Archiv*, 40 (6), 1084–6.

Eckert, R. (2009a) 'Der 9. Oktober: Tag der Entscheidung' in K.-D. Henke (ed.) *Revolution und Vereinigung 1989/90. Als in Deutschland die Realität die Phantasie überholte* (Munich: DTV), pp. 213–23.

Eckert, R. (2009b) 'Das "Erinnerungsjahr" 2009: 60 Jahre Bundesrepublik und 20 Jahre Friedliche Revolution. Ein Zwischenbericht', *Deutschland Archiv*, 42 (6), 1069–78.

Eckert, R. (2011) 'Nikolaikirche' in M. Donath and A. Thieme (eds) *Sächsische Mythen. Elbe – August – Eierschecke* (Leipzig: Edition Leipzig), pp. 321–33.

Eppelmann, R. and R. Grünbaum (2004) 'Sind wir die Fans von Egon Krenz? Die Revolution von 1989/90 war keine "Wende" ', *Deutschland Archiv*, 37 (5), 864–9.

Erll, A. and A. Nünning (eds) (2004) *Medien des kollektiven Gedächtnisses. Konstruktivität – Historizität – Kulturspezifität* (Berlin: de Gruyter).

Flacke, M. (ed.) (2001) *Mythen der Nationen: Ein europäisches Panorama* (Munich: Koehler & Amelang).

Führer, C. (2009) 'Die gewaltlose Revolution aktuell: Aufruf zu Friedensgebeten', *Publik-Forum*, April, Insert, xvi.

Geissler, R. (2011) 'Erinnern – aber richtig', *Die Zeit*, 5 January 2011, 10.

Jeismann, M. (2001) *Auf Wiedersehen Gestern. Die deutsche Vergangenheit und die Politik von morgen* (Stuttgart: Deutsche Verlagsanstalt).

Jesse, E. (2011) http://www.geschichtswerkstatt-jena.de/archiv_texte/der_begriff_wende_in_der_diskussion.pdf [date accessed 15 August 2011].

Jessen, R. (2009) 'Die Montagsdemonstrationen' in M. Sabrow (ed.) *Erinnerungsorte der DDR* (Munich: Beck), pp. 466–80.

Kielmannsegg, P. G. (2010) 'Die zweite Oktoberrevolution. Ein Glücksfall der europäischen Geschichte' in a reader produced by the Stadt Leipzig and circulated to interested parties, *Leipzig. Leipziger Freiheits- und Einheitsdenkmal*, 1–7.

Korff, G. (1990) 'Rote Fahnen und Bananen. Notizen zur politischen Symbolik im Prozess der Vereinigung von DDR und BRD', *Schweizerisches Archiv für Volkskunde*, 86, 130–60.

Kowalczuk, I.-S. (2009) *Endspiel. Die Revolution von 1989 in der DDR* (Munich: Beck).

Krutsch, P. (2009a) '"Wir brauchen kein Monument"', *Leipziger Volkszeitung*, 7 February.

Krutsch, P. (2009b) 'Erleuchtung der Revolutionsmeile', *Leipziger Volkszeitung*, 26 May, 15.

Kuhn, E. (1992) *Der Tag der Entscheidung: Leipzig, 9. Oktober 1989* (Berlin: Ullstein).

Kühnhardt, L. (1997) 'Umbruch – Wende – Revolution. Deutungsmuster des deutschen Herbstes 1989', *Aus Politik und Zeitgeschichte*, 40–41, 12–18.

Leipziger Thesen (2009) 'Die historische Erinnerung ist ein Mandat für Handeln in Gegenwart und Zukunft', *Deutschland Archiv*, 42 (5), 801–3.

Lila Offensive (2010) 'Aus den friedlichen Küchen der Revolution. Wider die feierliche Verklärung von "Wende" und Mauerfall', *Deutschland Archiv*, 43 (2), 210–12.

Mundus, D. (2009) *Leipzig 1989. A Chronicle* (Leipzig: Lehmstedt).

Münkler, H. (2009) *Die Deutschen und ihre Mythen* (Reinbek: Rowohlt).

Münkler, H. and J. Hacke (eds) (2009) *Wege in die neue Bundesrepublik. Politische Mythen und kollektive Selbstbilder nach 1989* (Frankfurt/Main: Campus).

Neubert, E. (1997) *Geschichte der Opposition in der DDR 1949–1989* (Berlin: Links).

Nooke, G. (2008) '"Die Helden kommen aus Leipzig". CDU-Politiker Günter Nooke über Friedliche Revolution und Einheitsdenkmal', *Leipziger Volkszeitung*, 22 December, 5.

Orbeck, M. (2011) 'Anrufer lehnen Denkmal ab', *Leipziger Volkszeitung*, 13 January, 19.

Raulien, A. (2009) 'Litfaßsäule als Sprachrohr', *Leipziger Volkszeitung*, 8 April.

Richter, M. (2007) 'Die Wende. Plädoyer für eine umgangssprachliche Benutzung', *Deutschland Archiv*, 40 (5), 861–8.

Richter, S. (2010) 'Die Erinnerung an 1989 und die Geschichtspolitik von 2009', *Deutschland Archiv*, 43 (1), 109–16.

Ruf aus Leipzig (2007) '40 + 20 = 60 Jahre Bundesrepublik', *Deutschland Archiv*, 40 (5), 859–60.

Schreier, A. (2009) 'Die gescheiterte Revolution', *telegraph. Ostdeutsche Zeitschrift*, 118/119, 4–8.

Seidel, K. (1996) *Die Kerze. Motivgeschichte und Ikonologie* (Hildesheim: Olms).

Stadt Leipzig (2009) *Press conference 'The Peaceful Revolution 20 years on'* (Leipzig: Press folder).

Stadt Leipzig (2011a) http://www.leipzig.de/herbst89 [date accessed 10 July 2011].

Stadt Leipzig (2011b) http://www.leipzig.de/de/buerger/politik/denkmal/ [date accessed 15 August 2011].

Stadt Leipzig (2011c) *Leipzig Herbst '89. Veranstaltungsprogramm rund um den 9. Oktober 2011* (Leipzig: Messedruck Leipzig GmbH).

Stiftung Friedliche Revolution (2011) http://www.stiftung-fr.de/Home.3.0.html [date accessed 12 August 2011].

Still not lovin' Germany (2009) http://antide2009.blogsport.de/ [date accessed 10 August 2011].

Part V

Memories in Private and Public

12
Re-Imaging the Niche: Visual Reconstructions of Private Spaces in the GDR

Gabriele Mueller

What did the GDR look like? Or more importantly for this chapter, how do we remember the look of the GDR? For most people, regardless of whether they lived in the GDR or not, this question would probably conjure up visual representations belonging to a well-known stock of media images which, through continuous repetition, have become iconic for the country and central to the production of historical knowledge.[1] Propelled forward by the growing mediatisation of history, a vast bank of images representing the GDR and in particular the fall of the Wall has been created since 1989. As a product of GDR memory discourse, this image arsenal reflects post-*Wende* remembrance culture in its division between the political and the private sphere, and between the often institutionally driven focus on the *Täterstaat* (perpetrator state) on the one hand and, on the other, a broader notion of *Alltagsgeschichte* (history of the everyday) and the visual representation of the material world of the GDR in private museums (see Chapter 8), in films and on television.

Even though historians now widely accept the study of *Alltagsgeschichte* as an indispensable complement to more traditional foci on political and economic structures, the process of narrating this *Alltagsgeschichte* within the context of GDR historiography remains problematic. Not only is the *Alltag* often thought of as a category that – due to its bottom-up approach to social analysis – is inherently uncritical and encourages a nostalgic glorification of the material world, but there is also disagreement among scholars as to whether such an approach is appropriate to the study of a 'thoroughly ruled society' ('durchherrschte Gesellschaft') (Faulenbach, 1997). These tensions are also evident in the contradictory use of the term *Nischengesellschaft* (niche society).

Originally used by Günter Gaus in 1983, it has been a central concept in the scholarly exploration of GDR *Alltagsgeschichte* as well as one of the dominant explanatory models in popular interpretations of East German society. Gaus (1983) describes the niche as an apolitical private sphere into which East Germans retreated in order to withdraw from a system that they opposed and from its public institutions and spaces. Thus, the niche allows the pursuit of individual interests beyond the reach of state control. More recently, scholars have questioned the term's usefulness. Richthofen (2009), for example, rejects it as simplistic and incapable of capturing the complexity of GDR society. She argues that social interaction was characterised by constant dialogue between the grassroots, intermediary and upper level functionaries, and that individuals were willing to integrate into, use and even manipulate structures and institutions to fulfil personal desires. Others criticise Gaus' assumption of the general public's opposition to the state, and scholars have often used the term to describe different phenomena and processes (Fulbrook, 1995; Palmowski, 2002; Betts, 2010). Nevertheless, the notion of the private niche has proven to be a pervasive paradigm. In public discourses it is particularly drawn upon because the focus on individual perspectives invites affective narratives and an emotional access to history while, at the same time, allowing for the potential of some agency and the display of *Eigen-Sinn*.[2]

This chapter looks at visual representations of the niche in order to trace shifts in the interpretation of individual agency and social interaction in GDR memory discourse. The following analysis discusses examples from GDR and post-*Wende* photography in comparison with visual reconstructions of the private sphere in museums and recent television productions. This comparative examination of images of the niche highlights first that the understanding of individual agency in the GDR has shifted, and second that television significantly contributes to the musealisation of the GDR and thus facilitates the transformation of heterogeneous experiential memories of the GDR into more homogenised forms of collective memory.

Documenting the private sphere in the GDR: Bernd Lasdin's *Zeitenwende*

Since the *Wende*, the term *Nischengesellschaft* has been used to characterise the organisation of the GDR in contrast to the West. However, Gaus (1983: 159) had conceptualised the GDR as a niche society in order to emphasise some similarities with the West as, in his opinion, all normal societies are to some extent niche societies. Indeed, Gaus's description of the withdrawal from politics into the private sphere was not restricted to GDR society. In the 1970s and 1980s, similar tendencies to embrace depoliticised individualism were observed in other East European countries as well as in the West (Betts, 2010). Cultural production in both German states also mediated these social developments; just as West German artists aspired to a 'New Subjectivity', in the GDR the 'withdrawal into the private sphere' became both a prevailing theme and an artistic strategy in the 1970s and 80s. Aiming for documentary realism, photographers and film directors focused on the private sphere and everyday relationships to probe changing behaviours, values and attitudes. Thus, the visual media in the GDR have left us with a rich source of images offering interpretations of the role of the private sphere that are much more complex than Gaus' description, and far from apolitical.

Bernd Lasdin's series of black-and-white photographs lend themselves to this discussion, as the work spans the two decades after unification.[3] In 1986, the photographer began what he called 'a sociological study'. He selected individuals and families in Mecklenburg to produce portraits of a representative cross-section of society. Roughly 10 and 20 years later, he returned to his subjects and repeated the process of creating a portrait following the same criteria and procedure as before. The resulting images were exhibited widely and published in the volumes *Zeitenwende* (*Time of Change*, 1998) and *Zeitenwenden* (*Times of Change*, 2009). Lasdin asked each person to select their favourite place and the pose for the portraits themselves, in order to minimise his own intervention in the composition of the image. These visual self-presentations were combined with a text written by the subject(s). Almost all participants chose a room in their homes and many of the photos are group portraits. In *Zeitenwende*, the first two portraits taken in 1987 and 1997 appear on a double page together with the individuals' own handwritten comments copied under the image. Thus, the spectator is left with the impression that most of the series' subjects staged their own portraits with focus, reflection and determination. How, then, did the E/east Germans present their 'niches'? The series projects a heterogeneous picture, highlighting on the one hand significant social, cultural and economic differences within the group selected, and on the other, a stark contrast between the relative prosperity and diversity displayed in many of the chosen private spaces and the often dilapidated and neglected streetscapes of well-known images of public spaces often seen in films and GDR photography of the 1980s.[4]

Studying the portraits from the vantage point of 2011, the most striking element is the lack of a unifying image of the GDR. The photographs show a willingness on the part of the subjects to shape their private spaces as the setting for their distinct individuality, and this notion of agency is confirmed through their active participation in the production process. While most family portraits are dominated by a round table in the foreground, bringing the family members together, different priorities are shown through the objects in the background, most often books, musical instruments, framed art or photographs, personal mementos, furniture or objects relating to the person's profession (see Figures 12.1 and 12.2). Many of the pictures differ from media representations of

Figure 12.1 Familie Brun: Marcel Brun, 59, Schriftsteller; Ingrid Brun, 40, Lektorin; Stephan Brun, 11, Schüler. Copyright: Bernd Lasdin.

Figure 12.2 Familie Helminiak: Carsta Helminiak, 24, Wirtschaftskaufmann; Sebastian Helminiak, 3. Copyright: Bernd Lasdin.

the GDR today in that they do not contain objects that allow the contemporary spectator to place the image clearly as one depicting the GDR *Alltag*. Importantly, in most images, the GDR specificity is not contained in the material world exhibited, but arises from the contradictions and tensions produced by the image's juxtaposition with the texts, which, through reference to social issues such as gender, family and work, take on a political dimension. If compared to Margit Emmerich's project *Wohnzimmer* (*Living Room*) of 1977 or Christian Borchert's *Familienportraits* (*Family Portraits*) of the early 1980s, similarities are clearly visible. In 1977 we already see the differentiation of society in terms of social status, education and corresponding individualisation. By the end of the 1980s, this trend had intensified: the differences had become more noticeable, fashions had changed, and living rooms were presented by their inhabitants as a reflection of their personal interests and values, often deliberately different from 'typical' living rooms and from official descriptions of GDR life.

Lasdin's *Zeitenwende* project does not primarily attempt to contribute to GDR memory discourse, but rather focuses on processes of social change to highlight breaks and continuities between the past and the present. The portraits do not try to recreate the GDR *Alltag* of the past; instead they capture one moment of the present. Nevertheless, the volume's method of juxtaposing the early portraits with the post-*Wende* images initiates memory processes and thus draws attention to and questions dominant positions of GDR memory discourse on several levels. First, even though the series of images covers roughly the same time frame for all the portraits' subjects, the images present a picture of a heterogeneous experience of the *Wende* which undermines general assumptions and myths of post-unification discourse, such as that the material world of the GDR disappeared overnight, or that the immense social changes affected the entire population to the same degree. Rather, most photographs suggest that the exhibited life models include determination as well as resistance to change. For example, ten years after the first photographs were taken, some subjects imitate the original pose at the same, unchanged location. In other images, changes in living standards and in the material environment seem deliberately emphasised and performed for the spectator while – at the same time – the accompanying texts ignore, question or even negate the individuals' embrace of consumer society. One such example shows the striking transformation of an outdated apartment into a room filled with antiquities, which is commented with the words 'Life goes on – getting worse' (Lasdin, 1998: 25).[5]

The private sphere is thus presented as a primary site of social activity where individuals constantly reflect on, determine and express the terms and level of their engagement with society. Second, unlike other media representations of GDR history, in *Zeitenwende* the experience of change is not tied to historical caesurae that have been established in public discourses. Rather, the portraits are snapshots of a moment in an individual life at a randomly chosen point in time. They reference important economic, social and cultural developments, but the evaluation of these changes has to be supplied by the viewers themselves, who look at the images within the context of their own (visual) memories and in comparison to dominant narratives of collective memory. A picture emerges of the niche that emphasises instances of *Eigen-Sinn*, highlights contradictions and disjunctures between individual and collective experiences and thus questions the notion of the unification process as a linear and coherent narrative of inexorable progress and modernisation.

Exhibiting the niche

With unification and the GDR's relegation to history, the East German niche has been re-created countless times in museums that attempt to put the history of the everyday on display. As early as 1993, museologists declared that the GDR belongs in the museum and that public institutions are necessary to describe social change within overarching contexts (Flacke, 1993). However, narrating GDR history in public museums has proved to be a contentious enterprise. Public museums, due to their educational mandate, try to provide useful future-oriented national narratives, authenticated through the museum's scientific methodology and its status as a public memory institution. Yet potential museum visitors will have widely differing experiences and expectations, and any attempt to narrate German post-war history inclusively, yet critically, remains difficult.[6] Even the museum's focus on the material, seemingly objective world of the GDR niche is seen as problematic; while, according to Scheunemann (2009), the scholarly attention to the political, social and cultural institutions of the GDR has provided important insights into the complexities of GDR society, the museal representation of GDR history has not kept pace with academic work and remains unsatisfactory as public museums either fail to capture these complexities or ignore GDR history entirely. This reluctance of public museums, in particular in the new *Bundesländer* (federal states), to include GDR history in their permanent exhibitions reflects the problematic transformation of diverse experiential memories into more homogenous forms of cultural memory.

Private museums, on the other hand, devote large spaces to the *Alltagsgeschichte* of the GDR, and during the last 20 years at least 15 private GDR museums have come into existence (see Chapter 8). Following a general trend in museum practices to increasingly favour experiential and affective approaches, they focus on the GDR's material world and aim at interactivity and entertainment. However, often these exhibitions are not professionally curated, nor do they attempt to present their collections and artefacts within their historical contexts. Therefore, instead of recognising them as valid contributions to a critical historiography, historians often see them as a tool to compensate for the experience of loss through the rediscovery of known objects (Scheunemann, 2009: 5), a process which allows the legitimisation and affirmation of individual biographies, but prevents critical analysis. Equally problematic is that the short period of time between the remembered past and the present has resulted in a musealisation of the material world which is partly still in use. By including objects in exhibitions whose value is still determined through their owner's everyday use, the object does not clearly signify the past as different from the experience of the present. The owners themselves are thus turned into exhibition pieces, and the transformation from present to past is institutionally predetermined. Therefore, this process is seen by some as 'culturally destructive' (Kuhn and Ludwig, 1997: 21).

The 1991 exhibition *Alltagsleben in der DDR* (*Everyday Life in the GDR*) at the Rheinische Freilichtmuseum may serve as an early example of the difficulties of musealising the GDR. For this exhibition, curators of the museum bought the complete living room and kitchen of an east German family which they then meticulously reconstructed in the museum space (Thomas-Ziegler, 1993). They hoped that this focus on the real living circumstances of one named family would have a greater emotional impact on visitors than statistics and figures, and that it would trigger reflection in order to help dispel prejudices. At the opening of the exhibition, the family who had donated the artefacts and accompanying personal documents appeared in their former living room, now located in a west German museum. The exhibition enraged both west and east Germans, albeit for different reasons, and frustrated the donor family, who felt misunderstood. Some visitors thought that this living room, which looked not too dissimilar to some west German homes, must have been a misrepresentation of the everyday life of an economically inferior place. Others objected to the perceived sell-out of this family, to their degradation to museum objects and to the exhibition space itself, which – through the use of grid-like separators between the rooms – could be read as a prison metaphor. Despite efforts to find a representative GDR family and to recreate their niche as authentically as possible, the exhibition did not fulfil the expectations of visitors who complained that 'the exhibition does not show the average living conditions of GDR citizens' (Thomas-Ziegler, 1993: 85). Misjudging preconceptions of their audience, the curators failed to identify what would have been accepted by their audience as 'typical' and 'representative' for the GDR everyday experience.

Since then many other museums have chosen a similar *mise-en-scène* approach to exhibiting the niche, often incorporating interactive aspects where visitors can enter re-created rooms and open drawers or sit on sofas. While these exhibitions often prove to be popular with the general public, the same reservations as mentioned above have been voiced by historians and museum experts (Scheunemann, 2009). These installations fail to convince them because they only intend to show rather than explain. They allow visitors to fill in the gaps based on their own memories and knowledge without relying on the institutional guidance demanded by Flacke. Even if carefully researched, the assemblages of objects remain strangely lifeless, first because the exhibited artefacts have not yet acquired an auratic presence (not least due to the fact that the objects can be handled because they are easily replaceable), and second because the *mise-en-scène* cannot display the essential force of the niche – deliberate social activity which gave shape to the unique personal experience of history.[7] If we assume that GDR niches were shaped by their inhabitants' desire to distance themselves from the typical, then this lack of critical approval in museums is not surprising, as museums of *Alltagsgeschichte* in general aim to display the typical and representative of a given period rather than the particular.

Musealising the niche on television screens

In their exhibition practices, private museums in particular increasingly rely on experiential and affective approaches that are often borrowed from the cinema. Film and television in turn have contributed significantly to the musealisation of the GDR. This convergence between the museum and television is not a new development. The museum and television are closely linked and share many representational and institutional practices: as visual media, they address the spectator through scopic regimes of representation and act as public institutions that preserve the past in images and organise it into coherent and often legitimising narratives contributing to the construction of national identity. An emphasis on emotional and accessible storytelling and the shift from history to memory are not only characteristic of television's approach to representing history, but have increasingly become priorities of museum practices. However, despite this convergence, the traditional notion of the museum as an antidote to trivial and fleeting visual entertainment offered by television is still very pervasive. Although both media present constructed versions of history and favour narrative clarity, the museum still makes a greater claim to historical 'truth' based on its perceived scientific authority and the transparency of its sources and research methodology. In contrast, television's preference for verisimilitude, accessibility and narrative realism are seen to be problematic, as the visual historical narrative avoids ambiguity and self-reflexivity and attempts to conceal the processes of representation.[8] This critical stance towards televised history finds its expression in the term musealisation, which, when used to assess media representations of the GDR, denotes processes concerning the preservation, collection and exhibition of images and objects outside of the museum space and on screen. Especially in relation to television, it mainly implies the de- and re-contextualisation of images and their commodification resulting in the distortion and misrepresentation of history. Therefore, critics often doubt the ability and willingness of televised history to contribute to the mediation of historical knowledge in meaningful ways. On the contrary, teenagers' frequently bemoaned ignorance of the GDR is often directly blamed on distorted and trivialised media images (see, for example, Flohr and Wensierski, 2007).

Nevertheless, in the run-up to the twentieth anniversary of the fall of the Wall, countless TV productions focused on the history of the GDR, such as: *Das Wunder von Berlin* (*The Miracle of Berlin*, Richter, 2008, ZDF), which tells the story of a young man who, under pressure from the Stasi, leaves his punk friends behind and experiences the *Wende* from inside the NVA; *Jenseits der Mauer* (*On the other Side of the Wall*, Fromm, 2009, ARD), a film about the forced adoption of a girl whose parents had fled to the West in the seventies; *Wir sind das Volk – Liebe kennt keine Grenzen* (*We are the People – Love knows no Boundaries*, Berger, 2008, Sat1), in which three narrative strands are interwoven and follow several people who oppose the GDR regime. Like many television programmes broadcast in 2009, all three films focus on the last few months of the GDR's existence. In contrast to many others, however, these three films were received positively in the media and were especially praised for their bottom-up approach to narrating everyday GDR history and the events of 1989. Critics mainly applauded the films for their 'authenticity and close reflection of reality' which, they thought, set them apart from the usual clichés served up by prime time television. On the basis of these qualities, commentators found the films eminently suitable 'as an introduction for a younger generation [...], that did not live through this period' (Sternburg, 2008). When the ARD production *Jenseits der Mauer* premiered at a special event at the Gewandhaus in Leipzig in the presence of the city's political and cultural dignitaries, it was introduced as follows: 'Remembering is necessary [...] in order to recall realities of the past and to tell the younger generation about it. Nothing is better suited than film to evoking the living conditions of the past' (Beermann, 2009).

These comments highlight the importance afforded to the visual media's contribution to memory discourses. As the films target a generation that has no embodied social memories of their own, but which has to learn about the past (Assmann, 2008: 52), television is accepted as a tool to facilitate the emergence of a 'disembodied and re-embodied trans-generational memory' (ibid.: 56) through its use of familiar visual signs and affectively charged narratives. Thus, for their visualisation of the East German niches, the directors relied on the image archives of the GDR that have grown as part of the post-*Wende* discourse and follow established patterns in composing GDR *mises-en-scène*. However, through their appropriation and repurposing of traditional museum practices the film-makers achieved two important goals. First, it allowed them to claim a greater degree of authenticity and thus lift their interpretations out of the realm of lightweight entertainment. Second, it resulted in a more homogeneous version of the 'niche' that eliminated contradictory elements and offered younger viewers the narrative closure that the *Wende* experience had withheld from the previous generation.

The producers of such films went to great lengths to assure the spectator of the museum-worthiness of their material by insisting on its status as a closed chapter which allows 'objective' study. The films' stories are situated firmly in a distant and mysterious past and fix the spectators' point of view from the outside. The trailers and previews promise new insights and previously unknown facts which have been unearthed through diligent historical work. This claim to historical accuracy and authenticity is supported by the contexts within which the films were shown. When *Jenseits der Mauer* was broadcast, for example, it was followed by a documentary presenting research about forced adoptions in the GDR. Similarly, *Wir sind das Volk* was shown on Sat 1 together with the documentation *Freiheit! Das Ende der DDR*, which presented a collection of witness interviews. For *Das Wunder von Berlin*, ZDF (2009) developed an elaborate interactive website with the help of historians and museum curators. It invited visitors to enter the space behind the Wall and, as in a museum, to explore different artefacts, documents and themes at their leisure. They could revisit scenes from the film, take in additional information and expand their background knowledge. Through the use of maps, the information was organised into clear thematic threads which could be followed up in more detail. These themes were tied to authentic places which were thus confirmed as sites of memory in written explanations. Elements of a more universal nature, which were not deemed representative of the unique GDR experience, were left out, and the main characteristics of this past were connected to scenes from the film. Just as in a museum, where the artefact is evidence and hypothesis at the same time, the film itself became an exhibition object and automatically commanded a greater degree of authenticity. However, through this juxtaposition of film scenes with historic places on the website, the richness of the *mise-en-scène* was reduced to a mere illustration of the 'real facts' of history, which were verified through the authority of the curator. Instead of increasing the viewer's autonomy, the prescribed routes on the map disciplined the spectator, restricted potential interpretative avenues and so guided the viewer to a preferred reading of history.

These meta-textual materials already point to an understanding of GDR *Alltag* that differs from Gaus' description. The film-makers clearly reject the notion of an apolitical niche and insist that authenticity means a GDR *Alltag* controlled by totalitarian oppression. Introducing the documentary *Freiheit! Das Ende der DDR*, which was broadcast together with *Wir sind das Volk*, Sat1 producer Korth explained: 'Of the GDR, there were only official images that had been approved of by the state [...]. The Stasi, for example, was invisible, as were the remand prisons. There were no authentic images of everyday life' (Sat1-Dokumentation). Comments like these highlight the role that the teams of all three films assign to their work in the process of producing and mediating historical knowledge. However, the ambition to fill the perceived gap and generate 'authentic' images of the GDR either shows a striking lack of reflection on their medium's inherent inability to directly reflect the original and authentic or, more likely, it hints at the film-makers' interpretation of the concept of 'authenticity': although they claim to offer an exact reconstruction of newly discovered historical facts, their main aim is the lifelike illustration of an agreed account of historical events and the re-creation of emotional experience through an encounter with the material world 'as it must have felt'. Therefore, while Lasdin's images of the private sphere mostly excluded visual elements with GDR specificity, it is these film-makers' goal to compose a world that corresponds to audiences' visual knowledge, which is shaped significantly by post-*Wende* discourse on television, and can be easily identified as belonging to the GDR past.

The films' representation of GDR spaces confirms the directors' interpretation of the niche as a realm shaped by and tied to the political system. Therefore, images of private spaces do not take up much room in comparison with encounters with police or demonstrations as, by its very everyday nature, the niche does not offer the desired excitement and emotional involvement. Instead, the films' iconography is dominated by public or institutional spaces such as prison cells, Stasi offices, army barracks and church halls, which are populated by police in riot gear, demonstrators, and Stasi agents spying on individuals in the public and semi-public sphere.

The private spaces we do see are either cramped apartments carefully composed in brown, grey and yellow hues or they are hiding places in gloomy basements and backyards marked by decades of neglect. The films offer a reading of the GDR *Alltag* which emphasises the repressive political structures and their permeation of all spheres of life. In contrast to Gaus' version of the niche, the private spaces depicted do not serve the films' characters as a refuge from the oppressive system or as an arena for social activity. On the contrary, the niche is constantly observed, raided, or in the form of family members or friends, infiltrated by the Stasi. Even seemingly innocent objects, such as private photographs or letters, connect the character's past to some form of Stasi activity, for example a snapshot taken by a friend who, in the end, turns out to be a Stasi spy (in *Das Wunder von Berlin*). While in Lasdin's images the *mise-en-scène* allows the spectator to discover traces of the inhabitant's agency and multiple layers of personality, here it stands in contrast to the individualism and rebellion of the main protagonists. Rather than a visual manifestation of the protagonists' *Eigen-Sinn*, the private spaces in the films illustrate the GDR population's inability to determine their own lives, and both the uniformity of the niches and their decrepitude and compromised privacy serve to explain the characters' desire to flee to the West. If the niche contains any objects of value, these are not tied to their social or cultural lives in the GDR, but are often West German consumer products, such as a pair of jeans or an old Volkswagen car.

In order to create a feeling of claustrophobia, fear, oppression, material backwardness and stagnation, the interiors of private spaces in the GDR do not show any change even if the storylines span almost 20 years. Often the camera lingers for a moment on an object or a product brand that has acquired a special meaning in GDR memory discourse and will be recognised by a viewer familiar with post-*Wende* films, such as a telephone or a Stern cassette recorder (see Figure 12.3). It almost seems as if the exaggerated and satirised world of *Sonnenallee* (*Sun Alley*, Haußmann, 1999) has become the 'authentic' accepted picture of the GDR. Appropriating the museum's encyclopaedic approach to representing history, the films condense all the visual elements which have become markers of GDR life in complex post-*Wende* discourse into one 'representative' tableau, which contains several layers of time and is clearly identifiable as the past.

Although the films' visual construction of the GDR returns to well-known patterns of representation and embraces a simplistic notion of

Figure 12.3 Reconstructing the material world of the GDR. Screen shot from *Jenseits der Mauer* (Fromm, 2009, Ziegler Film GmbH + Co.).

recent history, the films do contain an additional element which might have contributed to their favourable reception. All of the films use original footage taken from television at the time of the fall of the Wall as part of the diegesis, and despite the different stories, all of the texts include the same images: Genscher's speech at the Prague embassy, a group of people running across the border in Hungary, and Schabowski shuffling his papers and announcing the opening of the Wall. With their provenance and status as authentic historical documents established through continuous institutional repetition, these images serve as metonyms for the emotional experience of all the different characters who are watching them on television. In fact, all film narratives put enormous emphasis on the role of the West German media's coverage of the autumn demonstrations. With television sets in East German niches tuned to West German channels, the media images of the historical events provided East Germans with the courage and information needed to succeed. The significance of the television image is repeatedly established through parallel editing and *mise-en-scène*, and then reinforced through the dialogue, such as in *Wir sind das Volk*, in which West German television producers watch their own broadcast and anticipate the events thinking, 'When they see that in the East, twice that many will be on the streets next week'. In this way, the television image that mediates the historical event transforms into an authentic artefact. And, as in a museum environment, the exhibited artefacts are labelled, explained and interpreted from the vantage point of the present for the benefit of the spectator who cannot rely on personal memories to make sense of the past. Apart from celebrating the medium of television itself and affirming the power of the image, the films thus construct the 'peaceful revolution' as a joint German project. In this way, they offer a palatable founding myth of the new Germany based on visual evidence.

In competition with the institution of the museum, television thus claims a stake in the institutional dissemination of historical knowledge and contributes more effectively to the musealisation of the GDR niche. By stripping the niche of its contradictory functions and heterogeneous appearance and through the elimination of the niche as a site of individual autonomy and engagement with society, the films do not have to confront or explain the complexities of social interaction in the GDR and are able to narrate the end of the GDR as the inevitable and logical conclusion to the Cold War. Adopting museal strategies, the film-makers select visual elements to re-imagine the GDR niche which distinguish the narrated past clearly from the present, and which have already become easily recognisable symbols in the memory discourse. The films do not aim to convince their audiences of the validity of their version of history, but rather offer a visual representation of a 'settled' account of history for which audience agreement is taken as a given. By bringing their simplified, generic niches to life with affectively charged narratives, the films avoid ambiguities and irritations that might lessen the emotional impact or complicate questions of historical agency; thus they allow a new generation to experience history from a safe distance and to acquire emotional knowledge of a past they did not live through. In response to the public museum's hesitation in narrating GDR *Alltagsgeschichte*, television appropriates its institutional mandate and reconfirms its role as a dominant force in cultural memory discourse as it facilitates and forces the transformation of complex and contradictory social memories into a more homogenised and institutionally driven version of history.

Notes

1. While the transmission of knowledge has always been contingent upon different forms of media, increasingly the construction of historical consciousness and cultural knowledge is shaped by images and the visual media. The increasing importance of images on the one hand and the media on the other in the organisation and transmission of knowledge has been theorised by scholars from different disciplines, for example, Jay (2002) on the 'visual turn', Lundby (2009) on mediatisation and Friesen and Hug (2009) on 'the mediatic turn'.

2. The term is mainly used in German as its English equivalents "stubbornness" or "obstinacy" are not deemed to capture the concept sufficiently. The term 'Eigen-Sinn' was coined by Alf Lüdke and usually describes individual determination and agency in the negotiations between private and public spheres.
3. Lasdin's work can also serve as an example for the (still continuing) difficulties and contradictions which arise when GDR artists and their work are evaluated. While Lasdin's work is known internationally and has often been received positively, his involvement with the Stasi in the 1980s continues to impact on the way in which his work is viewed in his home town of Neubrandenburg.
4. See, for example, photographs of Halle streetscapes in the eighties by Helga Paris or, in cinema, images of Berlin in *Solo Sunny* (1980) by Konrad Wolf.
5. 'Es geht immer noch – schlimmer.'
6. The debate about the *Freiheits- und Einheitsdenkmal* may serve as one example for the difficulties in narrating recent German history (see Chapter 10).
7. There are significant differences in these museums' aims, approaches and educational ambition. Some museums collect indiscriminately and present objects seemingly without any concept, while others try to alleviate some of these problems (for example the 'Haus der Geschichte' in Wittenberg insists on guided tours to provide context and prohibits visitors from handling the exhibits).
8. For more detailed discussions of history on television, see, for example, the special issue on the topic in the *European Journal of Cultural Studies*, 10 (1), or L. Engell (2009).

References

Assmann, A. (2008) 'Transformations between History and Memory', *Social Research*, 75 (1), 49–72.

Beermann, J. (2009) *Grußwort zur Premiere von "Jenseits der Mauer"*, Sächsische Staatskanzlei, www.89-90.sachsen.de/13920.htm [date accessed 15 April 2011].

Betts, P. (2010) *Within Walls. Private Life in the German Democratic Republic* (Oxford: Oxford University Press).

Engell, L. (2009) '"Virtual History": Geschichte als Fernsehen', *Zeithistorische Forschungen*, 6 (3), www.zeithistorische-forschungen.de/16126041-Engell-3-2009 [date accessed 12 November 2009].

Faulenbach, B. (1997) 'Probleme der Musealisierung der DDR und ihrer Alltagsgeschichte' in G. Kuhn and A. Ludwig (eds) *Alltag und soziales Gedächtnis: Die DDR-Objektkultur und ihre Musealisierung* (Hamburg: Ergebnisse), pp. 26–41.

Flacke, M. (1993) 'Alltagsobjekte der ehemaligen DDR. Zur Sammeltätigkeit des DHM' in B. Faulenbach and F. J. Jelich (eds) *Probleme der Musealisierung der doppelten deutschen Nachkriegsgeschichte* (Essen: Klartext), pp. 57–62.

Flohr, M. and P. Wensierski (2007) 'Honeckers paradiesische Diktatur', *Spiegel Online*, 9 November, http://www.spiegel.de/schulspiegel/wissen/0,1518,516534,00.html [date accessed 14 November 2009].

Friesen, N. and T. Hug (2009) 'The Mediatic Turn: Exploring Concepts for Media Pedagogy' in K. Lundby (ed.) *Mediatization: Concepts, Changes, Consequences* (New York: Lang), pp. 61–81.

Fulbrook, M. (1995) *Anatomy of a Dictatorship* (Oxford: Oxford University Press).
Gaus, G. (1983) *Wo Deutschland liegt. Eine Ortsbestimmung* (Hamburg: Hoffmann und Campe).
Jay, M. (2002) 'That Visual Turn. The Advent of Visual Culture', *Journal of Visual Culture*, 1 (1), 87–92.
Kuhn, G. and A. Ludwig (1997) 'Sachkultur und DDR-Alltag. Versuch einer Annäherung' in G. Kuhn and A. Ludwig (eds) *Alltag und soziales Gedächtnis: Die DDR-Objektkultur und ihre Musealisierung* (Hamburg: Ergebnisse), pp. 13–24.
Lasdin, B. (1998) *Zeitenwende. Portraits aus Ostdeutschland 1986–1998* (Bremen: Edition Temmen).
Lasdin, B. (2009) *Zeitenwenden. Zwanzig Jahre im Leben eines Menschen* (Friedland: Steffen).
Lundby, K. (ed.) (2009) *Mediatization: Concepts, Changes, Consequences* (New York: Lang).
Palmowski, J. (2002) 'Between Conformity and Eigen-Sinn: New Approaches to GDR History', *German History*, 20 (4), 494–502.
Richthofen, E. von (2009) *Bringing Culture to the Masses. Control, Compromise and Participation in the GDR* (New York: Berghahn).
Sat1-Dokumentation: 'Freiheit! Das Ende der DDR' (2008), Digitalfernsehen, 29 September, http://www.digitalfernsehen.de/Sat-1-Dokumentation-Freiheit-Das-Ende-der-DDR.news_601102.0.html [date accessed 10 May 2010].
Scheunemann, J. (2009) 'Gehört die DDR ins Museum? Beobachtungen zur Musealisierung der sozialistischen Vergangenheit', *Gerbergasse 18*, 55 (4), http://www.geschichtswerkstatt-jena.de/index.php?id= a55 [date accessed 10 May 2010].
Sternburg, J. von (2008) 'Die nächste Generation', *Frankfurter Rundschau*, 26 January, 39.
Thomas-Ziegler, S. (1993) 'Alltagsleben in der DDR – Eine Ausstellung des Rheinischen Freilichtmuseums und Landesmuseums für Volkskunde in Kommern' in B. Faulenbach and F. J. Jelich (eds) *Probleme der Musealisierung der doppelten deutschen Nachkriegsgeschichte* (Essen: Klartext), pp. 85–91.
ZDF (2009) http://wundervonberlin.zdf.de/ZDFde/inhalt/24/0,1872,7125208,00.html?dr=1 [date accessed 10 May 2010].

13

Memories, Secrets and Lies: The Emotional Legacy of the GDR in Christian Schwochow's *Novemberkind* (2008)[1]

Owen Evans

The fall of the Berlin Wall heralded unalloyed optimism for the future in Germany, and yet, with the benefit of hindsight, the euphoric reactions to the events of 9 November 1989 masked an array of fundamental problems that would gradually start to manifest themselves. Many commentators speculated that the merging of the old and new *Bundesländer* (Federal states) would require a generation to bed in due to the speed of social, political and economic union, forecasts which themselves seem overly optimistic now. In truth, nobody could have imagined the depth of trauma that lay at the heart of the GDR, or what secrets and lies lay buried, the vast majority of which were recorded meticulously in the Stasi files that were eventually opened up in 1991. Faced with his dossier, British historian Timothy Garton Ash (1997: 10) remarked: 'What a gift to memory is a Stasi file. Far better than Proust's madeleine.' While that may be true for Garton Ash, who spent much time in the GDR but whose life and livelihood were never truly controlled by the state, for so many people the opening of the files, and the discoveries therein, proved traumatic and led to irrevocable family breakdowns. The extent to which people informed on their loved ones was shocking; in some cases, one wonders whether ignorance might not have been the better gift.

The corrosive effects on family lives of long-hidden secrets coming to light is central to Christian Schwochow's debut film *Novemberkind* (*November Child*, 2008). It recounts the story of Inga, a young librarian in the Mecklenburg town Malchow, who believes her mother, Anne, to have drowned in the Baltic in 1980 when she was a baby. Raised by her maternal grandparents and a beloved member of the community, Inga is blissfully unaware of the truth – that Anne abandoned her baby to escape to the West, to Konstanz – until Robert von der Mühlen, a west German creative writing professor, arrives in Malchow. Anne had briefly been his student and written about her guilt at having fled without her daughter. Captivated by her tale, Robert resolves to locate the young woman in order to check its veracity. He unleashes an emotional chain reaction as Inga slowly begins to realise that she is enmeshed in a conspiracy of silence within the community. She embarks upon a quest to find her mother and the truth. Unbeknownst to Inga, Robert plans to write her story, recording her quest but failing to reveal how much of the truth he knows.

In some respects, the story recalls Wolfgang Becker's *Good Bye Lenin!* (2003), where Alex eventually learns the truth behind his father's escape to the West and his mother's resultant breakdown. Schwochow, however, provides a much more searching archaeology of the secrets and lies that families harbour, offering nothing of the lighter relief that is found at the heart of Becker's effervescent film. *Novemberkind* is shot through with a sombre mood, its aesthetics marked by subdued autumnal colours and reinforced by the sparing use of a melancholic soundtrack. While Becker provides an effective snapshot of the dramatic pace of change as the Wall fell and the readjustments demanded of those swept up in events leading up to reunification, *Novemberkind* tenders a more detached contemporary appraisal of the legacy of the GDR, revealing how it remains problematic more than a generation on from the *Wende*. The painful memories have not faded; on the contrary, there are still many instances where awkward memories are being awoken or contested, and this is a matter for Germany as a whole.

In this respect, it is the star discourse encircling Anna Maria Mühe, the talented young actress who plays both female protagonists, which deepens the film's impact. Her success in tackling this demanding double role is made all the more poignant by the fact that her parents, the actors Jenny Gröllmann and Ulrich Mühe, became embroiled in a bitter public row. Shortly before their untimely deaths from cancer in 2006 and 2007 respectively, Mühe, justifiably renowned for his performance in Florian Henckel von Donnersmarck's *Das Leben der Anderen* (*The Lives of Others*, 2006), accused Gröllmann, a major GDR star, of having been a Stasi informant. In the media coverage of her dual role and the inevitable questions about her family that accompanied it, Mühe was naturally defensive about the tragic feud, noting that 'nothing will ever be written again about my parents without this reference [to the

Stasi row]. And I just do not want to take sides or to be a referee' (Beier and Beyer, 2008: 187).[2] Nevertheless, it is impossible to watch her performance without being struck by her physical resemblance to her parents, and thus reminded of their sad story. In view of *Novemberkind*'s thematic thrust, it is inevitable that one will reflect upon the impact of family secrets and contested memories within her own life. Mühe herself concedes that Schwochow wrote the film with her in mind, intimating that the fledgling director was not unaware of the impact his casting would have. *Novemberkind* thus articulates a particularly poignant German–German story and marks a significant contribution to contemporary memory debates in the reunified country a generation on from the fall of the Wall.

The present chapter will analyse *Novemberkind* and its representation of how the GDR's painful legacy continues to be felt in the new Germany. It will examine the way in which Inga endeavours to come to terms with her past and dislodges long-dormant memories in those she encounters on her quest to locate Anne. In this way, the film functions as a meditation on the role, and workings, of cultural memory within society and the debates it provokes about how communities should engage with the past. Annette Kuhn (2010: 303) has observed that cinema is 'peculiarly capable of bringing together personal experiences and larger systems and processes of cultural memory'. *Novemberkind* offers an apposite example of this conflation of memories, not just in its fictional narrative, but also its inherent authenticity deriving from the wounds inflicted by the GDR on Anna Maria Mühe's family long after the collapse of the Wall.

Novemberkind provides a sensitive depiction of individuals coming to terms with the East German past, and the differing impacts this *Aufarbeitung* (reworking of the past) has on their lives. Where it differs refreshingly from many of the earlier films to tackle this topic is in its refusal to adopt the now traditional pattern of reducing the GDR to the series of binaries which Silke Arnold-de Simine and Susannah Radstone identify as characteristic of representations of the country's past (see Chapter 1). By decoupling itself from this dominant reductionist approach, *Novemberkind* allows for a more differentiated engagement with this past, while also underlining the story's relevance for reunified Germany as a whole.[3] Unsurprisingly, Schwochow dismissed classifications of his film as an *Ostfilm*, and many critics cited his family background as evidence of its pan-German qualities. Born on the island of Rügen and raised in East Berlin before moving with his parents to

Hanover in 1989, the director moved back to Berlin as an adult and felt uncertain how to define his identity:

> What am I today, after eighteen years of German unity? A unified German? Is there such a thing? I fondly remember *Ferienlager* [GDR holiday camps], Spreewald gherkins and all the amusing customs and rituals, but the GDR was more than that. But what exactly? A country made up of those who worked for the Stasi on one hand and those who resisted on the other, as films today suggest? Yes, for sure. But not just that. Today we see the terrible and the curious things, and the past is reduced to an event. A picture of history emerges that will at some point have nothing more in common with the GDR.
>
> (cit. in Friedrich, 2008)

This personal perspective permeates the film, especially as Schwochow and his mother, Heide, a former GDR radio journalist, wrote the screenplay together.

Despite any protestations to the contrary, however, the film's impetus derives unequivocally from the GDR. Significantly, the film opens with a flashback sequence of the hunt for a Russian deserter, Jurij, in Malchow in 1980, which introduces the spectator to Anne, who ultimately finds, hides and falls in love with the young soldier. It unfolds as a tale of *Republikflucht* – escape from East Germany – as the young couple flee via Poland to the West, leaving Anne's baby daughter behind. Nevertheless, the ripples from these events are felt in contemporary Germany, underlining how this collision of past and present is not simply a matter for east Germans. This impression is reinforced structurally both by the continual narrative interplay between events in 1980, relayed in flashback, and the present day, as well as the dual role played by Anna Maria Mühe. When we first see Inga, she is plunging naked into a freezing lake, which anticipates Anne's grief-stricken attempt to drown herself in Lake Constance later in the film, and both characters leave Malchow to find happiness, albeit in radically different circumstances. Underpinned by structural and aesthetic parallels, the two periods sit in apposition throughout the film, in constant dialogue with each other, reflecting the way memory is animated by the interaction of the past on the present and the present on the past.

Inga becomes the agent for this dialogue. Stimulated by Robert's sudden incursion in her life, she embarks upon a journey to find the truth about what happened to Anne. She begins to free herself from the false memories that have been grafted onto her by her grandparents and perpetuated by friends and the community as a whole. Demanding why Kerstin, her mother's best friend, and the mother of her own best friend, Steffi, would want to let Inga believe her mother drowned in an accident in the Baltic, she is told: 'We just wanted to protect you'. This response is echoed later by her grandparents. Inga's quest to find her mother forces all those who have conspired to keep the truth from her to confront long-repressed memories. She interacts with these individuals – her grandparents, Kerstin, Jurij, Alexander, Robert – stimulating painful recollections in flashback for those with whom she comes into contact. This narrative device allows the spectator to begin to piece together the story of what happened, just as Inga is doing. In effect, therefore, both protagonist and spectator are undertaking research into memory.

This investigative engagement mirrors the methodological approach to memory that Patricia Hogwood proposes (see Chapter 2). She argues that political scientists are less interested in the veracity of memory than its impact on issues of social identity and behaviour. The inhabitants of Malchow construct a narrative to explain away Anne's flight to the West with Jurij in order to conform with state demands and be allowed to continue leading their lives untrammelled. This 'official' history gradually creates false memories of what happened, which are in turn inculcated into Inga and become a retrospective justification for their own complicity of silence. The response of Inga's grandparents to their daughter's escape, in particular, sheds light on the compromises people were forced, or chose, to make in the GDR. Inga's interrogation of her grandparents uncovers that they severed ties with their daughter to obviate a threat to her grandfather's job as the school headmaster. 'Did you sign something?' Inga demands accusingly, and the discomfited reaction her question elicits hints at the Stasi's interference. By representing what is remembered, but perhaps more importantly in this context what is suppressed, *Novemberkind*'s importance as a memory text documenting the problematic GDR legacy in the new Germany is reinforced.

The avoidance of any schematic representation of victimhood lends the film an important dimension as a more nuanced engagement with the GDR past. Compared to *The Lives of Others*, with its melodramatic representation of East Germany as an *Unrechtsstaat* (illegitimate state), *Novemberkind* generally adopts a more allusive approach to the depredations of life under the socialist dictatorship. Both protagonists might be seen as victims of circumstances generated by the GDR's repressive nature, yet the film reveals how much more complex, and convoluted, the reality was than the traditional schemata imposed on many GDR, and post-GDR, narratives which have tended to rely primarily on polarised absolutes. As Hogwood underlines, the majority of GDR citizens did not engage in public dissent and eked out an existence based on finding accommodation with the state by various means. She ponders, therefore, whether restrictions on travel constitute victimhood in the same way as imprisonment or persecution by the Stasi, for example. Certainly, there is little evidence that Anne's life was impinged upon unduly by the state *before* she encounters Jurij hiding in an outbuilding and falls in love. It is this unexpected personal connection, and the subsequent act of *Republikflucht*, which place her in opposition to the state and expose her parents to pressure from the authorities.

Novemberkind conveys with great subtlety the complex interweaving of state victimhood with the simple expediency of needing to live life in the GDR by negotiating a pathway between conformity and dissent.[4] Inga understandably feels betrayed by those close to her, yet it could be argued that the family concoct the story of her mother's accident to shelter her from the traumatic realisation that she was abandoned. Conversely, the lies might be adjudged simply as selfish pragmatism on the part of Inga's grandparents, lies that were much easier to perpetuate following the GDR's demise and Anne's continued absence. In this way, the film articulates a subtle warning against hasty condemnation of the characters' actions, demanding instead careful consideration of the circumstances and sensitivity towards the complicated nature of the GDR *Alltag* (everyday life).

Inga is an innocent victim of the ramifications of her mother's flight and the subsequent pressure on her grandparents, and the community at large, to expunge her mother from memory; this eradication is achieved, of course, by means of the false memory narrativised and implanted within the young girl. The poignancy of Anne's fate serves to temper Inga's sense of rejection as she comes to terms with the truth. Her mother's grief and bitter self-excoriation for abandoning her sick baby precipitate a mental collapse and suicide. The psychiatrist who treated her in the asylum explains: 'She suffered from the consequences of her escape. She wanted to cut herself off from the traumatic experience. She didn't want to have to remember any longer.' Inga is appalled when he explains that he did not believe Anne would have the strength to take her own life. 'You gave up on her,' Inga replies, displaying not bitterness for her mother's rejection of her, but compassion for what her mother must have undergone. Ultimately, the inability to come to terms with the past destroyed Anne. The tragic irony is striking: Anne wanted desperately to expunge the memory of what she had done, while Inga has lived her life hitherto with a false memory.

As painful as coming to terms with the truth proves for Inga, the process appears nevertheless to facilitate the possibility of forgiveness and redemption that eluded her mother. Inga comes to understand how it must have felt for Anne to be separated from her daughter, rejected by her family and unable to return home, the anguish of which is encapsulated in the poem she writes and which is inscribed on her gravestone in Konstanz: 'No one teaches me to forget./Were there any greeting from home/And if you could search for me,/Then I would be able to hope,/Just a little.' At the graveside, Inga remarks sadly: 'It is actually just as it has always been. My mother is dead'. The key difference is that Inga's voyage to Konstanz has granted her greater understanding of what befell her mother, and the circumstances that prevented her from rescuing her daughter or coming to find her after the Wall had fallen. It is a tragic tale of the psychological damage the GDR could inflict upon its people.

Growing up shaped by a state-sanctioned lie, Inga can be seen as a victim of her family's pragmatism. In his study of autobiography, Paul John Eakin (1999: 109) underlines the 'interpersonal, relational dimension of identity formation' and stresses, in particular, the importance of the family as the 'key environment in the individual's formation [...] which serves as the community's primary conduit for the transmission of its cultural values' (ibid.: 85). While the family may embody a positive influence in many contexts, *Novemberkind* underlines how the state's desire to penetrate every nook and cranny in the GDR could distort normal relationships because of the Stasi's 'malign exercise of power' (Fulbrook, 2005: 241).[5] Much has been made of the GDR as a 'society of niches' (see Chapter 12), a collection of private spaces populated by family and close friends, where one could allegedly speak more openly and voice criticism, thereby alleviating the pressure of having to conform in public. However, opening the Stasi files quickly revealed that even such enclosed private spaces were not as inviolate as they seemed.

No matter what the motives may have been for the creation, and perpetuation, of the lie about her mother's accident within the family, it has a detrimental effect upon Inga's identity formation. As Eakin (1999: 117) notes, 'we can think of the child's sense of self as emerging within a crucible of family stories and cultural scripts', so Inga's realisation that her life hitherto has been grounded in a fiction is psychologically devastating. Her dismay and disorientation is affectingly realised by Mühe's beautifully nuanced performance, her expressive features conveying Inga's emotional turmoil as the truth of all she has known begins to unravel. At the end of *Novemberkind*, she embarks upon a second journey, this time in possession of her mother's writings, presumably in order to find herself and create a more stable sense of identity than her family and environment have hitherto allowed.

At the film's conclusion, Inga's life is in transition, shorn of all the trappings that link her to the past, save the notes of the mother she believed had died in 1980. At last she can begin to rewrite the past and correct the false memory she has been given. Hogwood argues that political scientists pay particular attention to phenomena such as regime change and democratic transition, and in this context perceive victimhood as a temporary phase and the prelude to change. She thus provides an interesting prism through which to interpret Inga's experiences. Although perhaps not a victim in the traditional sense of the majority of GDR film narratives, Inga has nevertheless been confronted with the psychological damage inflicted by the GDR on the lives of her family. Hogwood's argument (Chapter 2: 44) that victimhood such as Inga's is a transitory state also reinforces the sense of optimism that prevails at the film's conclusion, that 'the emerging post-GDR identity is essentially forward-looking'. Indeed, Hogwood maintains that the east Germans themselves will learn to adapt to life in the new Germany, empowered by 'a continuous process of selection and rejection of memories'. The dynamic of normalisation will not be driven by the politicians.

In the context of *Novemberkind*, Inga abandons the false memories grafted onto her, assimilating in their place the suppressed memories of those she encounters in her quest to come closer to her mother. Crucially, she now has access to her mother's 'memoirs', albeit in inchoate form, and can begin to construct a more accurate picture of the past. Her personal quest for identity in the unified Germany might be seen as metaphorical for east Germans as a whole, in their search for a post-GDR identity in the manner Hogwood envisages. The biography of the director, Christian Schwochow, lends additional weight to this reading, as someone, like both Inga and Mühe, born into the GDR, raised in the unified Germany, and yet still with an identity moulded in significant ways by those early experiences.

One final important aspect of Inga's quest is her role as a catalyst for those she encounters. Casting Mühe in the double role emphasises how Inga's physical resemblance to Anne jolts people like Robert, Jurij and Alexander, stimulating in each case recollections of her mother in the form of flashbacks as the past collides with the present. Robert's amazement at her similarity to her mother, when first encountering her in the library, is underlined by the editing; a shot/reverse shot sequence that juxtaposes a POV (point-of-view) close-up of Inga's face with a POV shot of the professor's shocked reaction, before cutting seamlessly to the film's second flashback sequence of Anne finding Jurij hiding in the outhouse. It is not Robert's direct recollection of events, but memories acquired from his familiarity with Anne's own account of events; nevertheless, he sees Anne in her daughter, and in that moment he realises the veracity of her story.

In Stuttgart, Inga confronts Jurij eking out an existence in the railway sidings. He reacts as if he has seen a ghost, initially evading her questions. A series of flashbacks to Malchow, then to the last time he saw Anne in Konstanz, tell a sad tale of a love shattered by Anne's inability to reconcile herself to her grief about her baby and the authorities' refusal to let Inga join her mother. Jurij explains that he believes Anne is living with Alexander in Konstanz. As Anne's former boyfriend who left the GDR in 1979 on an exit visa, Alexander had arranged their escape via Poland in the mistaken belief that Anne wanted to be with him. It also transpires that Alexander is Inga's father, another revelation that further disconcerts her.

Her first meeting with Alexander at his clinic in Konstanz is poignant for both, reinforced by a similar shot/reverse shot construction to the scene in the library, emphasising her father's shock at his daughter's sudden appearance in his life. Refusing to acknowledge her at first, Alexander has flashbacks to events surrounding the escape he orchestrated, in which Anne's love of Jurij, and her exploitation of her former boyfriend, becomes evident. As with Jurij's flashbacks, it is the leitmotif of Anne's anguish about her daughter that resonates most. When Inga returns the following day, a contrite Alexander breaks the news of her mother's death in 1992, explaining that a letter he sent to her grandparents was returned unopened. The present then cuts to the final flashback montage documenting Anne's nervous breakdown. Alexander then presents his side of the love triangle, which underlines the extent to which the lack of freedom in the GDR had a damaging impact on the lives of all three people involved, as well as those around them, including Inga.

Whether Inga's impact on both men's lives will initiate a healing process commensurate with her own is unclear. The same doubt remains about her grandparents. Inga's confrontation forces them also to reflect upon the past, as well as the moment when Anne left her sick baby with them before fleeing without explanation and their subsequent breaking of contact with her. At the end of the film, Inga looks sadly, but with hints of some understanding, through the window at her grandparents, before slipping a letter into their postbox and embarking on her second journey. Still oblivious to the fate of their daughter, having severed ties with her and returned Alexander's letter unopened, one can only speculate about their reaction to what Inga has discovered. Of all the characters affected by Anne's decision to flee the GDR, it is arguably her parents for whom the truth will be the hardest to bear.

If the main dramatic thrust of *Novemberkind* originates from its exploration of the GDR past's impact on east Germans in the present, the film tellingly incorporates a west German perspective in the guise of Robert. We see present-day Malchow through his eyes in a series of POV shots from the taxi that reveal the town to be typical of many provincial communities in the new *Bundesländer*, still bearing scars of neglect and underinvestment. To the accompaniment of sparse incidental music, Robert's gaze lingers on the buildings he passes, dwelling on evidence of a lack of urban regeneration: derelict houses, facades in need of renovation, regimented old GDR apartment blocks. In contrast to major cities like Berlin, Leipzig and Dresden where the physical scars of the past are beginning to fade away, towns like Malchow are still in desperate need of investment. The lingering shot of a street name, 'Neue Heimat' (new home), thus appears deeply ironic. A close-up of Robert's face reveals a smile, which might intimate a supercilious fascination with the environment around him, a whole world away from his home. Nobody quite believes that he is genuinely on holiday in Mecklenburg in such a bleak November. When he proposes going on an excursion with Inga, she enquires wryly if he wants to see the 'blossoming landscapes', suggesting that he is perceived as a typical *Wessi*, with a patronising curiosity about the fate of east Germans in the new Germany.

In truth, his intention is much more specific. 'I have to find this girl,' he tells his long-suffering partner, Claire, on being discharged from hospital following a heart attack. He is resolved to base his first novel on this sad tale of the GDR and its aftermath. And it is this stranger from Konstanz who catalyses Inga's quest in the first place, although it is unclear to the young woman what his motives are. 'What are you doing here?' she asks him, shortly before he tells her the story of the Russian deserter, thereby stimulating her investigation. 'You come here and destroy everything!' she shouts in anguish, once the lies begin to unravel, little realising that this is what he had anticipated.

As several reviews of the film observed, there is something decidedly unwholesome and predatory in the way he appropriates Anne's story, feeding off it for his own gain. The film highlights Robert's act of plagiarism by attributing the opening flashback to him, juxtaposing scenes of the initial hunt for Jurij in 1980 with him writing the title of the novel/film on a blank sheet of paper in hospital in Konstanz in 2007. Having acquired this memory, he subsequently manipulates Inga by undermining her own 'false' memory, initiating a memory contest. Robert could be seen to have a positive impact on Inga, setting her on the path to the truth. But in essence, his voyeuristic observation of her reactions at each stage of her journey, recording them into a dictaphone for use in his novel, is motivated primarily by utterly selfish goals, preying on his young companion like a 'bloodsucker' (Knoben, 2008). The depth of Robert's immorality is rather fittingly exposed at her mother's grave in Konstanz, when Alexander explains that Anne's literature professor chose her poem for the headstone inscription and took possession of all her notes. At this moment, Inga realises that she has been Robert's unwitting muse. He has known all along, yet concealed, what befell her mother.

Although the sense that Robert has, in effect, been spying on Inga might evoke comparisons with the Stasi, the simple fact that he is a west German militates against such a reading. Conversely, it hints instead at a west German propensity to gorge upon tales of woe from the former GDR. Hanns-Georg Rodek (2008) posits that Robert's fascination with the Kaden family has:

> something vampiric about it, just like the west German media's interest in the horror of the East German dictatorship. Initially, the principal motivation may have derived from the anti-communist reflex, yet in the interim one simply has to admit that the east has the more interesting stories to tell.

Although Robert's fate at the end appears much more pessimistic than Inga's – his partner has left him, he will never complete his novel and, more significantly, any hope of a relationship with the young woman is dead – there is persistent evidence that an often ghoulish fascination with the painful legacy of the GDR in the old *Bundesländer* has continued unabated. There is no more apposite or poignant example than the media and public reaction to the row which Mühe's parents fought out in public.

Shortly after work on *The Lives of Others* had been completed in 2006, Ulrich Mühe revealed his dismay in an interview with the film's director that his wife had hidden her involvement with the Stasi from him during their marriage from 1984 to 1990. Gröllmann disputed her ex-husband's accusations, maintaining that she had never worked for the Stasi or signed any Stasi documentation, and was unwittingly classified as an informant. On that basis, she was successful in securing a legal injunction against Mühe being able to repeat his allegations in public; the incriminating passages were expunged from the interview in question. Gröllmann subsequently sued several newspapers for circulating the allegations about her work for the Stasi, but tragically she died of cancer in August 2006, before the court cases had begun. The following year Mühe also died of cancer.

In a sensitive summary of the row, Frank Pergande (2008) observed how the story of Gröllmann and Mühe was 'a typical product of the GDR about which someone who has never been caught up in such complex circumstances should avoid making hasty judgements'. But in reality, people took sides and have sustained the row long after the deaths of the protagonists. Many close to Gröllmann accused Mühe of seeking to exploit the past as publicity for his new film. In particular, Thomas B. Goguel, Gröllmann's first husband, denounced Mühe in an essay titled 'Film Promotion with Collateral Damage', collected in a volume about defamation (Müller, 2008). Nevertheless, as several commentators noted, Goguel made no mention of his own dealings with the Stasi as a high-ranking diplomat, which compromised his attempts to dispute the authenticity of Gröllmann's 500-page file. He was hardly an objective, or credible, witness. Nevertheless, Petra Weisenburger's documentary titled *Ich will da sein* (*I Want to Be There*, 2008), released shortly after her death, also claimed that Gröllmann was an innocent victim; and respected journalists such as David Ensikat (2007) wrote eloquently in her defence, suggesting that the only certainty possible about the contents of her file was 'that there is no certainty'.

Mühe had his supporters too, leaping to defend him from posthumous accusations that he had defamed his ex-wife. Pergande (2008) argued that in preparing himself for his role as Stasi officer Wiesler in von Donnersmarck's film, Mühe had also confronted his own past and 'the dark and painful sides of life in the GDR'. He had found out about Gröllmann's Stasi contacts in 2001 and written about his discovery initially in 2004: ' "The whole time [we were married] my wife cooperated with the Stasi. That was the GDR" ' (Müller, 2008). It seems axiomatic, therefore, that he should reflect upon his ex-wife's activities in the context of *The Lives of Others*.

In an article about the Gröllmann affair, Susanne Beyer outlines the way in which the opposing factions divided broadly into west/east camps, with east Germans generally supporting Gröllmann, who had less success after reunification, and west Germans rallying behind the better known Mühe. Beyer (2008: 156) also underlines how the media were similarly partisan, so that the 'perspective on both of these unfortunate heroes in this German drama has long been distorted'. While other articles refer to the formal assessment of the Gröllmann case by Marianne Birthler, then head of the Stasi authority, as 'beyond contestation' (Müller, 2008), albeit without evidence that the actor signed any formal accord, Beyer (2008: 156) essays a more nuanced interpretation of the file. She underlines that informant reports about the actor, which have recently come to light, invite a more differentiated reading of Gröllmann's Stasi contacts that militate against any attempt to view her through the victim/perpetrator prism. A picture begins to emerge of a woman whose parents had suffered at the hands of the Nazis for their communist beliefs. She was not easily cowed by the authorities and ultimately wanted to be left alone. Her dealings with the Stasi ended, significantly, when she met and married Mühe, an actor in whom the Stasi was very interested because of his outspokenly critical stance. It tellingly contradicts Mühe's assertion that his ex-wife had been spying during their marriage and demands a more careful assessment of Gröllmann's role. For Beyer, the new documents do not trivialise what happened, but intimate that Gröllmann was a largely 'harmless' informant who passed on 'theatre tittle-tattle': 'This "IM-Jeanne" wanted to cooperate a little bit, but otherwise just wanted to be left alone, she wanted to find the middle path' (ibid.: 158). In that regard, Gröllmann was not alone, and what Beyer manages to do is bring some important perspective to bear on this tragic post-GDR tale.

Schwochow achieves the same thing with the events at the heart of *Novemberkind*. It documents the difficult choices ordinary people had to make in a country that denied its citizens important freedoms and sought, often by insidious means, to coerce their compliance. What the Stasi files have revealed is the extent to which families were violated and damaged in a climate of paranoia and fear, and how the scars have often been deep and painful. But the film is especially careful to emphasise how the GDR's legacy is not just of concern to east Germans. The ripples from Anne's story travel far and wide. As Inga uncovers the truth, it is clear how many people have been affected in different ways. As moving as Anna Maria Mühe's performance is, there is little doubt that her parents' unfortunate row imbues *Novemberkind* with a deeper authenticity that demonstrates the corrosive effect memories, secrets and lies continue to exert upon those coming to terms with the GDR and its legacy today.

Notes

1. I should like to record my thanks to the British Academy for their financial support in funding a research trip to the *Kinemathek* in Berlin in 2011, which enabled me to carry out research for this chapter alongside research for a major monograph.
2. All translations from the German in this chapter are my own.
3. It is the *Ostalgie*/Stasi dichotomy that emerges most typically when one looks at the films which comprise the most successful canon of post-GDR films, namely Leander Haußmann's *Sonnenallee* (*Sun Alley*, 1999), the aforementioned *Good Bye, Lenin!* and *Das Leben der Anderen*.
4. Jurij risks execution if caught and Anne faces prison for aiding and abetting a deserter. *Republikflucht* itself was punishable by a long prison sentence, as is reflected in Hannes Stöhr's *Berlin is in Germany* (2001).
5. Mike Dennis (2000: 212) underlines how the Stasi's approach was predicated on a 'deep-seated paranoia, as exemplified by [Erich] Mielke's conviction that everyone was a potential security risk'.

References

Becker, W. (dir.) (2003) *Good Bye Lenin!*, Germany: X-Filme Creative Pool, Westdeutscher Rundfunk, Arte.

Beier, L.-O. von and S. Beyer (2008) '"Ich habe mir auferlegt, meine Eltern zu schützen"', *Der Spiegel*, 47, 186–8.

Beyer, S. (2008) 'Drama der freundlichen Frau', *Der Spiegel*, 25, 154–8.

Dennis, M. (2000) *The Rise and Fall of the German Democratic Republic 1945–1990* (Harlow: Pearson).

Donnersmarck, F. H. von (dir.) (2006) *Das Leben der Anderen*, Germany: Arte, Bayerischer Rundfunk, Creado Film, Wiedemann and Berg Filmproduktion.

Eakin, P. J. (1999) *How Our Lives Become Stories: Making Selves* (Ithaca, NY: Cornell University Press).

Ensikat, D. (2007) 'Der Quellentreue', *Der Tagesspiegel*, 30 March.

Friedrich, D. (2008) 'Mecklenburgische Forschungen', *Berliner Zeitung*, 20 November.

Fulbrook, M. (2005) *The People's State: East German Society from Hitler to Honecker* (New Haven: Yale University Press).

Garton Ash, T. (1997) *The File: A Personal History* (London: Harper Collins).

Haußmann, L. (dir.) (1999) *Sonnenallee*, Germany: Ö-Film, Sat-1, Boje Buck Produktion.

Knoben, M. (2008) 'Geschichte in Gesichtern', *Süddeutsche Zeitung*, 24 November.

Kuhn, A. (2010) 'Memory Texts and Memory Work: Performances of Memory in and with Visual Media', *Memory Studies*, 3 (4), 298–313.

Müller, U. (2008) 'Die verlorene Ehre des Ulrich M.', *Berliner Morgenpost*, 16 January.

Pergande, F. (2008) 'Die Schauspielerin, ihr Mann und ihr Liebhaber', *Frankfurter Allgemeine Sonntagszeitung*, 2 March.

Rodek, R. (2008) 'Die Anderen sind immer auch die Unseren', *Die Welt*, 19 November.

Schwochow, C. (dir.) (2008) *Novemberkind*, Germany: Cine Plus, Filmakademie Baden-Württemberg, Filmemacher Produktion, Laube Film, Sommerhaus Filmproduktionen, Südwestrundfunk.
Stöhr, H. (dir.) (2001) *Berlin is in Germany*, Germany: Deutsche Film- und Fernsehakademie Berlin, Filmboard Berlin-Brandenburg, Filmstiftung Nordrhein-Westfalen, Luna-Film, Ostdeutscher Rundfunk Brandenburg, ZDF.
Weisenburger, P. (dir.) (2008) *Ich will da sein*, Germany: Weisenburger Film.

14
Life in the Army: Reported, Represented, Remembered

Mark Allinson

Few would dispute that the Socialist Unity Party of Germany (SED) placed considerable emphasis on the militarisation of GDR society. Following the creation of the National People's Army (NVA) in 1956 and the introduction of conscription in 1962, the party urged the recruitment of career soldiers and promised privileges to those who served for longer than the 18 months of national service. The SED waged a propaganda battle to convince the population from kindergarten age upwards of the need to defend socialism, with a weapon if necessary. Additionally, the school curriculum included compulsory military education after 1978, while the paramilitary Society for Sport and Technology (GST) and the 'fighting groups of the working class' both enjoyed high status. In short, barely a family remained untouched by the GDR military. Wolfgang Kissel's 1992 film *Kinder, Kader, Kommandeure* (*Children, Cadres, Commanders*), constructed solely with excerpts from officially sanctioned state-produced documentary films, succinctly and persuasively captured this creeping militarisation of GDR society.

Yet despite the importance of the army experience, and notwithstanding the centrality of the SED's defence doctrine to the state's official ideology, the military is curiously underrepresented within the memory landscapes constructed around the GDR since its demise. Where military matters are prominent, the emphasis has often been on key policy issues, as in the controversy surrounding the NVA's supposed intervention in Czechoslovakia in 1968 and the trials of border guards who shot escapers at the Berlin Wall. While the nature of GDR everyday life and its reflection in *Ostalgie* have been the subject of heated debate, life in the armed forces has rarely been centre stage in these controversies. Rather, the GDR's military history has been of interest mainly to relatively self-contained groups. One such group consists of those with specialist interests in militaria, for whom a wide variety of books and DVDs document uniforms, equipment, units and regiments. For these enthusiasts, however, the key interest may be militaria in general rather than the GDR in particular. Building detailed knowledge of regimental insignia is quite separate from constructing a consensus about the experience of military life. The other principal group comprises career soldiers, particularly those who held political responsibility and identified, largely or wholly, with the political aims of their state.

While there is no shortage of sources around which to construct a collective memory of the GDR military, this chapter's principal concern is to understand first why this central theme has not found a broader audience, and second why it has been rather less instrumentalised than other topics in the debates surrounding the GDR's memory. Indeed, while not a taboo in the way that the military experience of the Third Reich was for decades, the GDR military experience has been subject to deliberate forgetting (see Leonhard, 2008), not only in the individual memories of many of those personally involved, but also in the strategy of the (west) German establishment during the 'inner unity' project discussed by Patricia Hogwood (Chapter 2) and thus in the emergent collective memory of the GDR.

Foundations for collective memories of the GDR armed forces

Despite the general absence of controversy about or broad interest in the military, numerous post-1990 texts could contribute to a collective memory of the GDR's armed forces. A bibliography for the period to 2010 runs to 83 pages (*Was war die NVA?* [*What was the NVA?*] 2010: 560–663). Yet the military is underrepresented in general overviews of GDR history. Even the 18 volumes of the Bundestag's first commission of enquiry on the GDR contain just two expert reports specifically devoted to the NVA. This is striking given the importance of the Bundestag enquiries (see also Enquete-Kommission, 1995) in establishing visions of the GDR past which accorded with (west) German priorities for the unification project, as Patricia Hogwood has noted above. One of the expert reports is a general overview of the army's structures and its integration into the Warsaw Treaty Organisation; the other concerns the politically controversial 'construction soldiers', certainly important, but a rather smaller fragment of the overall GDR experience than the mainstream army, which is not examined. The final report simply notes that the militarisation of GDR society and its role in stabilising SED rule did not form part of the enquiry (Bundestag-Drucksache Nr. 12/7820, 1994: 40).

Other prominent sources in determining mainstream memory and interpretations of the GDR are similarly reticent. Klaus Schroeder devotes only four and a half of 648 pages in his formidable *Der SED-Staat* (*The SED State*, 1998) specifically to the army, mostly to the top-down structures. Stefan Wolle's book on the later GDR, *Die heile Welt der Diktatur* (*The Perfect World of the Dictatorship*, 1998), has brief sections on nearly all the key GDR institutions, but none about the NVA. Equally, the army is absent as a stand-alone topic from the exhibition in Berlin's popular DDR-Museum (see Chapter 8) and is mentioned only fleetingly in the permanent exhibition and accompanying catalogue of Leipzig's Forum for Contemporary History, despite this museum's emphasis on everyday life in the GDR. While the popular media have considered the NVA, other topics have dominated. For the 1990–2010 period the archive of the weekly news magazine *Spiegel* finds ten times as many articles with the search term 'Stasi' as articles referencing the NVA. The GDR's armed forces are thus adjacent rather than central to broad-brush characterisations of the GDR; detailed discussions or evaluations are generally restricted to a relatively closed world, unlike the historical, polemical and literary representations of the Stasi. Yet the military is recorded in a variety of more specific sources, ranging from the rigorously academic to the highly personal.

Despite considerable academic interest in the GDR's armed forces there remains no post-1990 comprehensive or definitive history of the NVA to complement the essay collections and individual chapters and articles. The principal academic publications are those produced by the Office for Military History Research (MGFA) in Potsdam, a part of the *Bundeswehr* (German Federal Army), which, perhaps anxious to avoid the charge of writing partial, establishment history, places itself firmly within the 'scientific community' (MGFA, 2011). This body has notably issued a series of some 20 heavyweight academic tomes in the series 'Military History of the GDR', clearly aimed at a specialist audience of academics, students and the already interested public. The emphasis has been on documentation and monographs firmly based in the archival record. The *Bundeswehr* also has its own military museum under the supervision of an academic panel (discussed below). Less prominent is the output of the 'Working Group for the History of the NVA and the Integration of former NVA members into Society and the *Bundeswehr*' (AGGI) of the Eastern Regional Association of the German *Bundeswehr*, published on a website and in three collections of articles, generally unavailable in the shops. The AGGI, which disbanded in 2010 due to the increasing age of its active members, was concerned with historical research and documentation, but many of the articles in its compendia entitled *Was war die NVA?* (2010) are the records and opinions of former senior NVA officers. Notwithstanding its serious historical approach, the AGGI saw its work in evaluating the NVA's history as a contribution to the process of internal German unification, in the sense that east German voices should be heard alongside the dominant western narrative:

> Even though the NVA no longer exists, in another way it is still present. It lives on in the memory of those who served or worked in it. It is frequently the subject of comparisons, especially for the sons or grandsons of former NVA members now serving in the *Bundeswehr*. [...] Questions about the role of the NVA, its purpose, development and contradictions are ultimately questions about the people without whom it would not have existed, about the motivations for their actions and their biographies.
>
> (AGGI, 2011)

In practice, much AGGI output consisted of spirited defences of the NVA's activities and its members' motivations, often pitted against the foreign and military policy of Germany and the international community since 1990 (Kunze, 2010: 208–41). The AGGI also aimed to reflect the perspective of former NVA members in remembering and understanding their own past in a situation where, it contended, much contemporary history writing served the aim of delegitimising the GDR and was written without the involvement of those who had served in the NVA (Fischer, 2010: 9). Much as active regiments construct their own traditions, the NVA old guard has attempted to define clear traditions of its own, centred on the view of an army which preserved and secured peace on the principles of humanism, understanding between nations, antifascism and antimilitarism (Hanisch, 1992: 266).

Besides the AGGI's output, numerous memoirs by GDR army personnel have appeared since 1990 without an explicitly academic framework. Some, written by those who held political authority, seek to uphold their legitimacy against the perceived victors' justice of the post-unification period, even though some also express dissatisfaction and doubts about the practical experience of the GDR. Among this group, former defence minister Heinz Keßler has become a central figure for those defenders of the GDR's reputation in general and its armed forces in particular. Keßler was particularly feted around his ninetieth birthday, which saw the publication by a 'circle of friends' of a Festschrift in his honour (Freundeskreis Heinz Keßler, 2010), at the initiative of the GRH (the Society for Just and Humanitarian Support, which champions the rights of former Stasi and party officials), the Solidarity Committee for the Victims of Political Persecution in Germany and the German Communist Party (DKP), for which Keßler also stood as a candidate in the 2011 Berlin elections, helping the party to a 0.2% share of the vote. In the Festschrift, former comrades and political associates, including Margot Honecker, Egon Krenz and Hans Modrow, paid tribute to Keßler's antifascism, his GDR patriotism, and his support for the peoples of Cuba, Mozambique, Ethiopia and beyond. The impression of the upright, exemplary antifascist who fulfilled his duty in the face of the threat from unreconstructed imperialists in the West is intended to reflect on the GDR's armed forces as a whole. While the volume's circulation may have remained principally limited to already supportive circles, Keßler subsequently co-authored with Fritz Streletz (deputy GDR defence minister and deputy commander in chief of the Warsaw Treaty forces) a more mainstream book, *Ohne die Mauer hätte es Krieg gegeben* (*Without the Wall there would have been War*, 2011). This essentially regurgitates a combination of the SED's line on the Berlin Wall and the defence of Egon Krenz and others at their trials, but, reinforced by the authority of a senior insider, it casts doubt on received (western) interpretations. It is clear from the title alone that the GDR military and political establishment saved the peace in the Cold War.

While the memoirs of bigger names such as Keßler and Klaus-Dieter Baumgarten, head of the GDR border troops, have tended to appear with prominent presses such as *edition ost* and are widely distributed in (mainly east) German bookshops, the memoirs of lower ranking officers and ordinary soldiers normally appear with smaller outlets such as the Ludwig Press in Kiel or as self-publishing ventures, and are relatively poorly placed to contribute much to a broader memory landscape. However, NVA experiences sometimes appear in the autobiographies of public figures and reach a much broader public, for example in Jens Bisky's reflections on the GDR in *Geboren am 13. August* (*Born on the 13th of August*,[1] 2004), itself later referenced in academic work (e.g. Rogg, 2008), or within wider memory projects such as the observational films about the *Kinder von Golzow* (*Children of Golzow*).

A further source for the construction of collective memory are the various fora for former NVA members. Besides the Eastern Regional Association of the established and establishment German *Bundeswehr*

Association for former soldiers and staff, there are also free-standing websites and chatrooms, such as 'nva-forum' and 'forum-ddr-grenze', the latter under the motto 'If you don't know the past you won't understand the present'. These organisations and others run meetings for old comrades. The GRH has organised more than 20 events for former border guards, with one in 2009 notably being addressed by Egon Krenz. The National People's Army Tradition Association, founded as recently as 2008, has the goal of recording the 'armed forces' role in preserving peace in Europe during the Cold War' and 'encourages the cultivation of progressive military traditions' (Traditionsverband, 2011). It organised a widely reported event in March 2011 to mark the NVA's fifty-fifth anniversary. While such public occasions with prominent speakers resonate in the wider media (Schütz, 2009; MDR, 2010), these fora essentially attract a self-selecting membership and usually make little broad impact. Nonetheless, with over 4,000 registered users and nearly 250,000 chat room contributions by March 2009, the NVA-forum website clearly has an active clientele (NVA forum, 2009).

This broad range of information and comment on the NVA contributes variously to the memory landscape around the GDR army, but perhaps more influential have been fictional works, most notably Leander Haußmann's 2005 film *NVA*, and TV films such as *An die Grenze* (*To the Border*, 2007 and periodically repeated) or *Der Mauerschütze* (*Soldier at the Wall*,[2] 2010). Additionally, some novels centre on NVA experiences, notably Christoph Brumme's *Tausend Tage* (*Thousand Days*, 1997), and *Fassonschnitt* (*Short Back and Sides*, 1984) by Jürgen Fuchs. Both are out of print and less relevant to the contemporary memory landscape, but more recently Uwe Tellkamp's monumental *Der Turm* (*The Tower*, 2008) also devoted some of its many pages to impressions of the NVA. Beyond the mainstream, at least one novel, Frank Günther's *Der Tanz des Schützen Faber* (*The Dance of Soldier Faber*, 2007), is a memoir in fictional form by a 1980s conscript, published with a local press.

These are the principal public media upon which collective memory of the NVA might be constructed. With the exception of some of the purely academic work, all build on and interact with the personal memories of those who were directly involved with the GDR army. In principle, though to varying degrees, the five elements are present which Aleida Assmann (2008: 55–6) suggests may combine to 'transform ephemeral social memory into long-term collective memory':

> emplotment of events in a [...] narrative; visual and verbal signs that serve as aids of memory; institutions of learning and the

dissemination of mass media; sites and monuments that present palpable relics; commemoration rites that periodically reactivate the memory and enhance collective participation.

Evaluating the sources

Given the controversy which has surrounded so much of the presentation and memory of the GDR past, it is perhaps surprising that the diverse range of available sources collectively presents a reasonably homogenous picture of how the NVA was experienced by its soldiers. While questions surrounding the legitimacy or otherwise of the GDR's border regime and the politics of the Cold War remain vexed, these bigger political questions remain largely separate from, or at most adjacent to, memory of the NVA experience itself.

In many senses Haußmann's film *NVA* reflects this broad consensus around the army experience. Though produced unambiguously as comedy, in part as exaggerated caricature, the film's early sequences portray themes which recur in academic works, politicised discussions, and memoirs. These include the helplessness of new recruits faced with harsh military discipline; the sadistic behaviour of the *Entlassungskandidaten*, those conscripts counted as 'candidates for release' in the final six months of their service, towards the newer recruits, whether the brand new *Sprutze* ('squirts' in the soldiers' jargon) or the *Zwischenpisser* ('middle pissers') who had already served for six months; the fear of the infamous military prison at Schwedt from which the rebellious Krüger returns tamed and broken, itself belatedly the subject of a memoir (Auerswald, 2010); the boredom and emptiness of the inevitable political education; the idiocy of the commanding officers, taken to increasingly farcical proportions; the general inability and ineptness of the GDR's armed forces when practising military operations; and the sheer pointlessness of the entire experience in the conscripts' eyes. As the lead character, Henrik, reflects: 'Nobody knows why we are here, so we just count the days.' The film garnered mixed reviews, some critics regarding it as little more than a slapstick comedy, though the *Berliner Zeitung* newspaper noted that 'the dreariness of the GDR is again reconstructed here without exaggeration' (Westphal, 2005). The same reviewer felt that accidents with live ammunition were no laughing matter and that the film did not match her friends' and relations' reports of GDR army life. Peter Tannhoff (2010), author of the memoir *Sprutz*, concluded that Haußmann's film 'absolutely plays down the seriousness of the true situation' and denounced the romance in the film as 'unrealistic kitsch', but simultaneously wondered if many of the details in the film had been copied from his own book.

Yet probably no other presentation of the NVA has been consumed by so many Germans since the *Wende*. 786,000 saw it at cinemas in 2005 (Inside Kino, 2010), and many more will have seen subsequent television showings or the DVD. Notwithstanding criticisms of the film's lightweight tone, themselves reminiscent of the debates around *Sonnenallee* (*Sun Alley*, 1999) and *Good Bye, Lenin!* (2003), the essentials of army life as portrayed in *NVA* are common to the standard academic (e.g. Rogg, 2008), autobiographical and literary representations noted above. Indeed, the same details occur in memoirs covering the GDR's entire life-span (e.g. Awiszus, 2002; Grünitz, 2006; Tannhoff, 2008). While some former NVA conscripts regarded the film as unrealistic, echoing Tannhoff's views, a larger number believed the description was essentially accurate (Filmszene, 2010). The TV film *An die Grenze*, set in the mid-1970s, contains (like *NVA*) a love story, but also a much darker portrayal of the abuses perpetrated by the *Entlassungskandidaten* on their younger comrades, and a damning presentation of the officer class, this time not camped up for comedic effect. The film won the Adolf Grimme prize for drama in 2008, the jury praising in particular its realism (Grimme, 2008). Again, published historical sources confirm the specific information portrayed in the film, from the details of barracks life to military equipment that was often unfit for purpose; the unwillingness, inability, or both, of the officer class to exercise control over conscripts at the end of their military service; yet also the arbitrary orders of senior commanders; even the widespread belief that a substance called 'Hängolin' was added to the tea to curb the soldiers' sexual appetites (Ehlert and Rogg, 2004). The films also mirror the memoirs in their inclusion of humorous elements. Despite criticising the comedic approach of the Haußmann film, Tannhoff's memoir (2008: 131–2) includes a number of anecdotes, for instance about the soldiers ordered to remove leaves from trees at barracks before the arrival of a colonel general from Berlin, on the grounds that the army had decreed it was 'winter' and so it had better look like winter.

The films, memoirs and historians' accounts all testify to the blind eye regularly turned to shortcomings, and the regular sense that outward appearances were paramount. As Jens Bisky (2004: 166) put it:

> The NVA which I experienced resembled an army for show, trained for the amusement of old generals. If ever the order had arrived to mobilise without prior warning and as a complete surprise, the

> regiment would have made a sorry sight. [...] From headquarters the information filtered through which enabled us to get everything ready quietly in advance and to maintain appearances. The game was repeated according to the same rules at every level.

The high levels of alcohol consumption in the barracks, reported in every memoir, are further testimony to the absence of real control over the soldiers. The implications of the officers' lack of control are also clear in *An die Grenze*, when of all people the political officer, Dobbs, shoots himself, unable to exert control over either the soldiers in his classes or even his own wife, who taunts him by having an affair with a soldier under his nose. While this is clearly a dramatic device for TV effect, the historical record documents that suicides regularly occurred (Rogg, 2008: 361–5).

In sum, the fictional and non-fictional depictions and memoirs of life in the NVA largely present similar memories of the GDR's armed forces. Further, the substance of this depiction appears to accord plausibly with the personal memories of most of those actually involved. On this basis, and in the absence of prominent conflicting portrayals, there are strong foundations for the construction of a post-1990 collective memory of the GDR army which appears authentic. Nonetheless, disagreements about the political place of the GDR impinge on this broad consensus, while the light-hearted tone of films such as *NVA* disappoints or even angers both those who wish to defend the integrity of the army in which they served and those who wish to delegitimise the GDR in general. This chapter now turns to these disagreements of interpretation and the way they and other factors have limited the space accorded to the NVA in the overall memory landscape of the GDR.

The relative absence of the NVA from the GDR memory landscape

Given the broad consensus in the collective memory of the NVA, the subsidiary role played by the GDR military in the broad memory landscape requires explanation. The principal factors behind its virtual absence reflect a perceived normality of military life, and a general unwillingness to remember it, both on the part of many of the individuals concerned and the agencies which have otherwise dominated debates about the nature of the GDR. First, the broad consensus noted above has facilitated a collective memory of the NVA which is relatively stable and uncontentious. Arguably this allows a greater sense of closure and demands rather less space in the GDR memory landscape than other topics. Where controversies remain, they are linked to the broader and widely contested questions of the legitimacy of the state and SED rule.

Second, for the majority of the conscripts their period of service was to be endured, survived and then quickly forgotten. Peter Tannhoff's memoir (2008: 66) quotes a soldier declaring just before demobilisation: 'Never had a Schnuffi [gas mask], never had Lederol [protective uniform], neeeeeever had it, all this crap here, I never had it!', and on his own final release Tannhoff (ibid., 138) recalls himself and a comrade shouting just beyond the gate 'Never had it!!! Never had all this crap here!! Never was in the army!!! We were never there!'. In a similar vein, a blog on the Haußmann film includes Ollie's view: 'From autumn 78 to spring 80 I messed up a year and a half of my life but the odd thing is that looking back you only remember the funny things (the art of repression perhaps)' (Filmszene, 2010). Though it is somewhat paradoxical to recall a willingness to forget, as these writers have done, these comments reflect the desire of most former NVA and border guard conscripts, and many staff, not only to forget but actively to suppress the memory of what appeared to the majority of them as so much wasted, if not robbed, time from their young lives. Notwithstanding the ideological specifics of SED socialism, the GDR seems comparable in this sense to other states with armies built on conscription, particularly in peacetime. The lack of interest in political education reflected in all sources (Rogg, 2008: 388) suggests that the men spent their military service defending an ideal they largely did not share under the command of officers for whom they lacked respect. Clearly for some the military experience remains an exciting and worthwhile part of their biographies and it is this subset of the former soldiers which is most likely to participate in web fora and veterans' associations. The majority, however, seem less inclined to look back.

Third, the experience of army life has been a constant expectation for all young men in German states since well back into the nineteenth century. The GDR and the NVA thus conform to a well-established pattern which persisted until *Bundeswehr* conscription finally ended in 2011. In his review of Haußmann's *NVA*, Günter Schabowski (2005) commented that 'the larks are entirely reminiscent of West German barracks comedies'. Similarly, *Die Zeit*'s review of Brumme's *Tausend Tage* commented that the tale 'could in many respects also have been set in a *Bundeswehr* barracks' (Steinert, 1997). Though GDR border guards occasionally faced the urgent moral and practical dilemma of how to react when would-be escapers approached the border, for them and for their comrades in the regular army much of the GDR military experience otherwise largely resembled that of conscripts and soldiers elsewhere. The GDR texts noted above are comparable to accounts of military service in quite different circumstances. For example, Sven Regener's fictional tale (2004) of Frank Lehmann's experiences as an unwilling *Bundeswehr* conscript in 1980, based partly on the author's own experiences, contains farcical elements of soldiers' lives and incompetent officers presiding over apparently pointless operations. David Lodge's novel of British national service in the mid-1950s, *Ginger You're Barmy* (1984), also autobiographically based fiction, presents a remarkably similar picture ranging from humour to tragedy against a background of senseless activity. Memoirs and autobiographically based fiction reflect a sense that this was an expected fate for young men in many countries. In short, life in the NVA was less exceptional than other aspects of the GDR which diverged more notably from perceived norms, that is western norms, and is consequently less noteworthy or memorable.

Fourth, and perhaps as a consequence of the above, the film and literary representations and most of the memoirs by the NVA rank and file have been broadly unpolitical. The memoirs in particular are notable for concentrating on the experience itself with very little reference to SED rule, notwithstanding the frequent portrayals of the political education to which conscripts were subjected, such as the so-called 'infrared treatment' and the ban on consuming West German television and radio. Tannhoff (2010) concluded from his NVA experience that escape was the only answer to the GDR and sailed out in a hot air balloon shortly before the *Wende*. However, this was an unusual reaction. For the most part, the broadly unpolitical outlook on SED rule among NVA soldiers who have published memoirs reflects that of the general population from which they were drawn, but also the lack of ideological commitment during their service and a tendency to identify with *Bundeswehr* conscripts, seen by many in the NVA not as enemies but simply as workers also fulfilling their orders (as recorded in NVA Berlin, 1977: 51 and many other contemporary archival sources; Rogg, 2008: 215–6). The absence of a decidedly political edge to NVA memories also reduces the topic's prominence in the broader memory landscape.

Besides a general unwillingness on the part of those directly involved to recall their military service as individual memory, or actively to contribute to a collective memory by participating in veterans' parades or the like, those factors which have encouraged the instrumentalisation of memory within the 'normalisation' project undertaken after 1990 by the (west) German establishment are also generally absent. While the high politics of the closed borders and shootings of would-be emigrants lend themselves to condemnation, there is little else about the GDR military which seems exceptional, particularly by comparison with West Germany before 1990. In this the NVA differs markedly from the Stasi, the mismanaged command economy and the often arbitrary nature of SED rule, all far more central to the GDR debate.

Indeed, the surviving senior representatives of the GDR armed forces paint a relatively favourable picture of their own history by pointing to the contrast between the military activity of united Germany and the *Bundeswehr* since 1990, and that of the NVA, which participated in no wars or conflicts. This record also precludes the comparisons between the GDR and the Third Reich which have been utilised in other debates about memory and history (such as political repression, comparisons between the Stasi and the Gestapo), and is powerful in a country where pacifism is a significant political factor, as noted following Gerhard Schröder's re-election in 2002 on a platform of non-participation in the imminent war against Iraq. The elements of trauma and of victim/perpetrator relationships which have marked out much of memory studies are broadly absent from the NVA. There would, in any event, be serious difficulties of categorisation. Can uniformed and armed soldiers plausibly be presented as victims of SED rule? Yet, with the exception of those few border guards who shot escapers from conviction, they cannot plausibly be presented as perpetrators either.

Memory of the NVA experience has consequently been relatively non-politicised. The creation as early as 1990 of the Eastern Regional Association within the German *Bundeswehr* Association is an unusual example of full incorporation of the GDR past into an existing West German institution on the basis of broad equality. Within the Eastern Regional Association, former high ranking GDR military figures and military historians have been able to make a case that the NVA has left a positive legacy of antifascism and internationalism (e.g. Hanisch, 2001). However, this early example of inclusivity within a relatively closed body has also served to neutralise a history and a memory which could not easily be instrumentalised to delegitimise the GDR past, and might even prove politically embarrassing in the present. While even officers as senior as Baumgarten (2008: 218) were prepared to join, he was convinced that the aim was to 'keep us under control'.

Military issues may yet play a more central role in defining the GDR memory landscape. The heightened activity around Heinz Keßler perhaps represents a final attempt by the last generation of senior GDR military personnel to secure what they would regard as a fitting legacy for their life's work, while also in practice supporting the political agenda of the Left party by calling attention to united Germany's increasingly active military role. Keßler makes regular public appearances at events to mark NVA anniversaries and, in January 2011, to sign copies of his Festschrift at the annual Liebknecht–Luxemburg march to the socialists' cemetery in Berlin. However, despite the concerned press coverage about the public wearing of NVA uniforms at an event to mark the NVA's 55th anniversary in March 2011 (e.g. Hasselmann and Stollowsky, 2011), only some 100 former officers attended, rather fewer than the 400 who had attended a similar event in 2006 (Leonhard, 2008: 150). The Berlin Senator responsible for constitutional protection played down the significance of the event and its elderly participants in the *Traditionsverband*. In her view, the group was attempting to twist history, but this was insufficient to warrant observation (Abgeordnetenhaus, 2011: 6).

This policy of neutralisation has been continued in the new exhibition at the *Bundeswehr*'s Military History Museum in Dresden, based in the GDR's former military museum, and which opened in late 2011. Prior to its closure for comprehensive renovation the exhibition on the post-war period only extended to 1970. In the new exhibition, the museum locates the NVA within the wider framework of German and international military history. Rather than simply displaying uniforms and other militaria, the museum's aim is to demonstrate the 'varied forms of the exercise of power by society' as well as forms of state power in practice (Militärhistorisches Museum, 2011).

In conclusion, the collective memory of the GDR's armed forces throws up rather less controversy than other elements of the GDR past. This only partially explains the NVA's low status in the overall memory framework. Besides the unattractiveness for many participants of this enforced aspect of their biographies, the NVA's history is unsuitable for the instrumentalisation which has characterised so much else within the GDR debate since 1990. The GDR military experience was not unusual in the broader historical perspective, and the sometimes humorous portrayals of a pointless, poorly disciplined and often ineffectual institution do not support the general interpretation of the GDR as a repressive communist state, and also undermine the reputations of the military and party leadership. Though NVA uniforms resembled those of the Third Reich's *Wehrmacht*, there are few other compelling comparisons to be drawn; rather, the *Bundeswehr* is prone to damaging comparisons, both as an institution which, it is claimed, has retained rather more pre-1945 traditions (e.g. Hanisch, 1992: 263) and as an army which, unlike the NVA, is active in foreign campaigns. If, as Silke Arnold-de Simine and Susannah Radstone suggest in Chapter 1, the question is who benefits from certain memories of the GDR, the answer in the case of the army may be 'very few'. The place of the military in the collective memory of the GDR is accordingly slight.

Notes

1. 13 August is also a reference to the date on which the Berlin Wall was built in 1961.
2. *Der Mauerschütze* may also be translated as *Marksman*.

References

Abgeordnetenhaus Berlin (2011) Ausschuß für Verfassungsschutz, 23 March 2011 minutes, http://www.parlament-berlin.de/ados/16/VerfSch/protokoll/vfs16-034-ip.pdf [date accessed 5 August 2011].

AGGI (2011) http://www.aggi-info.de/ (homepage) [date accessed 2 August 2011].

Assmann, A. (2008) 'Transformations between history and memory', *Social Research*, 75 (1), 49–72.

Auerswald, K. (2010) *...sonst kommst du nach Schwedt! Bericht eines Militärstrafgefangenen* (Rudolstadt: Greifenverlag).

Awiszus, R. (2002) *Genosse Soldat! Kommen Sie mal zurück. Erlebnisse eines DDR-Soldaten* (self-published).

Baumgarten, K.-D. (2008) *Erinnerungen. Autobiographie des Chefs der Grenztruppen der DDR* (Berlin: edition ost).

Bisky, J. (2004) *Geboren am 13. August* (Hamburg: Rowohlt).

Brumme, C. (1997) *Tausend Tage* (Cologne: Kiepenheuer & Witsch).

Bundestag-Drucksache Nr. 12/7820 (1994) http://dip21.bundestag.de/dip21/btd/12/078/1207820.pdf [date accessed 1 September 2010].

Ehlert, H. and M. Rogg (2004) *Militär, Staat und Gesellschaft in der DDR. Forschungsfelder, Ergebnisse, Perspektiven* (Berlin: Links).

Enquete-Kommission (1995) *Aufarbeitung von Geschichte und Folgen der SED-Diktatur in Deutschland* (Baden-Baden: Nomos).

Filmszene (2010) 'NVA', http://www.filmszene.de/kino/n/nva.html [date accessed 3 September 2010].

Fischer, E. (2010) 'Vorwort' in *Was war die DDR. Zapfenstreich.*

Freundeskreis Heinz Keßler (2010) *Die Sache aufgeben, heißt sich selbst aufgeben. Festschrift für Heinz Keßler zum 90. Geburtstag*, 2nd edn (Berlin: Wiljo Heinen).

Fuchs, J. (1984) *Fassonschnitt* (Hamburg: Rowohlt).

Grimme (2008) '44. Adolf-Grimme-Preis 2008. Begründung der Jury', http://www.grimme-institut.de/html/index.php?id=722 [date accessed 2 September 2010].

Grünitz, H.-J. (2006) *Eingezogen. Ein Wehrpflichtiger der NVA erinnert sich*, 3rd edn (Kiel: Ludwig).

Günther, F. (2007) *Der Tanz des Schützen Faber* (Halle: Projekte).

Hanisch, W. (1992) 'In der Tradition von Müntzer, Scharnhorst, Engels und Thälmann? Zum Traditionsverständnis und zur Traditionspflege in der NVA' in M. Backerra (ed.) *Ein Rückblick für die Zukunft. Zeitzeugen berichten über ein Stück deutscher Militärgeschichte* (Cologne: Markus).

Hanisch, W. (2001) 'Was ist heute noch bewahrenswert aus der Traditionsauffassung der NVA?' in *Was war die NVA? Studien – Analysen – Berichte. Zur Geschichte der Nationalen Volksarmee*, http://www.aggi-info.de/SB_IH/SB1.html [date accessed 2 September 2010].

Hasselmann, J. and C. Stollowsky (2011) 'Aufmarsch einer Geistertruppe', *Tagesspiegel*, 7 March, http://www.tagesspiegel.de/berlin/aufmarsch-einer-geistertruppe-empoerung-ueber-nva-feier-im-tierpark/3921350.html [date accessed 5 August 2011].

Inside Kino (2010) 'Top 100 Deutschland 2005', http://www.insidekino.de/DJahr/D2005.htm [date accessed 2 September 2010].

Keßler, H. and F. Streletz (2011) *Ohne die Mauer hätte es Krieg gegeben* (Berlin: edition ost).

Kunze, M. (2010) 'Frieden schaffen ohne Waffen? Von der Illusion der Jahre 1989/1990 und der Realität 2009' in *Was war die NVA? Zapfenstreich.*

Leonhard, N. (2008) 'The National People's Army as an Object of (Non) Remembrance', *German Politics and Society*, 26 (4), 150–63.

Lodge, D. (1984) *Ginger You're Barmy* (London: Penguin).

MDR (2010) *exakt*, http://www.mdr.de/exakt/6828827.html [date accessed 2 September 2010].

MGFA (2011) 'Institut', http://www.mgfa-potsdam.de/html/institut_2005.php [date accessed 2 August 2011].

Militärhistorisches Museum (2011) 'Leitgedanken der Neugestaltung' and 'Neukonzeption Dauerausstellung', http://www.militaerhistorisches-museum.bundeswehr.de [date accessed 2 August 2011].

NVA Berlin (1977) 'Informationsbericht 6/77', Bundesarchiv-Militärarchiv DVP 4-3/12551, fols 45–51.

NVA forum (2009) 'Forumsgeschichte/Historie', www.nva-forum.de/index_f.htm [date accessed 31 August 2010].

Regener, S. (2004) *Neue Vahr Süd* (Frankfurt/Main: Eichborn).

Rogg, M. (2008) *Armee des Volkes? Militär und Gesellschaft in der DDR* (Berlin: Links).

Schabowski, G. (2005) 'Unfidel in der Castro-Kaserne', *Der Spiegel*, 26 September, 222.

Schroeder, K. (1998) *Der SED-Staat. Geschichten und Strukturen der DDR* (Munich: Bayerische Landeszentrale für politische Bildungsarbeit).

Schütz, J. (2009) 'Egon Krenz meldet sich zu Wort', *Sächsische Zeitung*, 24 October.

Steinert, H. (1997) 'Das brennende Ei', *Die Zeit*, 41. http://www.zeit.de/1997/41/Das_brennende_Ei [date accessed 27 June 2012].

Tannhoff, P. (2008) *Sprutz. In den Fängen der NVA*, 4th edn (Kiel: Ludwig).

Tannhoff, P. (2010) http://www.peter-tannhoff.de [date accessed 2 September 2010].

Tellkamp, U. (2008) *Der Turm* (Frankfurt/Main: Suhrkamp).

Traditionsverband Nationale Volksarmee (2011) 'Aufgaben und Ziele', www.traditionsverband-nva.de [date accessed 5 August 2011].

Was war die NVA? Zapfenstreich (2010) (Berlin: Selbstverlag der Arbeitsgruppe Geschichte der NVA und Integration ehemaliger NVA-Angehöriger in Gesellschaft und Bundeswehr im Landesverband Ost des Deutschen Bundeswehr Verbandes).

Westphal, A. (2005) 'Was nicht passt, wird passend gemacht', *Berliner Zeitung*, 28 September.

Wolle, S. (1998) *Die heile Welt der Diktatur. Alltag und Herrschaft in der DDR 1971–1989* (Berlin: Links).

Index

Note: **Bold** locators represents illustrations.

3 October, 166–7, 185
9 November, 12, 59, 166–7, 174–6, 179, 182–3, 214
9 October, 12, 179–80, 182–5, 187, 190–1
11 September 2001, 172
13 August, 233, 242
17 June, 191
20th July group, 56–7

Adorno, Theodor, 4
advertising, 44, 142, 184
After the Wall Network, 3, 8, 13–14, 19–20, 22
Ahbe, Thomas, 105
Alltag. *see* everyday life
amnesia, 24, 29, 95, 174
  selective, 132
  see also forgetting
Ampelmann, Ampelmännchen, 30, 107, 114, 160, 162
anniversaries, 1–3, 8, 14, 135, 152–3, 165–7, 172, 175, 179–81, 184, 190, 206, 234, 241
anthologies, 10, 68, 72–3, 75–6, 79–80
antifascism, 9–10, 51–2, 54–8, 60–1, 63–4, 170, 189, 232–3, 240
  see also resistance, antifascist
Antze, Paul, 31, 160
armed forces, 1, 13, 60, 154–5, 180, 229–42
  see also Bundeswehr (Federal Army); NVA (National People's Army)
Arnold-de Simine, Silke, 64, 103, 150, 161–2, 216, 242
Assmann, Aleida, 25–6, 29, 79, 165, 189, 234
Assmann, Jan, 25, 167, 189
Association of Victims of Stalinism, 159
Attewell, Nadine, 121
Aufarbeitung (re-working of the past), 4, 27, 149–55, 159–62, 164, 175, 216
autobiography, 6–7, 9–10, 26, 52, 54, 58–9, 60–4, 67–8, 73, 75–80, 220, 233, 236, 239
  see also life writing

Bach, Jonathan, 102
Bahr, Erhard, 120
Barenboim, Daniel, 119
Barthes, Roland, 78
Baumgarten, Klaus-Dieter, 233, 240
Becker, Wolfgang, 215
  Good Bye, Lenin!, 6, 215, 227, 236
Beethoven, Ludwig van, 124, 126
Beijing, 180
Belke, Julia, 104
Benjamin, Walter, 20–1, 31
Berdahl, Daphne, 103, 105, 144
Berlin, 1, 54, 85–6, 91–2, 101, 113, 144, 164, 169–70, 172, 174, 191, 212, 217, 223, 233, 236, 241
BStU, 137
  East, 84–5, 87, 89, 216
  literature, 83–6, 90–2, 94
  Musik-Biennale, 125
  Palace, 172
  Palast der Republik, 170
  Republic, 35, 87, 95, 173
  Sinfonieorchester, 119
  Staatsoper, 119, 129
  West, 84–5, 88–9, 116, 118
  see also memorials; monuments; museums
Berlin Wall, 22, 27, 84–6, 91, 112, 123–4, 133, 155, 165, 191, 207, 210, 229, 233
  building of, 242

Berlin Wall – *continued*
fall of, 19, 101, 104, 116, 122, 124, 165–7, 172, 179–80, 184, 187, 190–1, 197, 206, 210, 214–16, 220
'in the head/mind', 7, 86
Bertsch, Georg, 140
Besserwesserei, 140
Betts, Paul, 140, 142, 145
Beuys, Joseph
Wirtschaftswerte, 139, 141
Beyer, Susanne, 225–6
Birmingham Centre Popular Memory Group, 63, 102–3
Birth, Kevin, 150–1
Birthler, Marianne, 1–2, 226
Bisky, Jens, 233, 236
'blooming/blossoming landscapes', 124–5, 127, 223
Bolter, Jay David, 73, 77
Bonn, 125
see also museums
Borchert, Christian
Familienportraits, 201
border guards, 4, 155, 229, 233–4, 238, 240
Böthig, Peter, 84
Boym, Svetlana, 3, 11, 13, 30, 122, 128, 161
Brabazon, Tara, 102
Brandt, Willy, 116, 128
Brecht, Bertolt, 1, 120
Bredemeyer, Reiner, 117, 119, 120–2
Aufschwung OST, 125, **126**
Bagatellen für B., 126
Einmischung, 126
Wendepunkt, 124
Brubaker, Rogers, 116–17
Brumme, Christoph
Tausend Tage, 234, 238
Brussig, Thomas, 173
Bruyn, Günter de, 87
BStU (Office of the Federal Commissioner for the Stasi Files), 133, 137, 151
Bundestag special enquiry commissions, 4, 28, 37, 42, 230–1
Bundeswehr (Federal Army), 231–2, 238–41
AGGI, 231–2
Eastern Regional Association, 231, 233, 240
Bundeszentrale für politische Bildung (BpB; Federal Office for Political Education), 103–4, 153
Burke, Kenneth, 156
Burmeister, Brigitte, 86

capitalism, 8, 43–4, 76, 105, 133, 137, 183
contrast with socialism; communism
Capps, Lisa, 154
CDU (Christian Democratic Union), 28, 166
Chamisso, Adelbert von, 85, 87
Chansonwerkstatt, 1–2
Chipperfield, David, 187
church, 56, 175, 184, 187, 208
Evangelical, 72
Protestant, 180
cinema. *see* film
Classen, Christoph, 55
Clifford, James, 121–2
Clinton, Bill, 31
Cold War, 7, 37, 86, 125, 171, 211, 233–5
colonisation, 41, 117
Columbo, 62–3
commemoration, 3, 25, 51, 53, 55, 122, 136, 149, 176, 179–85, 189–90, 235
communism, 9, 52, 59, 72, 84, 103, 116, 136, 140, 190, 224, 226, 233, 241
composers, 11, 116–20, 122–5, 127–9
confectionary, 102, 107, 110, 114
Confino, Alon, 35, 45
Connerton, Paul, 42, 44, 191
consumerism, 28, 43–4, 202
consumer products, 14, 30, 39, 43–4, 102, 105, 107, 110, 114, 136–7, 139, 140, 142, 144–5, 149, 209
Cooke, Paul, 102–3, 105–6, 113–14
Council of Peace, 53, 62
CSU (Christian Social Union), 166

Cuba, 233
Czechoslovakia, 61, 229

Declaration of Human Rights, 123
Demokratischer Aufbruch (Democratic Awakening), 166
denazification, 55
Dennis, Mike, 227
Dessau, 176
diaries, 26, 68, 102
diaspora, 11, 24, 116–17, 120–1, 124, 128
  accidental, 116–17
  see also memory, diasporic
dictatorship, 5–6, 11, 27–8, 51, 79, 132, 136, 151–3, 155, 160–1, 164, 171, 185, 218, 224
  modern, 4
  SED, 38, 75, 149, 153, 175
  welfare, 4
Dittrich, Paul-Heinz, 117, 120
documentary films, 67, 179, 207, 229, 233
  Die Kinder von Golzow, 233
  Freiheit! Das Ende der DDR, 207–8
Donnersmarck, Florian Henckel von, 138
  Das Leben der Anderen, 6, 75, 137, 215, 218, 224–5, 227
doppelgänger, 10, 83–7, 89–95
Dostoyevsky, Fyodor
  The Double: A Petersburg Poem, 86
Drawert, Kurt, 94
  Ich hielt meinen Schatten für einen anderen und grüßte, 86
  Spiegelland, 86
Dresden, 223
  Semperoper, 119, 129
  Staatskappelle, 119
  see also museums
'dual past', 4
Dulles, Allen, 55–6
durchherrschte Gesellschaft (thoroughly ruled society), 197

Eakin, Paul John, 220
Eckert, Rainer, 186
ego-documents, 67
Eigen-Sinn, 4, 14, 198, 202, 209, 212
Eisler, Hanns, 120–1
Emmerich, Margit
  Wohnzimmer, 201
Engert, Jürgen, 166
Ensikat, David, 225
Erinnerungsgemeinschaft (memory community), 10, 29, 157–8, 161
Erll, Astrid, 68, 73, 77
Ethiopia, 233
everyday life, 4–5, 7, 9, 11, 22, 27–8, 30, 38–9, 52, 64, 71, 86, 102, 111, 132, 134–6, 140, 144–5, 155, 161, 175, 190, 197, 201–4, 208–9, 219, 229, 231
  Alltagsgeschichte (history of everyday life), 197–8, 203, 205, 211
  see also museums
exhibitions, 10, 57–8, 67, 139, 141–2, 169, **169**, 170, 179, 203–5, 207, 210, 231, 241
  Alltagsleben in der DDR, 204
  BStU, 133, 137
  Gewalt hinter Gittern, 68, 76–80
  Normiert, Möbliert, Variiert. Eine Ost-West-Berliner Wohnstudie um die 70er, 142–3
  SED. Schönes Einheits Design, 139–41, 145
  see also museums
exile, 11, 60, 117–18, 120, 122, 124
eyewitness, 6, 67–72, 76–80, 144
  archive (Zeitzeugenarchiv), 68, 70, 75–7

fascism, 57
FDJ (Free German Youth), 155
FDP (Free Democratic Party), 166, 172
film, 4–6, 24, 26, 75, 102, 139, 179, 197, 199, 205–10, 212, 216–17, 221, 227, 233, 236–7, 239
  Ostfilm, 216
  see also documentary films; television productions; *and under directors*
Flügge, Matthias, 175
forgetting, 9, 19, 31, 44–5, 85, 93–4, 142, 175–6, 230, 238
  prescriptive, 42, 44

Frankfurt, 119
Paulskirche, 172
Freud, Sigmund, 83, 89–90
FRG (Federal Republic of Germany), 12, 14, 35–8, 41–5, 74–6, 116–19, 125, 170, 172, 179, 183–5, 187–91
Friedliche Revolution. see peaceful revolution
Friedman, Jonathan, 150
Fries, Fritz Rudolf, 87
Fritzsche, Peter, 35, 45
Fuchs, Jürgen, 73, 75
Fassonschnitt, 234
Fühmann, Franz, 87
Führer, Christian, 183, 185

Gallinat, Anselma, 13, 27, 35, 132, 135, 143
Garton Ash, Timothy, 214
Gauck, Joachim, 1
Gaus, Günter, 198–9, 208–9
Gedenkstätte. *see* museums
generation, 2–3, 6, 10–11, 24, 26, 83, 94, 109, 117, 167, 170, 175, 190, 206–7, 211, 214–16, 240
genre, 9, 26, 52–4, 58, 63, 67, 80, 84, 90, 102, 120, 122
Genscher, Hans-Dietrich, 210
George, Heinrich, 72
Geschichtspolitik (politics of history), 189
Gestapo, 57, 64, 240
Gläser, Markus, 187
glasnost, 190
Goebbels, Joseph, 123
Goguel, Thomas B., 225
Goldmann, Friedrich, 117–18
Gorbachev, Mikhail, 126, 190
grand coalition, 28
Grass, Günter
Ein weites Feld, 86
Green Party, 28, 166
GRH (Society for Just and Humanitarian support), 233–4
Gröllmann, Jenny, 215, 224–6
Grotewohl, Otto, 72
Grundgesetz (federal constitution), 153, 190
Grusin, Richard, 73, 77

GST (Society for Sport and Technology), 229
Guffey, Elizabeth, 141
Günther, Frank
Der Tanz des Schützen Faber, 234

Halbwachs, Maurice, 22–3, 31, 189
Hanover, 188, 217
Haußmann, Leander
NVA, 234–8
Sonnenallee, 105–6, 209–10, 227, 236
Heimat, 104, 117, 158–9, 223
Hein, Christoph, 180
Hensel, Jana
Zonenkinder, 6
Heuer, Christian, 67
Hilbig, Wolfgang, 86–7
Hirsch, Marianne, 24, 26
Hoepker, Thomas, 142
Hoffmann, E.T.A, 87–90
Das öde Haus, 88
Das steinerne Herz, 87
Der Sandmann, 88, 90
Hogwood, Patricia, 101, 132, 162, 218–19, 221, 230
Holocaust, 24, 29, 39, 62, 164, 171, 189
see also memorials
Honecker, Erich, 56, 118, 123, 186
Honecker, Margot, 233
Hungary, 61, 210
Huyssen, Andreas, 121, 176

IM (unofficial informant), 226
Initiative 9. Oktober, 181, 185–7
Initiative Denkmal Deutsche Einheit, 166
internet forums, 5, 67, 234
Iraq, 240
Iron Curtain, 116
Ives, Charles, 123

Jahn, Roland, 1
Jean Paul, 87, 90
Jentsch, Ernst, 89
Jirgl, Reinhard, 94
Abtrünnig, 85
Johnson, Laurie Ruth, 83, 93, 95
Jolly, Margaretta, 57

Jordan, Jennifer, 175
journalism, 52, 54, 58–60, 64, 135, 154–6, 158, 162, 166, 174, 179, 182, 186, 188–9, 217, 225–6, 231–2, 235
Jung, Burkhard, 182
Junge, Ricarda
  Die komische Frau, 94

Kafka, Franz, 124
Kammen, Michael, 121
Kant, Immanuel, 90, 96
  Versuch über die Krankheiten des Kopfes, 92
Katzer, Georg, 117, 119–20, 128
  Aide mémoire, 123
  Landschaft mit steigender Flut, 127
  Les paysages fleurissants, 127
  Mein 1989, 122–4, 126–7, 129
  Mon 1789, 122–3
  Offene Landschaft mit obligatem Ton e, 127
Keßler, Heinz, 232–3, 240–1
Kissel, Wolfgang
  Kinder, Kader, Kommandeure, 229
Kleist, Heinrich von, 90, 93, 96
Knabe, Hubertus, 72–6, 79
Kochan, Günter, 117, 120
Kohl, Helmut, 124–5, 127
Kohl, Katrin, 144
Köhler, Horst, 181
Kondo, Dorinne, 158
Königsdorf, Helga, 86
Kordon, Klaus, 73, 75
Korff, Gottfried, 138, 184–5
Koselleck, Reinhard, 23
Kowalczuk, Ilko-Sascha, 190
KPD (Communist Party of Germany), 60–1, 233
Krämer, Sibylle, 68–70
Kremlin, 135
Krenz, Egon, 186, 233–4
Kuckhoff, Greta, 9–10, 51–64
  Vom Rosenkranz zur roten Kapelle: ein Lebensbericht, 61
Kuhn, Annette, 216

Lambek, Michael, 31, 160
Landeszentrale für politische Bildung (LpB; Regional Office for Political Education), 151–2
Landsberg, Alison, 6, 26
Lasdin, Bernd, 12, 200–1, 208–9, 212
  Zeitenwende, 198–9, 202
  Zeitenwenden, 199
Lazda, Irene, 144
Leipzig, 8, 71, 119, 137, 172, 174, 179–88, 190–1, 223
  Augustusplatz, 180–2, **181**, 184
  Freiheitsglocke (freedom bell), 181
  Friedensgebete (peace prayers), 180
  Gewandhaus, 181, 184, 206
  Lichtfest (festival of lights), 12, 179, 181, **181**, 182–3, 185, 187–8, 191
  Nikolaikirche, 180–1, 183, 187
  Nikolaiplatz, 176
  Oper, 129, 181
  Runde Ecke, 180, 182
  Wilhelm-Leuschner-Platz, 188
  see also museums; monuments
Lenin, Vladimir, 168
letters, 26, 51–8, 62, 64, 68, 72–3, 96, 166, 188, 209, 222–3
Lewerenz, Erika, 62
Liebknecht-Luxemburg march, 241
Liebmann, Irina, 94
life writing, 52–4, 58, 63, 67
  see also autobiography
Linke, Die, 114, 175
  see also PDS (Party of Democratic Socialism)
Liszt, Franz, 123
Lodge, David
  Ginger, You're Barmy, 239
Lowenthal, David, 121
LStU (Office of the Regional Commissioner for the Stasi Files), 151
Luhmann, Niklas, 83, 90

Magdeburg, 176
Maier, Charles, 121
Maizière, Lothar de, 166
Malchow, 214–15, 217–18, 222–3
  see also museums

Maron, Monika, 85
  Flugasche, 86
Marx, Karl, 168
Masur, Kurt, 184–5
Matthus, Siegfried, 117, 120
Mausbach, Florian, 166, 169
Mecklenburg, 124, 199, 214, 223
Melzer, Hannah, 59
memorials, 7, 21, 26, 151, 176, 187–8
  Hohenschönhausen, 68, 70, 72, 76, 80
  to the Holocaust, 164, 170–1
  see also monuments; museums
memory
  boom, 9, 20–2, 164, 179, 189
  collective: collective memory, 4, 9, 11, 22–23, 25, 27, 29–30, 34, 38–39, 128, 144, 149, 182, 185, 191, 198, 202, 230, 233–234, 237, 239, 241–242; memory collective, 34–5, 37–8, 42, 44–5
  communicative, 25–6, 29, 80
  community. *see* *Erinnerungsgemeinschaft* (memory community)
  cultural, 6–7, 25–6, 29, 43, 87, 93, 95, 132, 173, 203, 216
  diasporic, 116, 121–2
  dominant, 103, 106, 109, 112–14
  false, 24, 218–21, 224
  hyper-memory, 29
  national, 12, 122, 171
  political, 11–12, 165, 167, 171–2, 175–6
  popular, 38, 102–3, 106, 109, 113–14
  post-memory, 24
  prosthetic, 6, 23, 26
  selective, 9, 34, 36, 38, 44–5, 152
  social, 23, 54, 149–50, 167, 176, 207, 211, 234
Merkel, Angela, 166, 181
Merkel, Ina, 138, 140, 145
MfS (Ministry for State Security). *see* Stasi
Mielke, Erich, 73, 123, 227
Milla und Partner, 166, 174
Modrow, Hans, 233
Montaigne, Michel de, 92
monuments, 25, 32, 164, 166, 168, 170–1, 173–4, 176, 235
  antifascist, 170
  Freiheitsglocke (freedom bell), 181
  Freiheits- und Einheitsdenkmal (monument to freedom and unity), Berlin, 11–12, 164–77, **169**, 187, 191, 212
  Freiheits- und Einheitsdenkmal, Leipzig, 12, 174, 187–8, 191
  'Freudenmal' ('positive' monument), 171
  to Kaiser Wilhelm I, 172
  Mahnmal (monument as a warning), 170–2
  Prussian, 168
  socialist realist, 165, 168, 170
  see also memorials
Mozambique, 233
Mueller, Gabriele, 139, 142, 145
Mühe, Anna Maria, 215–17, 220–1, 224, 226
Mühe, Ulrich, 215, 224–6
Müller, Kurt, 72–3
Munich, 119
Münkler, Herfried, 189–90, 192
museums, 2, 5–7, 21, 26, 57–8, 67, 132–45, 151, 197–8, 203–7, 209–12
  DDR-Museum, Berlin, 7, 28, 133, 135–6, 141, 231
  DDR-Museum Malchow, 133, 136–7
  DDR-Museum 'Zeitreise', Dresden-Radebeul, 133–4, **134**, 137, 143–4
  Dokumentationszentrum Alltagskultur der DDR, Eisenhüttenstadt, 7, 28, 133, 136, 139, 145
  of everyday life/culture, 5, 11, 132–3, 135, 142, 144
  Gedenkstätte Bautzen, 76
  Gedenkstätte Hohenschönhausen, 6, 68, 70, 76, 80
  German Historical Museum, Berlin, 174
  Haus der Geschichte, Bonn, 142

Haus der Geschichte, Wittenberg, 212
memorial museums, 5
Military History Museum, Dresden, 241
Mitte Museum, Berlin, 143
Museum for German History, Berlin, 56–7
Museum in der 'Runden Ecke', Leipzig, 136–7
Rheinische Freilichtmuseum, 204
Zeitgeschichtliches Forum Leipzig, 132, 144–5, 186, 231
myth, 12, 122, 135, 174, 179, 187–92, 202, 211

Naficy, Hamid, 118
nationalism, 116, 128, 158, 172, 186
negative, 170–1
National Socialism, 4, 14, 27, 37–40, 42–3, 55, 106
Nazi, 52–3, 55–6, 60–1, 171, 189, 226
see also National Socialism; resistance, anti–Nazi
Neumann, Bernd, 28, 175
niche, 12, 197–9, 202–5, 207–11, 220
Nischenglück, 29
Nietzsche, Friedrich, 95, 129
Nischengesellschaft (niche society). *see* niche
Nooke, Günter, 166, 169–71
Nooteboom, Cees, 94
Nora, Pierre, 21
normalisation, 9, 34, 39–45, 164, 221, 239
nostalgia, 1, 6, 10, 13–14, 27, 31, 39, 63, 93–4, 101–2, 110, 121–2, 127, 132, 149–50, 153–6, 159–62, 197
popular, 151
reflective, 3, 11, 30, 32, 116, 122, 128, 161
restorative, 3, 13, 30, 32, 122, 161
western, 109, 110
see also Ostalgie, ostalgic
Nünning, Ansgar, 26
Nuremberg, 62
NVA (National People's Army), 206, 229–42

Ochs, Elinor, 154
Office for Military History Research, 231
Ohler, Norman, 91, 94
Mitte, 92–3
Olias, Günter, 127
Olick, Jeffrey, 23, 31
oppression, 10, 28, 40–1, 67–8, 74, 76, 91, 101, 103, 123, 136–7, 208–9
Ossi, 7, 14, 107, 114–15
Ostalgie, ostalgic, 2, 5–7, 9–11, 14, 22, 27–8, 30–1, 38–9, 43, 45, 101–15, 122, 128, 132–3, 145, 149, 160, 227, 229

Pamuk, Orhan
The White Castle, 86
Parei, Inka, 94
Die Schattenboxerin, 91
Paris, Helga, 212
path dependence, 34, 41–2, 45
PDS (Party of Democratic Socialism), 103, 114, 166–7, 173, 175
see also Linke, Die
peaceful revolution, 8, 12, 122, 165–8, 170, 173–4, 179, 181, 183–91, 211
Peitsch, Helmut, 52
perestroika, 126, 190
Pergande, Frank, 225
photography, 12–13, 26, 77–8, 102, 136–7, 140–2, 154, 198–200, 202, 209, 212
Pieper, Cornelia, 172
Pioneer organisation, 1, 136
Plantinga, Carl R., 69
pogrom, 59
popular culture, 7, 42, 102
popular music, 1, 102, 143
posthistoire, 21
Potsdam, 28, 231
Prague, 210
prison
Cottbus, 71
Hoheneck, 71
Höhenschönhausen, 68, 73, 75–6, 79
public v. private, 12, 14, 26, 54, 197, 199, 212

radio, 51–6, 58, 62, 64, 93, 217, 239
Radstone, Susannah, 64, 103, 150, 161–2, 216, 242
Ramelsberger, Annette, 135, 138, 142
Rávic-Strubel, Antje
  Fremd Gehen: Ein Nachtstück, 94
Red Orchestra, 52–3, 55–7, 59–62, 64
re-enactment, 12, 23, 182, 191
Regener, Sven, 239
Reinhardt, Helmut, 60
repression, 4, 7, 19, 24, 27, 30, 37, 74, 85, 91, 93, 158, 170, 209, 218, 238, 240–1
resistance, 5, 9–12, 28, 41–2, 53, 56–7, 59, 60–1, 105–6, 120, 143–4, 155, 180, 185, 202, 217
  antifascist, 52, 55, 58, 60, 63, 64
  anti-Nazi, 51, 55, 61
reunification., *see* unification
revolution, 93, 122, 124, 126
  1848, 172
  1917, 190
  1989. *see* peaceful revolution
  Copernican, 90, 92
're-working' the past. *see Aufarbeitung* (re-working of the past)
Richthofen, Esther von, 198
Rigney, Ann, 73, 77
Rodek, Hanns-Georg, 224
Romanticism, 10, 83, 87, 90–1, 95, 125
Rudd, Kevin, 31
Rügen, 216
Rushdie, Salman, 13

Sabrow, Martin, 4–5
Sabrow Report, 28–9
Samuel, Raphael, 141
Sandmann, 102
Santner, Eric, 26
Schabowski, Günter, 135, 138, 210, 238
Schenker, Friedrich, 117
  ...ins Endlose..., 124
Scheunemann, Jan, 203
Schlager (popular songs). *see* popular music
Schlesinger, Klaus, 88, 92, 94
  Alte Filme, 91, 96
  Berliner Traum, 84
  'Die Spaltung des Erwin Racholl', 85
  Trug, 10, 83–7, 89, 91–5
Schneider, Frank, 118
Schneider, Peter, 7, 86
Schnitzler, Arthur, 93
Schoenberg, Arnold, 120
Schønwandt, Michael, 119
Schorlemmer, Friedrich, 183
Schröder, Gerhard, 240
Schroeder, Klaus, 231
Schubert, Franz
  Die Winterreise, 126
Schulz, Tilo, 187
Schumann, Robert, 125–6, **126**
Schwerter zu Pflugscharen, 175, 184
Schwochow, Christian
  Novemberkind, 12, 214–2, 226
Scribner, Charity, 139–40
second class citizens, 41
Second World War, 11, 51, 117, 120, 123, 171
SED (Socialist Unity Party), 14, 30, 35, 37–8, 40–3, 57, 75, 111, 137, 149, 152–3, 155, 157, 162, 172, 175, 179–80, 185–6, 190–1, 229, 231, 233, 238–40
Sinopli, Giuseppe, 119
socialism, 7–9, 44, 57, 60–1, 76, 101, 103, 106–8, 110–113, 133, 136–7, 149, 152–6, 158, 161–2, 168, 183, 218, 229, 238, 241
  post-socialism, 9, 39–40, 42, 103, 162
Solidarity Committee for the Victims of Political Persecution in Germany, 233
Sontag, Susan, 23, 30
Soviet special camp, 72–3
Soviet Union, 42, 51, 53, 55, 60, 64, 116, 136, 157
Soviet Zone, 53
SPD (Social Democratic Party), 28, 166–8, 170
Stanley, Liz, 54, 57

Stasi, 1, 7, 14, 27, 67, 69, 71, 73–4, 76, 78–80, 103, 133, 136–7, 155, 157, 159, 180, 206, 208–9, 212, 215–20, 224–7, 231, 233, 240
files, 1, 2, 4, 71, 133, 151, 214, 220, 226
prison, 6, 68
Steimle, Uwe, 102
Stephan, Hans-Joachim, 134, 143
Stiftung Friedliche Revolution, 183
Stöhr, Hannes
Berlin is in Germany, 227
Stötzner, Andreas, 187
Streletz, Fritz, 233

Tannhoff, Peter, 236, 238–9
Sprutz, 235
television, 23, 26, 76–7, 102, 138, 197, 205–8, 210–212, 234, 236–7, 239
television productions, 12, 114, 139, 142, 145, 179, 198, 234
An die Grenze, 234, 236–7
Das Wunder von Berlin, 206–7, 209
Der Mauerschütze, 234, 242
Jenseits der Mauer, 206–7, **210**
Wir sind das Volk – Liebe kennt keine Grenzen, 206–8, 210
Tellkamp, Uwe
Der Turm, 234
Thälmann, Ernst, 168
Theobald, John, 104, 109
Thierse, Wolfgang, 170–1
Thompson, Peter, 7
totalitarianism, 4, 52, 74, 117, 128, 149, 152, 156, 160, 190, 208
tourism, 28, 30, 136, 181, 183
trauma, 12, 24, 26, 31, 39, 59, 67, 116, 160, 214, 219–20, 226, 240
Turkey, 86, 116
TV. *see* television

Ulbrich, Reinhard
Spur der Broiler, 39
Ulbricht, Walter, 56
unification, 4, 13–14, 27, 30, 35, 37, 41–3, 94–5, 101, 103–4, 108, 114, 116–18, 124, 128, 144, 149, 154, 167–8, 170, 172, 183–4, 186–7, 189, 191, 199, 202–3, 215, 226, 230, 232
Unrechtsstaat (illegitimate state), 6, 27–8, 218

victimhood, 4, 7–9, 27–9, 31, 34, 39–41, 45, 56, 67, 69, 71–2, 74–5, 79–80, 137, 150, 154–5, 159, 164–5, 171, 218–19, 220–1, 225–6, 240
perpetrator v. victim, 7–8, 27–29, 150, 154–155, 226, 240
Vierneisel, Beatrice, 60

Waldheim, 59–61
Warsaw Treaty Organisation, 230, 233
Webber, Andrew, 91
Wehrmacht, 123, 241
Weimar constitution, 172
Weisenburger, Petra
Ich will da sein, 225
Weltbühne, Die, 58, 60
Wende, 1–3, 8, 10–12, 14, 43, 72, 78, 83, 86–7, 90, 92, 94–5, 120–2, 125–8, 135, 137, 139, 144–5, 186–7, 190, 197–9, 202, 206–9, 215, 236, 239
Wessi, 7, 14, 223
Wolf, Christa, 86–7, 94
Wolf, Konrad
Solo Sunny, 212
Wolle, Stefan, 231

Yugoslavia, 116

5. Teil: Zusammenfassung der Ergebnisse und Ausblick 353
A. Zusammenfassung der Ergebnisse 353
I. Breitenwirkung und Veröffentlichung der Rechtsprechung des BFH, Reaktionsmöglichkeiten der Exekutive und Legislative auf die Rechtsprechung des BFH 353
II. Untersuchung der steuerlichen Nichtanwendungsgesetzgebung und Typologisierung der steuerlichen Nichtanwendungsgesetze 354
III. Verfassungsrechtliche Würdigung der steuerlichen Nichtanwendungsgesetzgebung 355
IV. Rechtspolitische Würdigung der steuerlichen Nichtanwendungsgesetzgebung 357
B. Ausblick 357

Anhang 361
A. Geschäftsordnung über die Regelungen zur Zusammenarbeit des Bundes mit den Ländern nach § 21a FVG 361
I. Bund-Länder-Gremien 361
II. Einberufung und Ablauf der Sitzungen 362
III. Allgemeine fachliche Weisungen und Herausgabe von BMF-Schreiben 365
B. Untersuchung ergangener Nichtanwendungsgesetze 367
I. Nichtanwendungsgesetze gegen Entscheidungen des BFH 367
1. Nichtanwendungsgesetze der Abgabenordnung 367
2. Nichtanwendungsgesetze der Finanzgerichtsordnung 412
3. Nichtanwendungsgesetze des EG-Amtshilfe-Gesetzes 416
4. Nichtanwendungsgesetze der Einkommensteuer 418
5. Nichtanwendungsgesetze der Außensteuer 628
6. Nichtanwendungsgesetze der Umwandlungsteuer 635
7. Nichtanwendungsgesetze der Körperschaftsteuer 644
8. Nichtanwendungsgesetze der Gewerbesteuer 663
9. Nichtanwendungsgesetze der Erbschaftsteuer 673
10. Nichtanwendungsgesetze der Bewertung 683

11. Nichtanwendungsgesetze der Grundsteuer ... 687
12. Nichtanwendungsgesetze der Umsatzsteuer ... 691
13. Nichtanwendungsgesetze der Grunderwerbsteuer ... 705
14. Nichtanwendungsgesetze der Versicherungsteuer ... 710
II. Nichtanwendungsgesetze gegen Entscheidungen der Finanzgerichte ... 712

Literaturverzeichnis ... 721

Lebenslauf ... 741

Vorwort

Die vorliegende Arbeit wurde im Wintersemester 2016/2017 von der Juristischen Fakultät der Ruhr-Universität Bochum zum Promotionsverfahren zugelassen.

Redaktionsschluss der vorliegenden Druckfassung ist der 31. 03. 2016. Sie enthält die bis zu diesem Zeitpunkt ergangene Rechtsprechung, im BGBl verkündete Nichtanwendungsgesetze und Literatur.

Die Erstellung dieser Arbeit wäre ohne die Hilfe verschiedener Personen nicht möglich gewesen.

Zuvorderst zu nennen ist mein Doktorvater Prof. Dr. Roman Seer. Als ich mit ihm über die Thematik der Nichtanwendungsgesetze als mögliches Dissertationsthema gesprochen habe, hat er sofort seine Bereitschaft zur Betreuung der Arbeit erklärt. Für diese Bereitschaft und die weitere Unterstützung des Dissertationsvorhabens danke ich sehr herzlich. Ebenso danke ich ihm für die Aufnahme und Veröffentlichung dieser Arbeit in der von ihm herausgegebenen Reihe der Bochumer Schriften zum Steuerrecht.

Herrn Richter am BFH Prof. Dr. Matthias Loose habe ich für die zügige Erstellung des Zweitgutachtens zu danken. Ebenso verdanke ich ihm meine erste wissenschaftliche Publikation mit einem gemeinsamen Aufsatz über „Die Bindungswirkung des § 10a GewStG im Rahmen von Gesellschafterwechseln bei Personengesellschaften", der in der Finanzrundschau (FR) 2008, 864 veröffentlicht worden ist.

Herrn Vorsitzenden Richter am BFH a. D. Prof. Dr. Heinz-Jürgen Pezzer möchte ich erwähnen, weil er mit seinem Aufsatz „Finanzgerichtsbarkeit im gewaltengeteilten Verfassungsstaat" in Deutsches Steuerrecht (DStR) 2004, 525 bei mir das Interesse für die Frage geweckt hat, wie die Finanzverwaltung und der Gesetzgeber auf die Judikatur des BFH reagieren. Damit hat er mir, ohne es zu wissen, den Weg zu meinem Dissertationsthema gewiesen.

Herrn Ministerialrat Wilhelm Friedrich Rehrmann habe ich zu danken, weil er mir während meiner Referendariatsstage im Ministerium der Finanzen des Landes Nordrhein-Westfalen einen Einblick ermöglicht hat, welche Fragen für die Finanzverwaltung wesentlich sind, wenn diese über die allgemeine Anwendbarkeit der BFH-Rechtsprechung zu entscheiden hat.

Herr Leitender Regierungsdirektor a. D. Hans Brunswig ist ebenfalls zu nennen. Er hat es mir in seiner Eigenschaft als Vorsteher des Finanzamtes Dortmund-Ost durch die Gewährung einer Teilzeittätigkeit ermöglicht, ein Studium der Rechtswissenschaften aufnehmen zu können. Dies war in Anbetracht der

Gemengelage in der Finanzverwaltung des Landes Nordrhein-Westfalen keine Selbstverständlichkeit. Umso mehr weiß ich dies zu schätzen und ohne das rechtswissenschaftliche Studium wäre diese Arbeit keine Realität.

Der Konrad-Adenauer-Stiftung e. V. bin ich zu Dank verpflichtet, da sie mich durch die Gewährung eines Stipendiums in der Zeit meines Studiums und in der Zeit der Promotion ideell und finanziell unterstützt hat.

Jan-Marcel Drossel danke ich für manch kurzweiliges Gespräch während des Verfassens der Arbeit im Zentralen Rechtswissenschaftlichen Seminar der Ruhr-Universität Bochum und für seine inhaltlichen Anmerkungen zu meinem Promotionsthema.

Dr. Lars Lubisch verdient Erwähnung. Neben inhaltlichen Anmerkungen zur vorliegenden Arbeit haben wir gemeinsam unser juristisches Studium an der Ruhr-Universität Bochum absolviert und sind auch darüber hinaus stets in Kontakt geblieben.

Dortmund, im Februar 2018

Jendrik Suck

Abkürzungsverzeichnis

2. StÄndG 1973	Zweites Steueränderungsgesetz 1973
a. A.	andere Auffassung
ABl. EU	Amtsblatt der Europäischen Union
Abs.	Absatz
AcP	Archiv für die civilistische Praxis (Zeitschrift)
a. D.	außer Dienst
AEAO	Anwendungserlass zur Abgabenordnung
AEUV	Vertrag über die Arbeitsweise der Europäischen Union
a. F.	alte Fassung
AIFM-StAnpG	Gesetz zur Anpassung des Investmentsteuergesetzes und anderer Gesetze an das AIFM-Umsetzungsgesetz (AIFM-Steuer-Anpassungsgesetz)
AktG	Aktiengesetz
AltEinkG	Gesetz zur Neuordnung der einkommensteuerrechtlichen Behandlung von Altervorsorgeaufwendungen und Altersbezügen (Alterseinkünftegesetz)
AmtshilfeRLUmsG	Gesetz zur Umsetzung der Amtshilferichtlinie sowie zur Änderung steuerlicher Vorschriften (Amtshilferichtlinie- Umsetzungsgesetz)
Anl.	Anlage
Anm.	Anmerkung
AO	Abgabenordnung
AOÄG	Gesetz zur Änderung der Reichsabgabenordnung und anderer Gesetze
AöR	Archiv des öffentlichen Rechts (Zeitschrift)
Apr.	April
Art.	Artikel
AStG	Gesetz über die Besteuerung bei Auslandsbeziehungen (Außensteuergesetz)
Aufl.	Auflage
Aug.	August
AuR	Arbeit und Recht (Zeitschrift)
Az.	Aktenzeichen
BAB	Bundesautobahn

DStZ	Deutsche Steuer-Zeitung (Zeitschrift)
DStZ/A	Deutsche Steuer-Zeitung/Ausgabe A (Zeitschrift)
DVBl	Deutsches Verwaltungsblatt (Zeitschrift)
DWS	Deutsches wissenschaftliches Institut der Steuerberater
EDV	Elektronische Datenverarbeitung
EGMR	Europäischer Gerichtshof für Menschenrechte
EFG	Entscheidungen der Finanzgerichte (Zeitschrift)
EG	Europäische Gemeinschaft
EGAHiG	EG-Amtshilfe-Gesetz
EGAO 1977	Einführungsgesetz zur Abgabenordnung
Einf.	Einführung
EMRK	Konvention zum Schutz der Menschenrechte und Grundfreiheiten (Europäische Menschenrechtskonvention)
ErbStG	Erbschaft- und Schenkungsteuergesetz
ErbStR	Erbschaftsteuer-Richtlinien
ESt	Einkommensteuer
EStDV	Einkommensteuer-Durchführungsverordnung
EStG	Einkommensteuergesetz
EStR	Einkommensteuer-Richtlinien
EStRG	Gesetz zur Reform der Einkommensteuer, des Familienlastungsausgleichs und der Sparförderung (Einkommensteuerreformgesetz)
EU	Europäische Union
EUAHiG	EU-Amtshilfegesetz
EuGH	Europäischer Gerichtshof
EU-Kommission	Europäische Kommission
EURLUmsG	Gesetz zur Umsetzung von EU-Richtlinien in nationales Steuerrecht und zur Änderung weiterer Vorschriften (Richtlinien-Umsetzungsgesetz)
EUV	Vertrag über die Europäische Union
f	folgende
FA	Finanzamt
Feb.	Februar
FDP	Freie Demokratische Partei
ff	fortfolgende
FG	Finanzgericht
FGO	Finanzgerichtsordnung